Agora Paperback Editions

GENERAL EDITOR: ALLAN BLOOM

*Introduction to
the Reading of Hegel*

Agora Paperback Editions
GENERAL EDITOR: ALLAN BLOOM

Plato's Dialogue on Friendship: An Interpretation of the Lysis, *with a New Translation,* by David Bolotin

Introduction to the Reading of Hegel: Lectures on the Phenomenology of Spirit, by Alexandre Kojève

Medieval Political Philosophy, edited by Ralph Lerner and Muhsin Mahdi

The Roots of Political Philosophy: Ten Forgotten Socratic Dialogues, by Thomas L. Pangle

Politics and the Arts, by Jean-Jacques Rousseau

INTRODUCTION
TO THE READING OF
HEGEL

BY ALEXANDRE KOJÈVE

LECTURES ON THE

Phenomenology of Spirit

ASSEMBLED BY RAYMOND QUENEAU

Edited by Allan Bloom

Translated from the French by
James H. Nichols, Jr.

Cornell University Press

ITHACA AND LONDON

Published in French under the title *Introduction à la Lecture de Hegel*
(2d ed.; Paris: Gallimard, 1947)

English translation first published by Basic Books, Inc.

First published 1980 by Cornell University Press
First printing, Agora Paperback Editions, Cornell Paperbacks, 1980

Published by arrangement with Basic Books, a division of
HarperCollins Publishers, Inc. All rights reserved.

ISBN-13: 978-0-8014-9203-7 (pbk. : alk. paper)
Library of Congress Catalog Card Number 80-66908
Printed in the United States of America

Cornell University Press strives to use environmentally responsible suppliers and
materials to the fullest extent possible in the publishing of its books. Such materials
include vegetable-based, low-VOC inks and acid-free papers that are recycled,
totally chlorine-free, or partly composed of nonwood fibers. For further
information, visit our website at www.cornellpress.cornell.edu.

Paperback printing   20 19 18 17 16 15 14 13 12 11

Alexandre Kojève

1902–1968

Gentlemen! We find ourselves in an important epoch, in a fermentation, in which Spirit has made
a leap forward, has gone beyond its previous concrete form and acquired a new one. The whole
mass of ideas and concepts that have been current
until now, the very bonds of the world, are dis-
solved and collapsing into themselves like a vision
in a dream. A new emergence of Spirit is at hand;
philosophy must be the first to hail its appearance
and recognize it, while others, resisting impotently,
adhere to the past, and the majority unconsciously
constitute the matter in which it makes its appearance. But philosophy, in recognizing it as what is
eternal, must pay homage to it.

Hegel, *Lectures at Jena* of 1806,
final speech

The courage of truth, faith in the power of Spirit,
are the first condition of philosophy. Man, because
he is Spirit, can and must consider himself worthy
of everything that is most sublime. He can never
overestimate the greatness and power of his spirit.
And if he has this faith, nothing will be so recal-
citrant and hard as not to reveal itself to him.

Hegel, 1816

EDITOR'S INTRODUCTION

Queneau's collection of Kojève's thoughts about Hegel constitutes one of the few important philosophical books of the twentieth century—a book, knowledge of which is requisite to the full awareness of our situation and to the grasp of the most modern perspective on the eternal questions of philosophy. A hostile critic has given an accurate assessment of Kojève's influence:

> Kojève is the unknown Superior whose dogma is revered, often unawares, by that important subdivision of the "animal kingdom of the spirit" in the contemporary world—the progressivist intellectuals. In the years preceding the second world war in France, the transmission was effected by means of oral initiation to a group of persons who in turn took the responsibility of instructing others, and so on. It was only in 1947 that by the efforts of Raymond Queneau, the classes on the *Phenomenology of Spirit* taught by Alexandre Kojève at the *École des Hautes Études* from 1933–1939 were published under the title, *Introduction to the Reading of Hegel.* This teaching was prior to the philosophico-political speculations of J. P. Sartre and M. Merleau-Ponty, to the publication of *les Temps modernes* and the new orientation of *Esprit*, reviews which were the most important vehicles for the dissemination of progressivist ideology in France after the liberation. From that time on we have breathed Kojève's teaching with the air of the times. It is known that intellectual progressivism itself admits of a subdivision, since one ought to consider its two species, Christian (*Esprit*) and atheist (*les Temps modernes*); but this distinction, for reasons that the initial doctrine enables one to clarify, does not take on the importance of a schism. . . . M. Kojève is, so far as we know, the first . . . to have attempted to constitute the intellectual and moral *ménage à trois* of Hegel, Marx and Heidegger which has since that time been such a great success. [Aimé Patri, "Dialectique du Maître et de l'Esclave," *Le Contrat Social*, V, No. 4 (July–August 1961), 234.]

Kojève is the most thoughtful, the most learned, the most profound of those Marxists who, dissatisfied with the thinness of Marx's account of the human and metaphysical grounds of his teaching, turned to Hegel as the truly philosophic source of that teaching. Although he made no effort at publicizing his reflections, the superior force of his interpretations imposed them willy-nilly on those who heard him. For this reason, anyone who wishes to understand the sense of that mixture of Marxism and Existentialism which characterizes contemporary radicalism must turn to Kojève. From him one can learn both the implications and the necessary presuppositions of historicist philosophy; he elaborates what the world must be like if terms such as freedom, work, and creativity are to have a rational content and be parts of a coherent understanding. It would, then, behoove any follower of the new version of the left who wishes to think through the meaning of his own action to study that thinker who is at its origin.

However, Kojève is above all a philosopher—which, at the least, means that he is primarily interested in the truth, the comprehensive truth. His passion for clarity is more powerful than his passion for changing the world. The charm of political solutions does not cause him to forget the need to present an adequate account of the rational basis of those solutions, and this removes him from the always distorted atmosphere of active commitment. He despises those intellectuals who respond to the demands of the contemporary audience and give the appearance of philosophic seriousness without raising the kinds of questions which would bore that audience or be repugnant to it. A certain sense of the inevitability of this kind of abuse—of the conversion of philosophy into ideology—is, perhaps, at the root of his distaste for publication. His work has been private and has, in large measure, been communicated only to friends. And the core of that work is the careful and scholarly study of Hegel.

Because he is a serious man, Kojève has never sought to be original, and his originality has consisted in his search for the truth in the thought of wise men of the past. His interpretation has made Hegel an important alternative again, and showed how much we have to learn from him at a time when he seemed no longer of living significance. Kojève accomplished this revival of interest in Hegel not by adapting him to make him relevant, but by showing that contemporary concerns are best understood in the permanent light of Hegel's teaching. Kojève's book is a model of textual interpretation; the book is suffused with the awareness that it is of pressing concern to find out precisely what such a thinker meant, for he may well know much more than we do about the things that we need to know. Here scholarship is in the service of philosophy, and Kojève gives us a glimpse of the power of great minds and respect for the humble and unfashionable business of spending years studying an old book. His own teaching is but the distillation of more than six years devoted to nothing but reading a single book, line by line. INTRODUCTION TO THE READING OF HEGEL constitutes the most authoritative interpretation of Hegel.

Such a careful and comprehensive study which makes sense of Hegel's very difficult texts will be of great value in America where, though his influence has been great and is ever greater, very few people read, let alone understand, him. He has regularly been ignored by academic positivists who are put off by his language and are unaware of the problems involved in their own understanding of science and the relation of science to the world of human concern. Hegel is now becoming popular in literary and artistic circles, but in a superficial form adapted to please dilettantes and other seekers after the sense of depth who wish to use him rather than understand him. Kojève presents Hegel's teaching with a force and rigor which should counterpoise both tendencies.

What distinguishes Kojève's treatment of Hegel is the recognition that for Hegel the primary concern is not the knowledge of anything outside himself—be it of nature or history—but knowledge of himself, that is, knowledge of what the philosopher is and how he can know what he knows. The philosopher must be able to explain his own doings; an explanation of the heavens, of animals, or of nonphilosophic men which does not leave room for, or does not talk about, the philosopher is radically incomplete because it cannot account for the possibility of its own existence as knowledge. The world known by philosophy must be such that it supports philosophy and makes the philosopher the highest or most complete kind of human being.

Kojève learned from Hegel that the philosopher seeks to know himself or to possess full self-consciousness, and that, therefore, the true philosophic endeavor is a coherent explanation of all things that culminates in the explanation of philosophy. The man who seeks any other form of knowledge, who cannot explain his own doings, cannot be called a philosopher. Discussion of the rational state is only a corollary of the proof that the world can be known or is rational. Kojève insists that Hegel is the only man who succeeded in making this proof, and his interpretation of the *Phenomenology* expands and clarifies Hegel's assertion that reality is rational and hence justifies rational discourse about it. According to Kojève, Hegel is the fulfillment of what Plato and Aristotle could only pray for; he is the modern Aristotle who responded to—or, better, incorporated—the objections made to Aristotelian philosophy by modern natural and human science. Kojève intransigently tries to make plausible Hegel's claim that he had achieved absolute wisdom. He argues that without the possibility of absolute wisdom, all knowledge, science, or philosophy is impossible.

It may indeed be doubted whether Kojève is fully persuasive to the modern consciousness, particularly since he finds himself compelled to abandon Hegel's philosophy of nature as indefensible and suggests that Heidegger's meditation on being may provide a substitute for it. The abandoned philosophy of nature may well be a necessary cosmic support for Hegel's human, historical teaching. One might ask whether Kojève is not really somewhere between Hegel and Heidegger, but it should be added that Kojève himself leads the reader to this question, which is a proper theme of philosophical reflection. Kojève describes the character of wisdom even if he does not prove it has been actualized.

Now, the most striking feature of Kojève's thought is his insistence—fully justified—that for Hegel, and for all followers of Hegel, history is completed, that nothing really new can again happen in the world. To most of us, such a position seems utterly paradoxical and wildly implausible. But Kojève easily shows the ineluctable necessity of this consequence for anyone who understands human life to be historically determined, for anyone who believes that thought is relative to time—that is, for most modern men. For if thought is historical, it is only at the end of history that this fact can be known; there can only be knowledge if history at some point stops. Kojève elaborates the meaning of this logical necessity throughout the course of the book and attempts to indicate how a sensible man could accept it and interpret the world in accordance with it. It is precisely Marx's failure to think through the meaning of his own historical thought that proves his philosophical inadequacy and compels us to turn to the profounder Hegel.

If concrete historical reality is all that the human mind can know, if there is no transcendent intelligible world, then, for there to be philosophy or science, reality must have become rational. The Hegelian solution, accepted by Kojève, is that this has indeed happened and that the enunciation of the universal, rational principles of the rights of man in the French Revolution marked the beginning of the end of history. Thereafter, these are the only acceptable, viable principles of the state. The dignity of man has been recognized, and all men are understood to participate in it; all that remains to do is, at most, to realize the state grounded on these principles all over the world; no antithesis can undermine this synthesis, which contains within itself all the valid possibilities. In this perspective Kojève interprets our situation; he paints a powerful picture of our problems as those of post-historical man with none of the classic tasks of history to perform, living in a universal, homogeneous state where there is virtual agreement on all the fundamental principles of science, politics, and religion. He characterizes the life of the man who is free, who has no work, who has no worlds to conquer, states to found, gods to revere, or truths to discover. In so doing, Kojève gives an example of what it means to follow out the necessity of one's position manfully and philosophically. If Kojève is wrong, if his world does not correspond to the real one, we learn at least that either one must abandon reason —and this includes all science—or one must abandon historicism. More common-sensical but less intransigent writers would not teach us nearly so much. Kojève presents the essential outlines of historical thought; and, to repeat, historical thought, in one form or another, is at the root of almost all modern human science.

It is concerning the characterization of man at the end of history that one of the most intriguing difficulties in Kojève's teaching arises. As is only to be expected, his honesty and clarity lead him to pose the difficulty himself. If Hegel is right that history fulfills the demands of reason, the citizen of the final state should enjoy the satisfaction of all reasonable human aspirations; he should be a free, rational being, content with his situation and exercising all of his powers, emancipated from the bonds of prejudice and oppression. But looking around us, Kojève, like every other penetrating observer, sees that the completion of the human task may very well coincide with the decay of humanity, the rebarbarization or even reanimalization of man. He addresses this problem particularly in the note on Japan added to the second edition (pp. 159–162). After reading it, one wonders whether the citizen of the universal homogeneous state is not identical to Nietzsche's Last Man, and whether Hegel's historicism does not by an inevitable dialectic force us to a more somber and more radical historicism which rejects reason. We are led to a confrontation between Hegel and Nietzsche and perhaps, even further, toward a reconsideration of the classical philosophy of Plato and Aristotle, who rejected historicism before the fact and whom Hegel believed he had surpassed. It is the special merit of Kojève to be one of the very few sure guides to the contemplation of the fundamental alternatives.

ALLAN BLOOM

Ithaca, New York

[Shortly after the completion of this statement I learned that Alexandre Kojève had died in Brussels in May, 1968.]

TRANSLATOR'S NOTE

The original French edition of *Introduction à la Lecture de Hegel* consists of notes and transcripts of lectures, delivered by Alexandre Kojève from 1933 to 1939 at the École des Hautes Études, collected and edited by the poet and novelist Raymond Queneau, of the Académie Goncourt. Its first chapter (and the first in this translation) was written by Kojève and published in the January 14, 1939, issue of *Mesures*. The present translation includes slightly under one half of the original volume: the passages translated correspond to pp. 9–34, 161–195, 265–267, 271–291, 336–380, 427–443, 447–528, and 576–597 of the French text. The selections for this edition were made with two goals in mind: to present the outlines of Kojève's interpretation of the *Phenomenology of Spirit*, and to present the most characteristic aspects of his own thought.

The translation tries to preserve as much as possible of Kojève's style and terminology, which are determined at least in part by his careful attempt to preserve and explain the meaning of Hegel's own precise terminology. Some of the oddities consequently present in the translation should perhaps be mentioned. Many of Kojève's translations of Hegelian terms are not the customary ones, but represent his interpretation of their meaning. For example, he renders *Moment, Sein* (in one of its meanings), and *Wesen* as *élément-constitutif, être-donné,* and *réalité-essentielle;* these interpretations are maintained in the English as "constituent-element," "given-being," and "essential-reality." Kojève often translates single words of Hegel by several words joined with hyphens; this has sometimes been followed in the translation, but at other times (when great awkwardness or confusion might result) it has not. Kojève's use of capitalization has been preserved throughout. Kojève has also invented several French words, thus making it necessary to invent some English ones, such as "thingness" for *chosité* (for *Dingheit*) and "nihilate" for *néantir*. Of course, it is often impossible to use consistently one translation for each French term. To give two of many examples: *supprimer* (for *Aufheben*) has usually been translated "overcome," but sometimes "do away with"; and *Sentiment de soi* (for *Selbst-Gefühl*) has been translated "Sentiment of self," but sometimes *sentiment* is translated "feeling."

Page and line references to Hegel's *Phenomenology of Spirit* are to the Hoffmeister edition (Hamburg, Felix Meiner Verlag, 1952). Citations of other works of Hegel are from the Lasson-Hoffmeister edition (Leipzig: Felix Meiner Verlag, 1905–).

I should like to express my thanks to Kenley and Christa Dove, who kindly made available for this edition their translation of Kojève's "Structure of the *Phenomenology of Spirit*" and their correlation of the page and line references to J. B. Baillie's English translation [*The Phenomenology of Mind* (New York: Macmillan, 1931), 2nd ed.], which will be of great usefulness to the English reader (see Appendix). I am obliged to the Danforth Foundation for a summer grant that enabled me to complete the revision of the translation. Finally, I should like to thank my mother for her considerable help with various stages of the manuscript.

JAMES H. NICHOLS, JR.

CONTENTS

INTRODUCTION
TO THE READING OF
HEGEL

Absence of recognition/misrecognition is
(social) death for Hegel.

Time - social.

Marx - only humans can imagine + realize
(cognitively + then as concretely).
This is what Slave does thro' work

Sartre - gaze of the other pins you down,
curtails your freedom, misrecognised.

End of history - full recognition, mutual
certainty, absolute freedom, incorporates
Otherness.

'Recognition' in pa. but so it stable outside
the clinic, in the social? What group
analyses offer?

Master/Slave as allegory

Korean philosopher on capitalism

Jessica Benjamin uses Hegel - mutual recognition
critiqued for two - may want to be undone

1

IN PLACE OF AN INTRODUCTION*

Hegel . . . erfasst die *Arbeit* als das
Wesen, als das sich bewährende
Wesen des Menschen.

Karl Marx

[Man is Self-Consciousness. He is conscious of himself, conscious
of his human reality and dignity; and it is in this that he is essentially different from animals, which do not go beyond the level of
simple Sentiment of self. Man becomes conscious of himself at the
moment when—for the "first" time—he says "I." To understand
man by understanding his "origin" is, therefore, to understand
the origin of the I revealed by speech.

[Now, the analysis of "thought," "reason," "understanding,"
and so on—in general, of the cognitive, contemplative, passive
behavior of a being or a "knowing subject"—never reveals the
why or the how of the birth of the word "I," and consequently of
self-consciousness—that is, of the human reality. The man who
contemplates is "absorbed" by what he contemplates; the "knowing subject" "loses" himself in the object that is known. Contemplation reveals the object, not the subject. The object, and not
the subject, is what shows itself to him in and by—or better, as—
the act of knowing. The man who is "absorbed" by the object
that he is contemplating can be "brought back to himself" only
by a Desire; by the desire to eat, for example. The (conscious)
Desire of a being is what constitutes that being as I and reveals it
as such by moving it to say "I. . . ." Desire is what transforms
Being, revealed to itself by itself in (true) knowledge, into an

---

* A translation with commentary of Section A of Chapter IV of the *Phenomenology of Spirit*, entitled: "Autonomy and Dependence of Self-Consciousness:
Mastery and Slavery."

The commentary is in brackets. Words joined by hyphens correspond to a
single German word.

"object" revealed to a "subject" by a subject different from the object and "opposed" to it. It is in and by—or better still, as—"his" Desire that man is formed and is revealed—to himself and to others—as an I, as the I that is essentially different from, and radically opposed to, the non-I. The (human) I is the I of a Desire or of Desire.

[The very being of man, the self-conscious being, therefore, implies and presupposes Desire. Consequently, the human reality can be formed and maintained only within a biological reality, an animal life. But, if animal Desire is the necessary condition of Self-Consciousness, it is not the sufficient condition. By itself, this Desire constitutes only the Sentiment of self.

[In contrast to the knowledge that keeps man in a passive quietude, Desire dis-quiets him and moves him to action. Born of Desire, action tends to satisfy it, and can do so only by the "negation," the destruction, or at least the transformation, of the desired object: to satisfy hunger, for example, the food must be destroyed or, in any case, transformed. Thus, all action is "negating." Far from leaving the given as it is, action destroys it; if not in its being, at least in its given form. And all "negating-negativity" with respect to the given is necessarily active. But negating action is not purely destructive, for if action destroys an objective reality, for the sake of satisfying the Desire from which it is born, it creates in its place, in and by that very destruction, a subjective reality. The being that eats, for example, creates and preserves its own reality by the overcoming of a reality other than its own, by the "transformation" of an alien reality into its own reality, by the "assimilation," the "internalization" of a "foreign," "external" reality. Generally speaking, the I of Desire is an emptiness that receives a real positive content only by negating action that satisfies Desire in destroying, transforming, and "assimilating" the desired non-I. And the positive content of the I, constituted by negation, is a function of the positive content of the negated non-I. If, then, the Desire is directed toward a "natural" non-I, the I, too, will be "natural." The I created by the active satisfaction of such a Desire will have the same nature as the things toward which that Desire is directed: it will be a "thingish" I, a merely living I, an animal I. And this natural I, a function of the natural object, can be revealed to itself and to others only as Sentiment of self. It will never attain Self-Consciousness.

[For there to be Self-Consciousness, Desire must therefore be directed toward a non-natural object, toward something that goes beyond the given reality. Now, the only thing that goes beyond the given reality is Desire itself. For Desire taken as Desire—i.e., before its satisfaction—is but a revealed nothingness, an unreal emptiness. Desire, being the revelation of an emptiness, the presence of the absence of a reality, is something essentially different from the desired thing, something other than a thing, than a static and given real being that stays eternally identical to itself. Therefore, Desire directed toward another Desire, taken as Desire, will create, by the negating and assimilating action that satisfies it, an I essentially different from the animal "I." This I, which "feeds" on Desires, will itself be Desire in its very being, created in and by the satisfaction of its Desire. And since Desire is realized as action negating the given, the very being of this I will be action. This I will not, like the animal "I," be "identity" or equality to itself, but "negating-negativity." In other words, the very being of this I will be becoming, and the universal form of this being will not be space, but time. Therefore, its continuation in existence will signify for this I: "not to be what it is (as static and given being, as natural being, as 'innate character') and to be (that is, to become) what it is not." Thus, this I will be its own product: it will be (in the future) what it has become by negation (in the present) of what it was (in the past), this negation being accomplished with a view to what it will become. In its very being this I is intentional becoming, deliberate evolution, conscious and voluntary progress; it is the act of transcending the given that is given to it and that it itself is. This I is a (human) individual, free (with respect to the given real) and historical (in relation to itself). And it is this I, and only this I, that reveals itself to itself and to others as Self-Consciousness.

[Human Desire must be directed toward another Desire. For there to be human Desire, then, there must first be a multiplicity of (animal) Desires. In other words, in order that Self-Consciousness be born from the Sentiment of self, in order that the human reality come into being within the animal reality, this reality must

5

be essentially manifold. Therefore, man can appear on earth only within a herd. That is why the human reality can only be social. But for the herd to become a society, multiplicity of Desires is not sufficient by itself; in addition, the Desires of each member of the herd must be directed—or potentially directed—toward the Desires of the other members. If the human reality is a social reality, society is human only as a set of Desires mutually desiring one another as Desires. Human Desire, or better still, anthropogenetic Desire, produces a free and historical individual, conscious of his individuality, his freedom, his history, and finally, his historicity. Hence, anthropogenetic Desire is different from animal Desire (which produces a natural being, merely living and having only a sentiment of its life) in that it is directed, not toward a real, "positive," given object, but toward another Desire. Thus, in the relationship between man and woman, for example, Desire is human only if the one desires, not the body, but the Desire of the other; if he wants "to possess" or "to assimilate" the Desire taken as Desire—that is to say, if he wants to be "desired" or "loved," or, rather, "recognized" in his human value, in his reality as a human individual. Likewise, Desire directed toward a natural object is human only to the extent that it is "mediated" by the Desire of another directed toward the same object: it is human to desire what others desire, because they desire it. Thus, an object perfectly useless from the biological point of view (such as a medal, or the enemy's flag) can be desired because it is the object of other desires. Such a Desire can only be a human Desire, and human reality, as distinguished from animal reality, is created only by action that satisfies such Desires: human history is the history of desired Desires.

[But, apart from this difference—which is essential—human Desire is analogous to animal Desire. Human Desire, too, tends to satisfy itself by a negating—or better, a transforming and assimilating—action. Man "feeds" on Desires as an animal feeds on real things. And the human I, realized by the active satisfaction of its human Desires, is as much a function of its "food" as the body of an animal is of its food.

[For man to be truly human, for him to be essentially and really different from an animal, his human Desire must actually win out over his animal Desire. Now, all Desire is desire for a value. The supreme value for an animal is its animal life. All the Desires of an animal are in the final analysis a function of its desire to preserve its life. Human Desire, therefore, must win out over this desire for preservation. In other words, man's humanity "comes to light" only if he risks his (animal) life for the sake of his human Desire. It is in and by this risk that the human reality is created and revealed as reality; it is in and by this risk that it "comes to light," i.e., is shown, demonstrated, verified, and gives proofs of being essentially different from the animal, natural reality. And that is why to speak of the "origin" of Self-Consciousness is necessarily to speak of the risk of life (for an essentially nonvital end).

[Man's humanity "comes to light" only in risking his life to satisfy his human Desire—that is, his Desire directed toward another Desire. Now, to desire a Desire is to want to substitute oneself for the value desired by this Desire. For without this substitution, one would desire the value, the desired object, and not the Desire itself. Therefore, to desire the Desire of another is in the final analysis to desire that the value that I am or that I "represent" be the value desired by the other: I want him to "recognize" my value as his value. I want him to "recognize" me as an autonomous value. In other words, all human, anthropogenetic Desire—the Desire that generates Self-Consciousness, the human reality—is, finally, a function of the desire for "recognition." And the risk of life by which the human reality "comes to light" is a risk for the sake of such a Desire. Therefore, to speak of the "origin" of Self-Consciousness is necessarily to speak of a fight to the death for "recognition."

[Without this fight to the death for pure prestige, there would never have been human beings on earth. Indeed, the human being is formed only in terms of a Desire directed toward another Desire, that is—finally—in terms of a desire for recognition. Therefore, the human being can be formed only if at least two of these Desires confront one another. Each of the two beings endowed with such a Desire is ready to go all the way in pursuit of its satisfaction; that is, is ready to risk its life—and, consequently, to put the life of the other in danger—in order to be "recognized" by the other, to impose itself on the other as the supreme value; accordingly, their meeting can only be a fight to the death. And it is only in and by such a fight that the human reality is begotten, formed, realized, and revealed to itself and to others. Therefore, it is realized and revealed only as "recognized" reality.

[However, if all men—or, more exactly, all beings in the process of becoming human beings—behaved in the same manner, the fight would necessarily end in the death of one of the adversaries, or of both. It would not be possible for one to give way to the other, to give up the fight before the death of the other, to "recognize" the other instead of being "recognized" by him. But if this were the case, the realization and the revelation of the human being would be impossible. This is obvious in the case of the death of both adversaries, since the human reality—being essentially Desire and action in terms of Desire—can be born and maintained only within an animal life. But it is equally impossible when only one of the adversaries is killed. For with him disappears that other Desire toward which Desire must be directed in order to be a human Desire. The survivor, unable to be "recognized" by the dead adversary, cannot realize and reveal his humanity. In order that the human being be realized and revealed as Self-Consciousness, therefore, it is not sufficient that the nascent human reality be manifold. This multiplicity, this "society," must in addition imply two essentially different human or anthropogenetic behaviors.

[In order that the human reality come into being as "recognized" reality, both adversaries must remain alive after the fight. Now, this is possible only on the condition that they behave differently in this fight. By irreducible, or better, by unforeseeable or "undeducible" acts of liberty, they must constitute themselves as unequals in and by this very fight. Without being predestined to it in any way, the one must fear the other, must give in to the other, must refuse to risk his life for the satisfaction of his desire for "recognition." He must give up his desire and satisfy the desire of the other: he must "recognize" the other without being "recognized" by him. Now, "to recognize" him thus is "to recognize" him as his Master and to recognize himself and to be recognized as the Master's Slave.

[In other words, in his nascent state, man is never simply man. He is always, necessarily, and essentially, either Master or Slave. If the human reality can come into being only as a social reality, society is human—at least in its origin—only on the basis of its implying an element of Mastery and an element of Slavery, of "autonomous" existences and "dependent" existences. And that is why to speak of the origin of Self-Consciousness is necessarily to speak of "the autonomy and dependence of Self-Consciousness, of Mastery and Slavery."

[If the human being is begotten only in and by the fight that ends in the relation between Master and Slave, the progressive realization and revelation of this being can themselves be effected only in terms of this fundamental social relation. If man is nothing but his becoming, if his human existence in space is his existence in time or as time, if the revealed human reality is nothing but universal history, that history must be the history of the interaction between Mastery and Slavery: the historical "dialectic" is the "dialectic" of Master and Slave. But if the opposition of "thesis" and "antithesis" is meaningful only in the context of their reconciliation by "synthesis," if history (in the full sense of the word) necessarily has a final term, if man who becomes must culminate in man who has become, if Desire must end in satisfaction, if the science of man must possess the quality of a definitively and universally valid truth—the interaction of Master and Slave must finally end in the "dialectical overcoming" of both of them.

[However that may be, the human reality can be begotten and preserved only as "recognized" reality. It is only by being "recognized" by another, by many others, or—in the extreme—by all others, that a human being is really human, for himself as well as for others. And only in speaking of a "recognized" human reality can the term *human* be used to state a truth in the strict and full sense of the term. For only in this case can one reveal a reality in speech. That is why it is necessary to say this of Self-Consciousness, of self-conscious man:] Self-Consciousness exists *in* and *for itself* in and by the fact that it exists (in and for itself) for another Self-Consciousness; i.e., it exists only as an entity that is recognized.

. . . .

This pure concept of recognition, of the doubling of Self-Consciousness within its unity, must now be considered as its evolution appears to Self-Consciousness [i.e., not to the philosopher who speaks of it, but to the self-conscious man who recognizes another man or is recognized by him.]

In the first place, this evolution will make manifest the aspect of the inequality between the two Self-Consciousnesses [i.e., between the two men who confront one another for the sake of recognition], or the expansion of the middle-term [which is the mutual and reciprocal recognition] into the two extremes [which are the two who confront one another]; these are opposed to one another as extremes, the one only recognized, the other only recognizing. [To begin with, the man who wants to be recognized by another in no sense wants to recognize him in turn. If he succeeds, then, the recognition will not be mutual and reciprocal: he will be recognized but will not recognize the one who recognizes him.]

To begin with, Self-Consciousness is simple-or-undivided Being-for-itself; it is identical-to-itself by excluding from *itself* everything *other* [than itself]. Its essential-reality and its absolute object are, for it, *I* [I isolated from everything and opposed to everything that is not I]. And, in this *immediacy*, in this *given-being* [i.e., being that is not produced by an active, creative process] of its Being-for-itself, Self-Consciousness is *particular-and-isolated*. What is other for it exists as an object without essential-reality, as an object marked with the character of a negative-entity.

But [in the case we are studying] the other-entity, too, is a Self-Consciousness; a human-individual comes face to face with a human-individual. Meeting thus *immediately*, these individuals exist for one another as common objects. They are *autonomous* concrete-forms, Consciousnesses submerged in the *given-being* of *animal-life*. For it is as animal-life that the merely existing object has here presented itself. They are Consciousnesses that have not yet accomplished *for one another* the [dialectical] movement of absolute abstraction, which consists in the uprooting of all immediate given-being and in being nothing but the purely negative-or-negating given-being of the consciousness that is identical-to-itself.

Or in other words, these are entities that have not yet manifested themselves to one another as pure *Being-for-itself*—i.e., as *Self-Consciousness*. [When the "first" two men confront one another for the first time, the one sees in the other only an animal (and a dangerous and hostile one at that) that is to be destroyed, and not a self-conscious being representing an autonomous value.] Each of these two human-individuals is, to be sure, subjectively-certain of himself; but he is not certain of the other. And that is why his own subjective-certainty of himself does not yet possess truth [i.e., it does not yet reveal a reality—or, in other words, an entity that is objectively, intersubjectively, i.e., universally, recognized, and hence existing and valid]. For the truth of his subjective-certainty [of the idea that he has of himself, of the value that he attributes to himself] could have been nothing but the fact that his own Being-for-itself was manifested to him as an autonomous object; or again, to say the same thing: the fact that the object was manifested to him as this pure subjective-certainty of himself; [therefore, he must find the private idea that he has of himself in the external, objective reality.] But according to the concept of recognition, this is possible only if he accomplishes for the other (just as the other does for him) the pure abstraction of Being-for-itself; each accomplishing it in himself both by his own activity and also by the other's activity.

[The "first" man who meets another man for the first time already attributes an autonomous, absolute reality and an autonomous, absolute value to himself: we can say that he believes himself to be a man, that he has the "subjective certainty" of being a man. But his certainty is not yet knowledge. The value that he attributes to himself could be illusory; the idea that he has of himself could be false or mad. For that idea to be a truth, it must reveal an objective reality—i.e., an entity that is valid and exists not only for itself, but also for realities other than itself. In the case in question, man, to be really, truly "man," and to know that he is such, must, therefore, impose the idea that he has of himself on beings other than himself: he must be recognized by the others (in the ideal, extreme case, by all the others). Or again, he must transform the (natural and human) world in which he is not recognized into a world in which this recognition takes place. This transformation of the world that is hostile to a human project into a world in harmony with this project is called "action," "activity." This action—essentially human, because humanizing and anthropogenetic—will begin with the act of imposing oneself on the "first" other man one meets. And since this other, if he is (or more exactly, if he wants to be, and believes himself to be) a human being, must himself do the same thing, the "first" anthropogenetic action necessarily takes the form of a fight: a fight to the death between two beings that claim to be men, a fight for

11

pure prestige carried on for the sake of "recognition" by the adversary. Indeed:]

The *manifestation* of the human-individual taken as pure abstraction of Being-for-itself consists in showing itself as being the pure negation of its objective-or-thingish mode-of-being—or, in other words, in showing that to be for oneself, or to be a man, is not to be bound to any determined *existence*, not to be bound to the universal isolated-particularity of existence as such, not to be bound to life. This manifestation is a *double* activity: activity of the other and activity by oneself. To the extent that this activity is activity *of the other*, each of the two men seeks the death of the other. But in that activity of the other is also found the second aspect, namely, the *activity by oneself*: for the activity in question implies in it the risk of the life of him who acts. The relation of the two Self-Consciousnesses, therefore, is determined in such a way that they come to light—each for itself and one for the other—through the fight for life and death.

[They "come to light"—that is, they prove themselves, they transform the purely subjective certainty that each has of his own value into objective, or universally valid and recognized, truth. Truth is the revelation of a reality. Now, the human reality is created, is constituted, only in the fight for recognition and by the risk of life that it implies. The truth of man, or the revelation of his reality, therefore, presupposes the fight to the death. And that is why] human-individuals are obliged to start this fight. For each must raise his subjective-certainty of *existing for self* to the level of truth, both in the other and in himself. And it is only through the risk of life that freedom comes to light, that it becomes clear that the essential-reality of Self-Consciousness is not *given-being* [being that is not created by conscious, voluntary action], nor the *immediate* [natural, not mediated by action (that negates the given)] mode in which it first comes to sight [in the given world], nor submersion in the extension of animal-life; but that there is, on the contrary, nothing given in Self-Consciousness that is anything but a passing constituent-element for it. In other words, only by the risk of life does it come to light that Self-Consciousness is nothing but pure *Being-for-itself*. The human-individual that *has* not dared-to-risk his life can, to be sure, be recognized as a *human-person*; but he has not attained the truth of this fact of being recognized as an autonomous Self-Consciousness. Hence, each of the two human-individuals must have the death of the other as his goal, just as he risks his own life. For the other-entity is worth no more to him than himself. His essential-reality [which is his recognized, human reality and dignity] manifests itself to him as an other-entity [or another man, who does not recognize him and is therefore independent of him]. He is outside of himself [insofar as the other has not "given him back" to himself by recognizing him, by revealing that he has recognized him, and by showing him that he (the other) depends on him and is not absolutely other than he]. He must overcome his being-outside-of-himself. The other-entity [than he] is here a Self-Consciousness existing as a given-being and involved [in the natural world] in a manifold and diverse way. Now, he must look upon his other-being as pure Being-for-itself, i.e., as absolute negating-negativity. [This means that man is human only to the extent that he wants to impose himself on another man, to be recognized by him. In the beginning, as long as he is not yet actually recognized by the other, it is the other that is the end of his action; it is on this other, it is on recognition by this other, that his human value and reality depend; it is in this other that the meaning of his life is condensed. Therefore, he is "outside of himself." But his own value and his own reality are what are important to him, and he wants to have them in himself. Hence, he must overcome his "other-being." This is to say that he must make himself recognized by the other, he must have in himself the certainty of being recognized by another. But for that recognition to satisfy him, he has to know that the other is a human being. Now, in the beginning, he sees in the other only the aspect of an animal. To know that this aspect reveals a human reality, he must see that the other also wants to be recognized, and that he, too, is ready to risk, "to deny," his animal life in a fight for the recognition of his human being-for-itself. He must, therefore, "provoke" the other, force him to start a fight to the death for pure prestige. And having done this, he is obliged to kill the other in order not to be killed himself. In these circumstances, then, the fight for recognition can end only in the death of one of the adversaries—or of both together.] But this proving oneself by death does away with the truth [or revealed objective reality] that was supposed to come from it; and, for that very reason, it also does away with the subjective-certainty of oneself as such. For just as animal-life is the *natural* position of Consciousness, i.e., autonomy without absolute negating-negativity, so is death the *natural* negation of Consciousness, i.e., negation without autonomy, which negation, therefore, continues to lack the significance required by recognition. [That is to say: if both adversaries perish in the fight, "consciousness" is completely done away with, for man is nothing more than an inanimate body after his death. And if one of the adversaries remains alive but kills the other, he can no longer be recognized by the other; the man who has been defeated and killed does not recognize the victory of the conqueror. Therefore, the victor's certainty of his being and of his value remains subjective, and thus has no "truth."] Through death, it is true, the subjective-certainty of the fact that both risked their lives and that each despised his own and the other's life has been established. But this certainty has not been established for those who underwent this struggle. Through death, they do away with their consciousness, which resides in that foreign entity, natural existence. That is to say, they do away with themselves. [For man is real only to the extent that he lives in a natural world. This world is, to be sure, "foreign" to him; he must "deny" it, transform it, fight it, in order to realize himself in it. But without this world, outside of this world, man is nothing.] And they are done away with as *extremes* that want to exist for self [i.e., consciously, and independently of the rest of the universe]. But, thereby, the essential constituent-element—i.e., the splitting up into extremes of opposed determinate things—disappears from the play of change. And the middle-term collapses in a dead unity, broken up into dead extremes, which merely exist as given-beings and are not opposed [to one another in, by, and for an action in which one tries "to do away with" the other by "establishing" himself and to establish himself by doing away with the other.] And the two do not give themselves reciprocally to one another, nor do they get themselves back in return from one another through consciousness. On the contrary, they merely leave one another free, indifferently, as things. [For the dead man is no longer anything more than an unconscious thing, from which the living man turns away in indifference, since he can no longer expect anything from it for himself.] Their murderous action is abstract negation. It is not negation [carried out] by consciousness, which overcomes in such a way that it *keeps* and *preserves* the overcome-entity and, for that very reason, survives the fact of being overcome. [This "overcoming" is "dialectical." "To overcome dialectically" means to overcome while preserving what is overcome; it is sublimated in and by that overcoming which preserves or that preservation which overcomes. The dialectically overcome-entity is annulled in its contingent (stripped of sense, "senseless") aspect of natural, given ("immediate") entity, but it is preserved in its essential (and meaningful, significant) aspect; thus mediated by negation, it is sublimated or raised up to a more "comprehensive" and comprehensible mode of being than that of its immediate reality of pure and simple, positive and static given, which is not the result of creative action (i.e., of action that negates the given).

[Therefore, it does the man of the Fight no good to kill his adversary. He must overcome him "dialectically." That is, he must leave him life and consciousness, and destroy only his autonomy. He must overcome the adversary only insofar as the adversary is opposed to him and acts against him. In other words, he must enslave him.]

In that experience [of the murderous fight] it becomes clear to Self-Consciousness that animal-life is just as important to it as pure self-consciousness. In the immediate Self-Consciousness [i.e., in the "first" man, who is not yet "mediated" by this contact with the other that the fight creates], the simple-or-undivided I [of isolated man] is the absolute object. But for us or in itself [i.e., for the author and the reader of this passage, who see man as he has been definitively formed at the end of history by the accomplished social inter-action] this object, i.e., the I, is absolute mediation, and its essential constituent-element is abiding autonomy. [That is to say, real and true man is the result of his inter-action with others; his I and the idea he has of himself are "mediated" by recognition obtained as a result of his action. And his true autonomy is the autonomy that he *maintains* in the social reality by the effort of that action.] The dissolution of that simple-or-undivided unity [which is the isolated I] is the result of the first experience [which man has at the time of his "first" (murderous) fight]. By this experience are established: a pure Self-Consciousness [or an "abstract" one, since it has made the "abstraction" of its animal life

15

by the risk of the fight—the victor], and a Consciousness that [being in fact a living corpse—the man who has been defeated and spared] does not exist purely for itself, but rather for another Consciousness [namely, for that of the victor]: i.e., a Consciousness that exists as a *given-being*, or in other words, a Consciousness that exists in the concrete-form of *thingness*. Both constituent-elements are essential—since in the beginning they are unequal and opposed to one another and their reflection into unity has not yet resulted [from their action], they exist as two opposed concrete-forms of Consciousness. The one is autonomous Consciousness, for which the essential-reality is Being-for-itself. The other is dependent Consciousness, for which the essential-reality is animal-life, i.e., given-being for an other-entity. The former is the *Master*, the latter—the *Slave*. [This Slave is the defeated adversary, who has not gone all the way in risking his life, who has not adopted the principle of the Masters: to conquer or to die. He has accepted life granted him by another. Hence, he depends on that other. He has preferred slavery to death, and that is why, by remaining alive, he lives as a Slave.]

The Master is Consciousness existing *for itself*. And he is no longer merely the [abstract] concept of Consciousness, but a [real] Consciousness existing for itself, which is mediated with itself by *another* Consciousness, namely, by a Consciousness to whose essential-reality it belongs to be synthesized with *given-being*, i.e., with thingness as such. [This "Consciousness" is the Slave who, in binding himself completely to his animal-life, is merely one with the natural world of things. By refusing to risk his life in a fight for pure prestige, he does not rise above the level of animals. Hence he considers himself as such, and as such is he considered by the Master. But the Slave, for his part, recognizes the Master in his human dignity and reality, and the Slave behaves accordingly. The Master's "certainty" is therefore not purely sub-jective and "immediate," but objectivized and "mediated" by an-other's, the Slave's, recognition. While the Slave still remains an "immediate," natural, "bestial" being, the Master—as a result of his fight—is already human, "mediated." And consequently, his behavior is also "mediated" or human, both with regard to things and with regard to other men; moreover, these other men, for him, are only slaves.] The Master is related to the following two constituent-elements: on the one hand, to a *thing* taken as such, i.e., the object of Desire; and, on the other hand, to the Consciousness for which thingness is the essential-entity [i.e., to the Slave, who, by refusing the risk, binds himself completely to the things on which he depends. The Master, on the other hand, sees in these things only a simple means of satisfying his desire; and, in satisfying it, he destroys them]. Given that: (1) the Master, taken as concept of self-consciousness, is the immediate relation of *Being-for-itself*, and that (2) he now [i.e., after his victory over the Slave] exists at the same time as mediation, i.e., as a Being-for-itself that exists for itself only through an other-entity [since the Master is Master only by the fact of having a Slave who recognizes him as Master]; the Master is related (1) immediately to both [i.e., to the thing and to the Slave], and (2) in a mediated way to each of the two through the other. The Master is related *in a mediated way to the Slave*, viz., by *autonomous given-being*; for it is precisely to this given-being that the Slave is tied. This given-being is his chain, from which he could not abstract in the fight, in which fight he was revealed—because of that fact—as dependent, as having his autonomy in thingness. The Master, on the other hand, is the power that rules over this given-being; for he revealed in the fight that this given-being is worth nothing to him except as a negative-entity. Given that the Master is the power that rules over this given-being and that this given-being is the power that rules over the Other [i.e., over the Slave], the Master holds—in this [real or active] syllogism—that Other under his domination. Likewise, the Master is related *in a mediated way to the thing*, viz., *by the Slave*. Taken as Self-Consciousness as such, the Slave, too, is related to the thing in a negative or negating way, and he overcomes it [dialectically]. But—for him—the thing is autonomous at the same time. For that reason, he cannot, by his act-of-negating, finish it off to the point of the [complete] annihilation [of the thing, as does the Master who "consumes" it]. That is, he merely *transforms it by work* [i.e., he prepares it for consumption, but does not consume it himself]. For the Master, on the other hand, the *immediate* relation [to the thing] comes into being, through that mediation [i.e., through the work of the Slave who transforms the natural thing, the "raw material," with a view to its consumption (by the Master)], as pure negation of the object, that is, as

Enjoyment. [Since all the effort is made by the Slave, the Master has only to enjoy the thing that the Slave has prepared for him, and to enjoy "negating" it, destroying it, by "consuming" it. (For example, he eats food that is completely prepared)]. What Desire [i.e., isolated man "before" the Fight, who was alone with Nature and whose desires were directed without detour toward that Nature] did not achieve, the Master [whose desires are directed toward things that have been transformed by the Slave] does achieve. The Master can finish off the thing completely and satisfy himself in Enjoyment. [Therefore, it is solely thanks to the work of another (his Slave) that the Master is free with respect to Nature, and consequently, satisfied with himself. But, he is Master of the Slave only because he previously freed himself from Nature (and from his own nature) by risking his life in a fight for pure prestige, which—as such—is not at all "natural."] Desire cannot achieve this because of the autonomy of the thing. The Master, on the other hand, who introduced the Slave between the thing and himself, is consequently joined only to the aspect of the thing's dependence, and has pure enjoyment from it. As for the aspect of the thing's autonomy, he leaves it to the Slave, who transforms the thing by work.

In these two constituent-elements the Master gets his recognition through another Consciousness; for in them the latter affirms itself as unessential, both by the act of working on the thing and by the fact of being dependent on a determinate existence. In neither case can this [slavish] Consciousness become master of the given-being and achieve absolute negation. Hence it is given in this constituent-element of recognition that the other Consciousness overcomes itself as Being-for-itself and thereby does itself what the other Consciousness does to it. [That is to say, the Master is not the only one to regard the Other as his Slave; this Other also considers himself as such.] The other constituent-element of recognition is equally implied in the relation under consideration; this other constituent-element is the fact that this activity of the second Consciousness [the slavish Consciousness] is the activity proper of the first Consciousness [i.e., the Master's]. For everything that the Slave does is, properly speaking, an activity of the Master. [Since the Slave works only for the Master, only to satisfy the Master's desire and not his own, it is the Master's desire that acts in and through the Slave.] For the Master, only Being-for-itself is the essential-reality. He is pure negative-or-negating power, for which the thing is nothing; and consequently, in this relation of Master and Slave, he is the pure essential activity. The Slave, on the other hand, is not pure activity, but nonessential activity. Now, for there to be an authentic recognition, there must also be the third constituent-element, which consists in the Master's doing with respect to himself what he does with respect to the other, and in the Slave's doing with respect to the Other what he [the Slave] does with respect to himself. It is, therefore, an unequal and one-sided recognition that has been born from this relation of Master and Slave. [For although the Master treats the Other as Slave, he does not behave as Slave himself; and although the Slave treats the Other as Master, he does not behave as Master himself. The Slave does not risk his life, and the Master is idle.

[The relation between Master and Slave, therefore, is not recognition properly so-called. To see this, let us analyze the relation from the Master's point of view. The Master is not the only one to consider himself Master. The Slave, also, considers him as such. Hence, he is recognized in his human reality and dignity. But this recognition is one-sided, for he does not recognize in turn the Slave's human reality and dignity. Hence, he is recognized by someone whom he does not recognize. And this is what is insufficient—what is tragic—in his situation. The Master has fought and risked his life for a recognition without value for him. For he can be satisfied only by recognition from one whom he recognizes as worthy of recognizing him. The Master's attitude, therefore, is an existential impasse. On the one hand, the Master is Master only because his Desire was directed not toward a thing, but toward another desire—thus, it was a desire for recognition. On the other, when he has consequently become Master, it is as Master that he must desire to be recognized; and he can be recognized as such only by making the Other his Slave. But the Slave is for him an animal or a thing. He is, therefore, "recognized" by a thing. Thus, finally, his Desire is directed toward a thing, and not—as it seemed at first—toward a (human) Desire. The Master, therefore, was on the wrong track. After the fight that made him a Master, he is not what he wanted to be in starting that fight: a man recognized by another man. Therefore: if man can be satisfied only by recognition, the man who behaves as a Master will never be satisfied. And since—in the beginning—man is either Master or Slave, the satisfied man will necessarily be a Slave; or more exactly, the man who has been a Slave, who has passed through Slavery, who has "dialectically overcome" his slavery. Indeed:]

Thus, the nonessential [or slavish] Consciousness is—for the Master—the object that forms the *truth* [or revealed reality] of the subjective-certainty he has of himself [since he can "know" he is Master only by being recognized as such by the Slave]. But it is obvious that this object does not correspond to its concept. For in the Master's fulfilling himself, something entirely different from an autonomous Consciousness has come into being [since he is faced with a Slave]. It is not such an autonomous Consciousness, but all to the contrary, a dependent Consciousness, that exists for him. Therefore, he is not subjectively certain of his *Being-for-itself* as of a truth [or of a revealed objective reality]. His truth, all to the contrary, is nonessential Consciousness, and the non-essential activity of that Consciousness. [That is to say, the Master's "truth" is the Slave and the Slave's Work. Actually, others recognize the Master as Master only because he has a Slave; and the Master's life consists in consuming the products of slavish Work, and in living on and by this Work.]

Consequently, the *truth* of autonomous Consciousness is *slavish Consciousness*. This latter first appears, it is true, as existing *outside* of itself and not as the truth of Self-Consciousness [since the Slave recognizes human dignity not in himself, but in the Master, on whom his very existence depends]. But, just as Mastery showed that its essential-reality is the reverse or perversion of what it wants to be, so much the more will Slavery, in its fulfillment, probably become the opposite of what it is immediately; as *repressed* Consciousness it will go within itself and reverse and transform itself into true autonomy.

[The complete, absolutely free man, definitively and completely satisfied by what he is, the man who is perfected and completed in and by this satisfaction, will be the Slave who has "overcome" his Slavery. If idle Mastery is an impasse, laborious Slavery, in contrast, is the source of all human, social, historical progress. History is the history of the working Slave. To see this, one need only consider the relationship between Master and Slave (that is, the first result of the "first" human, social, historical contact), no longer from the Master's point of view, but from the Slave's.]

We have seen only what Slavery is in its relation to Mastery. But Slavery is also Self-Consciousness. What it is as such, in and for itself, must now be considered. In the first place, it is the Master that is the essential-reality for Slavery. *The autonomous Consciousness existing for itself* is hence, for it, *the truth* [or a revealed reality], which, however, *for it*, does not yet exist *in it*. [The Slave is subordinated to the Master. Hence the Slave esteems, recognizes, the value and the reality of "autonomy," of human freedom. However, he does not find it realized in himself; he finds it only in the Other. And this is his advantage. The Master, unable to recognize the Other who recognizes him, finds himself in an impasse. The Slave, on the other hand, recognizes the Other (the Master) from the beginning. In order that mutual and reciprocal recognition, which alone can fully and definitively realize and satisfy man, be established, it suffices for the Slave to impose himself on the Master and be recognized by him. To be sure, for this to take place, the Slave must cease to be Slave: he must transcend himself, "overcome" himself, as Slave. But if the Master has no desire to "overcome"—and hence no possibility of "overcoming"—himself as Master (since this would mean, for him, to become a Slave), the Slave has every reason to cease to be a Slave. Moreover, the experience of the fight that made him a Slave predisposes him to that act of self-overcoming, of negation of himself (negation of his given I, which is a slavish I). To be sure, in the beginning, the Slave who binds himself to his given (slavish) I does not have this "negativity" in himself. He sees it only in the Master, who realized pure "negating-negativity" by risking his life in the fight for recognition.] However, Slavery *in fact* has *in itself* this truth [or revealed reality] of pure negating-negativity and of *Being-for-itself*. For it has *experienced* this essential-reality within itself. This slavish Consciousness was afraid not for this or that, not for this moment or that, but for its [own] entire essential-reality: it underwent the fear of death, the fear of the absolute Master. By this fear, the slavish Consciousness melted internally; it shuddered deeply and everything fixed-or-stable trembled in it. Now, this pure universal [dialectical] movement, this absolute liquefaction of every stable-support, is the simple-or-undivided essential-reality of Self-

Consciousness, absolute negating-negativity, *pure Being-for-itself*. Thus, this Being-for-itself exists *in* the slavish Consciousness. [The Master is fixed in his Mastery. He cannot go beyond himself, change, progress. He must conquer—and become Master or preserve himself as such—or die. He can be killed; he cannot be transformed, educated. He has risked his life to be Master. Therefore, Mastery is the supreme given value for him, beyond which he cannot go. The Slave, on the other hand, did not want to be a Slave. He became a Slave because he did not want to risk his life to become a Master. In his mortal terror he understood (without noticing it) that a given, fixed, and stable condition, even though it be the Master's, cannot exhaust the possibilities of human existence. He "understood" the "vanity" of the given conditions of existence. He did not want to bind himself to the Master's condition, nor does he bind himself to his condition as a Slave. There is nothing fixed in him. He is ready for change; in his very being, he is change, transcendence, transformation, "education"; he is historical becoming at his origin, in his essence, in his very existence. On the one hand, he does not bind himself to what he is; he wants to transcend himself by negation of his given state. On the other hand, he has a positive ideal to attain; the ideal of autonomy, of Being-for-itself, of which he finds the incarnation, at the very origin of his Slavery, in the Master.] This constituent-element of Being-for-itself also exists *for slavish Consciousness*. For in the Master, Being-for-itself is, for it [the slavish Consciousness], its object. [An object that it knows to be external, opposed, to it, and that it tends to appropriate for itself. The Slave knows what it is to be free. He also knows that he is not free, and that he wants to become free. And if the experience of the Fight and its result predispose the Slave to transcendence, to progress, to History, his life as a Slave working in the Master's service realizes this predisposition.] In addition, slavish Consciousness is not only this universal dissolution [of everything fixed, stable, and given], taken *as such*; in the Master's service, it accomplishes this dissolution *in an objectively real way* [i.e., concretely]. In service [in the forced work done in the service of another (the Master)], slavish Consciousness [dialectically] overcomes its attachment to natural existence in all the *particular-and-isolated* constituent-elements, and it eliminates this existence by work. [The Master forces the Slave to work. And by working, the Slave becomes master of Nature. Now, he became the Master's Slave only because—in the beginning—he was a slave of Nature, joining with it and subordinating himself to its laws by accepting the instinct of preservation. In becoming master of Nature by work, then, the Slave frees himself from his own nature, from his own instinct that tied him to Nature and made him the Master's Slave. Therefore, by freeing the Slave from Nature, work frees him from himself as well, from his Slave's nature: it frees him from the Master. In the raw, natural, given World, the Slave is slave of the Master. In the technical world transformed by his work, he rules—or, at least, will one day rule—as absolute Master. And this Mastery that arises from work, from the progressive transformation of the given World and of man given in this World, will be an entirely different thing from the "immediate" Mastery of the Master. The future and History hence belong not to the warlike Master, who either dies or preserves himself indefinitely in identity to himself, but to the working Slave. The Slave, in transforming the given World by his work, transcends the given and what is given by that given in himself; hence, he goes beyond himself, and also goes beyond the Master who is tied to the given which, not working, he leaves intact. If the fear of death, incarnated for the Slave in the person of the warlike Master, is the *sine qua non* of historical progress, it is solely the Slave's work that realizes and perfects it.]

However, the feeling of absolute power that the Slave experienced as such in the fight and also experiences in the particularities of service [for the Master whom he fears] is as yet only dissolution effected *in itself*. [Without this sense of power—i.e., without the terror and dread inspired by the Master—man would never be Slave and consequently could not attain the final perfection. But this condition "in itself"—i.e., this objectively real and necessary condition—is not sufficient. Perfection (which is always conscious of itself) can be attained only in and by work. For only in and by work does man finally become aware of the significance, the value, and the necessity of his experience of fearing absolute power, incarnated for him in the Master. Only after having worked for the Master does he understand the necessity of the fight between Master and Slave and the value of the risk and terror that it implies.] Thus, although the terror inspired by the Master is the beginning of wisdom, it can only be said that in this terror Consciousness exists *for itself*, but is not yet *Being-for-itself*. [In mortal terror man becomes aware of his reality, of the value that the simple fact of living has for him; only thus does he take account of the "seriousness" of existence. But he is not yet aware of his autonomy, of the value and the "seriousness" of his liberty, of his human dignity.] But through work Consciousness comes to itself. [In work, i.e.] in the constituent-element that corresponds to Desire in the Master's consciousness, it seemed, it is true, that the nonessential relation to the thing was what fell to the lot of the slavish Consciousness; this is because the thing preserves its autonomy. [It seemed that, in and by work, the Slave is enslaved to Nature, to the thing, to "raw material"; while the Master, who is content to consume the thing prepared by the Slave and to enjoy it, is perfectly free with respect to it. But this is not the case. To be sure] the [Master's] Desire has reserved for itself the pure act-of-negating the object [by consuming it] and has thereby reserved for itself the unmixed sentiment-of-self-and-of-one's-dignity [experienced in enjoyment]. But for the same reason this satisfaction itself is but a passing phase, for it lacks the *objective* aspect—i,e., the *stable support*. [The Master, who does not work, produces nothing stable outside of himself. He merely destroys the products of the Slave's work. Thus his enjoyment and his satisfaction remain purely subjective: they are of interest only to him and therefore can be recognized only by him; they have no "truth," no objective reality revealed to all. Accordingly, this "consumption," this idle enjoyment of the Master's, which results from the "immediate" satisfaction of desire, can at the most procure some pleasure for man; it can never give him complete and definitive satisfaction.] Work, on the other hand, is *repressed* Desire, an *arrested* passing phase; or, in other words, it forms-and-educates. [Work transforms the World and civilizes, educates, Man. The man who wants to work—or who must work—must repress the instinct that drives him "to consume" "immediately" the "raw" object. And the Slave can work for the Master—that is, for another than himself—only by repressing his own desires. Hence, he transcends himself by working—or, perhaps better, he educates himself, he "cultivates" and "sublimates" his instincts by repressing them. On the other hand, he does not destroy the thing as it is given. He postpones the destruction of the thing by first trans-forming it through work; he prepares it for consumption—that is to say, he "forms" it. In his work, he trans-forms things and trans-forms himself at the same time: he forms things and the World by transforming himself, by educating himself; and he educates himself, he forms himself, by transforming things and the World. Thus,] the negative-or-negating relation to the object becomes a *form* of this object and gains *permanence*, precisely because, for the worker, the object has autonomy. At the same time, the *negative-or-negating* middle-term—i.e., the forming *activity* [of work]—is the *isolated-particularity* or the pure Being-for-itself of the Consciousness. And this Being-for-itself, through work, now passes into what is outside of the Consciousness, into the element of permanence. The working Consciousness thereby attains a contemplation of autonomous given-being such that it contemplates *itself* in it. [The product of work is the worker's production. It is the realization of his project, of his idea; hence, it is he that is realized in and by this product, and consequently he contemplates himself when he contemplates it. Now, this artificial product is at the same time just as "autonomous," just as objective, just as independent of man, as is the natural thing. Therefore, it is by work, and only by work, that man *realizes* himself *objectively* as man. Only after producing an artificial object is man himself really and objectively more than and different from a natural being; and only in this real and objective product does he become truly conscious of his subjective human reality. Therefore, it is only by work that man is a supernatural being that is conscious of its reality; by working, he is "incarnated" Spirit, he is historical "World," he is "objectivized" History.

[Work, then, is what "forms-or-educates" man beyond the animal. The "formed-or-educated" man, the completed man who is satisfied by his completion, is hence necessarily not Master, but Slave; or, at least, he who has passed through Slavery. Now, there is no Slave without a Master. The Master, then, is the catalyst of the historical, anthropogenetic process. He himself does not participate actively in this process; but without him, without his presence, this process would not be possible. For, if the history of man is the history of his work, and if this work is historical, social, human, only on the condition that it is carried out against the worker's instinct or "immediate interest," the work must be carried out in the service of another, and must be a forced work, stimulated by fear of death. It is this work, and only this work, that frees—i.e., humanizes—man (the Slave). On the one hand, this work creates a real objective World, which is a non-natural World, a cultural, historical, human World. And it is only in this World that man lives an essentially different life from that of animals (and "primitive" man) in the bosom of Nature. On the other hand, this work liberates the Slave from the terror that tied him to given Nature and to his own innate animal nature. It is by work in the Master's service performed in terror that the Slave frees himself from the terror that enslaved him to the Master.]

Now, the forming [of the thing by work] contains not only the positive significance that the slavish Consciousness, taken as pure *Being-for-itself*, becomes an *entity that exists as a given-being* [that is to say, work is something more than the action by which man creates an essentially human technical World that is just as real as the natural World inhabited by animals]. The forming [of the thing by work] has a further negative-or-negating significance that is directed against the first constituent-element of the slavish Consciousness; namely, against fear. For in the act of forming the thing, the negating-negativity proper of Consciousness—i.e., its Being-for-itself—comes to be an Object [i.e., a World] for Consciousness only by the fact that Consciousness [dialectically] overcomes the opposed *form* that exists as a [natural] given-being. Now, this objective *negative-entity* is precisely the foreign essential-reality before which slavish Consciousness trembled. Now, on the contrary, this Consciousness destroys that foreign negative-entity [in and by work]. Consciousness establishes *itself* as a negative-entity in the element of permanency; and thereby it becomes a thing *for itself*, an *entity-existing-for-itself*. In the Master, *Being-for-itself* is, for the slavish Consciousness, *an other* Being-for-itself; or again, Being-for-itself exists there only *for the slavish Consciousness*. In fear, Being-for-itself [already] exists *in the slavish Consciousness itself*. But in the act of forming [by work], Being-for-itself is constituted for slavish Consciousness as *its own*, and slavish Consciousness becomes aware of the fact that it itself exists in and for itself. The form [the idea or project conceived by the Consciousness], by being *established outside* [of the Consciousness, by being introduced—through work—into the objective reality of the World], does not become, for the [working] Consciousness, an other-entity than it. For it is precisely that form that is its pure Being-for-itself; and, in that form, this Being-for-itself is constituted for it [the Consciousness] as truth [or as revealed, conscious, objective reality. The man who works recognizes his own product in the World that has actually been transformed by his work: he recognizes himself in it, he sees in it his own human reality, in it he discovers and reveals to others the objective reality of his humanity, of the originally abstract and purely subjective idea he has of himself.] By this act of finding itself by itself, then, the [working] Consciousness becomes *its own meaning-or-will*; and this happens precisely in work, in which it seemed to be *alien meaning-or-will*.

[Man achieves his true autonomy, his authentic freedom, only after passing through Slavery, after surmounting fear of death by work performed in the service of another (who, for him, is the incarnation of that fear). Work that frees man is hence necessarily, in the beginning, the forced work of a Slave who serves an all-powerful Master, the holder of all real power.]

For that reflection [of Consciousness into itself], the [following] two constituent-elements [first, that] of terror, and [second, that] of service as such, as well as the educative-forming [by work], are equally necessary. And, at the same time, the two elements are necessary in a universal way. [On the one hand,] without the discipline of service and obedience, terror remains in the formal domain and is not propagated in the conscious objective-reality of existence. [It is not sufficient to be afraid, nor even to be afraid while realizing that one fears death. It is necessary to live in terms of terror. Now, to live in such a way is to serve someone whom one fears, someone who inspires or incarnates terror; it is to serve a Master (a real, that is, a human Master, or the "sublimated" Master—God). And to serve a Master is to obey his laws. Without this service, terror could not transform existence, and existence, therefore, could never go beyond its initial state of terror. It is by serving another, by externalizing oneself, by binding oneself to others, that one is liberated from the enslaving dread that the idea of death inspires. On the other hand,] without the educative-forming [by work], terror remains internal-or-private and mute, and Consciousness does not come into being for itself. [Without work that transforms the real objective World, man cannot really transform himself. If he changes, his change remains "private," purely subjective, revealed to himself alone, "mute," not communicated to others. And this "internal" change puts him at variance with the World, which has not changed, and with the others, who are bound to the unchanged World. This change, then, transforms man into a madman or a criminal, who is sooner or later annihilated by the natural and social objective reality. Only work, by finally putting the objective World into harmony with the subjective idea that at first goes beyond it, annuls the element of madness and crime that marks the attitude of every man who—driven by terror—tries to go beyond the given World of which he is afraid, in which he feels terrified, and in which, consequently, he could not be satisfied.] But, if the Consciousness forms [the thing by work] without having experienced absolute primordial terror, it is merely its vain intention or self-will; for the form or the negating-negativity of that Consciousness is not negating-negativity *in itself*; and consequently its act-of-forming cannot give it consciousness of itself as the essential-reality. If the Consciousness has not endured absolute terror, but merely some fear or other, the negative-or-negating essential-reality remains an external-entity for it, and its [own] substance is not entirely infected by this essential-reality. Since all the fulfillments-or-accomplishments of its natural consciousness have not vacillated, that Consciousness still belongs—*in itself*—to determined given-being. Its intention or self-will [*der eigene Sinn*] is then stubborn-capriciousness [*Eigensinn*]: a freedom that still remains within the bounds of Slavery. The pure form [imposed on the given by this work] cannot come into being for that Consciousness, as essential-reality. Likewise, considered as extension over particular-and-isolated entities, this form is not [a] universal educative-forming; it is not absolute Concept. This form, on the contrary, is a skillfulness that dominates only certain things, but does not dominate universal power and the totality of objective essential-reality.

[The man who has not experienced the fear of death does not know that the given natural World is hostile to him, that it tends to kill him, to destroy him, and that it is essentially unsuited to satisfy him really. This man, therefore, remains fundamentally bound to the given World. At the most, he will want to "reform" it—that is, to change its details, to make particular transformations without modifying its essential characteristics. This man will act as a "skillful" reformer, or better, a conformer, but never as a true revolutionary. Now, the given World in which he lives belongs to the (human or divine) Master, and in this World he is necessarily Slave. Therefore, it is not reform, but the "dialectical," or better, revolutionary, overcoming of the World that can free him, and—consequently—satisfy him. Now, this revolutionary transformation of the World presupposes the "negation," the non-accepting of the given World *in its totality*. And the origin of this absolute negation can only be the absolute dread inspired by the given World, or more precisely, by that which, or by him who, dominates this World, by the Master of this World. Now, the Master who (involuntarily) engenders the desire of revolutionary negation is the Master of the Slave. Therefore, man can free himself from the given World that does not satisfy him only if this World, in its totality, belongs properly to a (real or "sublimated") Master. Now, as long as the Master lives, he himself is always enslaved by the World of which he is the Master. Since the Master transcends the given World only in and by the risk of his life, it is only his death that "realizes" his freedom. As long as he lives, therefore, he never attains the freedom that would raise him above the given World. The Master can never detach himself from the World in which he lives, and if this World perishes, he perishes with it. Only the Slave can transcend the given World (which is subjugated by the Master) and not perish. Only the Slave can transform the World that forms him and fixes him in slavery and create a World that he has formed in which he will be free. And the Slave achieves this only through forced and terrified work carried out in the Master's service. To be sure, this work by itself does not free him. But in transforming the World by this work, the Slave transforms himself, too, and thus creates the new objective conditions that permit him to take up once more the liberating Fight for recognition that he refused in the beginning for fear of death. And thus in the long run, all slavish work realizes not the Master's will, but the will—at first unconscious—of the Slave, who—finally—succeeds where the Master—necessarily—fails. Therefore, it is indeed the originally dependent, serving, and slavish Consciousness that in the end realizes and reveals the ideal of autonomous Self-Consciousness and is thus its "truth."]

2

SUMMARY OF THE FIRST SIX CHAPTERS
OF THE *PHENOMENOLOGY OF SPIRIT*

*Complete Text of the First Three Lectures
of the Academic Year 1937–1938*

We still have the last two chapters of the *Phenomenology of Spirit* to read. Chapter VII is entitled "Religion"; Chapter VIII, "Das absolute Wissen," absolute Knowledge. This "absolute Knowledge" is nothing other than the complete System of Hegelian philosophy or "Science," which Hegel expounded later in the *Encyclopaedia of Philosophical Sciences*. In Chapter VIII, then, the problem is not to develop the *content* of absolute Knowledge. It is concerned only with this Knowledge itself, as a kind of "faculty." It is concerned with showing what this *Knowledge* must be, what the Man must be who is endowed with a Knowledge that permits him completely and adequately to reveal the *totality* of existing Being. In particular, it will be concerned with differentiating this absolute philosophical Knowledge from *another* Knowledge, which also claims to be absolute—the Knowledge implied in the Christian revelation and the theology that follows from it. Therefore, one of the principal themes of Chapter VIII is the comparison between Hegelian philosophy or "Science" and the Christian religion.

Now, in order to understand fully the essential character of these two phenomena and of the relations between them, one must consider them in their genesis.

The genesis of Christianity, of the "absolute *Religion*," starting from the most "primitive" religion, is described in Chapter VII. As for the genesis of Hegel's philosophy, one can say that the whole *Phenomenology*—and particularly Chapters I through VI, which we have already read—is nothing but a description of the genesis that culminates in the production of the *Phenomenology*, which itself *describes* this *genesis* of philosophy and thus makes it possible by *understanding* its possibility. Chapters I through VI, which show how and why Man could finally reach absolute Knowledge, also complete the analysis of the Christian or absolute *Religion* given in Chapter VII. According to Hegel—to use the Marxist terminology—Religion is only an ideological superstructure that is born and exists solely in relation to a *real* substructure. This substructure, which supports both Religion and Philosophy, is nothing but the totality of human *Actions* realized during the course of universal history, that History in and by which Man has *created* a series of specifically *human Worlds*, essentially different from the natural World. It is these social Worlds that are reflected in the religious and philosophical ideologies, and therefore—to come to the point at once—*absolute* Knowledge, which reveals the *totality* of Being, can be realized only at the *end* of History, in the *last* World created by Man.

To understand what absolute Knowledge is, to know how and why this Knowledge has become possible, one must therefore understand the whole of universal history. And this is what Hegel has done in Chapter VI.

However, to understand the edifice of universal history and the process of its construction, one must know the materials that were used to construct it. These materials are men. To know what *History* is, one must therefore know what Man who realizes it is. Most certainly, man is something quite different from a brick. In the first place, if we want to compare universal history to the construction of an edifice, we must point out that men are not only the bricks that are used in the construction; they are also the masons who build it and the architects who conceive the plan for it, a plan, moreover, which is progressively elaborated during the construction itself. Furthermore, even as "brick," man is essentially different from a material brick: even the human brick changes during the construction, just as the human mason and the human architect do. Nevertheless, there is something in Man, in every man, that makes him suited to participate—passively or actively—in the realization of universal history. At the *beginning* of this History, which ends finally in absolute Knowledge, there are, so to speak, the necessary and sufficient conditions. And Hegel studies these conditions in the first four chapters of the *Phenomenology*.

Finally, Man is not only the material, the builder, and the architect of the historical edifice. He is also the one *for* whom this edifice is constructed: he lives in it, he *sees* and *understands* it, he *describes* and *criticizes* it. There is a whole category of men who do not actively participate in the historical construction and who are content to live in the constructed edifice and to *talk* about it. These men, who live somehow "above the battle," who are content to *talk* about things that they do not create by their *Action*, are Intellectuals who produce intellectuals' *ideologies*, which they take for philosophy (and pass off as such). Hegel describes and criticizes these ideologies in Chapter V.

Therefore, once again: the whole of the *Phenomenology*, summarized in Chapter VIII, must answer the question, "What is absolute Knowledge and how is it possible?"; that is to say: what must Man and his historical evolution be, so that, at a certain moment in that evolution, a human *individual*, by chance having the name of Hegel, sees that he has an *absolute* Knowledge—i.e., a Knowledge that reveals to him no longer a particular and momentary *aspect* of Being (which he mistakes for the totality of Being), but Being in its integral *whole*, as it is in and for itself?

Or again, to present the same problem in its Cartesian aspect: the *Phenomenology* must answer the question of the philosopher who believes he can attain the definitive or absolute truth: "I think, therefore I *am*; but *what* am I?"

The Cartesian reply to the philosophers' question, "What am I?" —the reply, "I am a thinking being"—does not satisfy Hegel.

Certainly, he must have said to himself, "I *am* a thinking being. But what interests me above all is that I am a *philosopher*, able to reveal the definitive *truth*, and hence endowed with an *absolute* Knowledge—that is, a *universally* and *eternally* valid Knowedge. Now, if *all* men are 'thinking beings,' I *alone*—at least for the moment—possess this Knowledge. By asking myself 'what am I?' and by answering 'a thinking being,' I therefore understand nothing, or very little, of myself.

"I am not only a thinking being. I am the bearer of an absolute Knowledge. And this Knowledge is actually, at the moment when

I think, incarnated in me, Hegel. Therefore, I am not only a thinking being; I am also—and above all—Hegel. What, then, is this Hegel?"

To begin with, he is a man of flesh and blood, who *knows* that he is such. Next, this man does not float in empty space. He is seated on a chair, at a table, writing with a pen on paper. And he *knows* that all these objects did not fall from the sky; he knows that those things are products of something called human *work*. He also knows that this work is carried out in a human *World*, in the bosom of a Nature in which he himself participates. And this World is present in his mind at the very moment when he writes to answer his "What am I?" Thus, for example, he hears sounds from afar. But he does not hear mere *sounds*. He *knows* in addition that these sounds are cannon shots, and he knows that the cannons too are products of some *Work*, manufactured in this case for a *Fight* to the death between men. But there is still more. He knows that he is hearing shots from Napoleon's cannons at the Battle of Jena. Hence he knows that he lives in a World in which Napoleon is acting.

Now, this is something that Descartes, Plato, and so many other philosophers did *not* know, *could* not know. And is it not because of this that Hegel attains that absolute Knowledge to which his predecessors *vainly* aspired?

Perhaps. But why then is it *Hegel* who attains it, and not some other of his contemporaries, all of whom know that there is a man named Napoleon? But *how* do they know him? Do they *truly* know him? Do they know *what* Napoleon is? Do they *understand* him?

Now, in fact, what is it to "understand" Napoleon, other than to understand him as the one who perfects the ideal of the French Revolution by *realizing* it? And can one understand this idea, this Revolution, without understanding the ideology of the *Aufklärung*, the Enlightenment? Generally speaking, to understand Napoleon is to understand him in relation to the whole of anterior historical evolution, to understand the whole of universal history. Now, almost none of the philosophers contemporary with Hegel posed this problem for himself. And none of them, except Hegel, resolved it. For Hegel is the only one able to accept, and to justify, Napoleon's existence—that is, to "deduce" it from the first principles of his philosophy, his anthropology, his conception of history. The others consider themselves obliged to condemn Napoleon, that is, to condemn the historical *reality*; and their philosophical systems—by that very fact—are all condemned by that reality.

Is he not this *Hegel*, a thinker endowed with an *absolute* Knowledge, because on the one hand, he *lives* in Napoleon's time, and, on the other, is the *only* one to *understand* him?

This is precisely what Hegel says in the *Phenomenology*.

Absolute Knowledge became—*objectively*—possible because in and by Napoleon the *real* process of historical evolution, in the course of which man *created* new Worlds and *transformed* himself by creating them, came to its end. To reveal *this* World, therefore, is to reveal *the* World—that is, to reveal being in the *completed* totality of its spatial-temporal existence. And—*subjectively*—absolute Knowledge became possible because a man named Hegel was able to understand the *World* in which he lived and to understand *himself* as living in and understanding this World. Like each of his contemporaries, Hegel was a microcosm, who incorporated in *his* particular being the completed *totality* of the spatial-temporal realization of *universal* being. But he was the only one to *understand* himself as this whole, to give a correct and complete answer to the Cartesian question, "What am I?" By understanding himself through the understanding of the *totality* of the anthropogenetic historical process, which ends with Napoleon and his contemporaries, and by understanding this process through his understanding *of himself*, Hegel caused the completed whole of the universal real process to penetrate into his individual consciousness, and then he penetrated this consciousness. Thus this consciousness became just as total, as universal, as the process that it revealed by understanding itself; and this fully self-conscious consciousness *is* absolute Knowledge, which, by being developed in discourse, will form the content of absolute *philosophy* or Science, of that *Encyclopaedia of the Philosophical Sciences* that contains the sum of all possible knowledge.

Descartes' philosophy is insufficient because the answer that it gives to the "What am I?" was insufficient, incomplete from the beginning. To be sure, Descartes *could* not realize absolute, Hegelian philosophy. At the moment when he lived, history was not yet completed. Even if he had *fully* understood himself, then, he would have conceived only a *part* of the human reality, and his system founded on this understanding of himself would necessarily be insufficient and false, to the extent that it lays claim to *totality*, as every system worthy of the name must. But it must also be said that Descartes—for reasons that Hegel explains—erred in answering his initial question. And that is why his answer, "I am a *thinking* being," is not only too summary, but also false, because it is one-sided.

Starting with "I think," Descartes fixed his attention only on the "think," completely neglecting the "I." Now, this I is essential. For Man, and consequently the Philosopher, is not only Consciousness, but also—and above all—*Self*-Consciousness. Man is not only a being that *thinks*—i.e., reveals Being by *Logos*, by *Speech* formed of words that have a *meaning*. He reveals in addition—also by Speech—the being that *reveals* Being, the being that he himself is, the revealing being that he *opposes* to the revealed being by giving it the name *Ich* or *Selbst*, I or Self.

To be sure, there is no human existence without *Bewusstsein*, without *Consciousness* of the external world. But for there *truly* to be human existence, capable of becoming a *philosophic* existence, there must also be *Self*-Consciousness. And for there to be *Self*-Consciousness, *Selbst-bewusstsein*, there must be this *Selbst*, this specifically human thing that is revealed by man and reveals itself when man says, "I. . . ."

Before analyzing the "*I think*," before proceeding to the Kantian theory of *knowledge*—i.e., of the relation between the (conscious) *subject* and the (conceived) object, one must ask what this subject is that is revealed in and by the *I* of "I think." One must ask when, why, and how man is led to say "I. . . ."

For there to be Self-Consciousness, there must—first of all—be Consciousness. In other words, there must be revelation of Being by Speech, if only by the one word *Sein*, Being—revelation of a Being that will later be called "*objective, external, non*-human being," "World," "Nature," and so on, but for the moment is still *neutral*, since as yet there is no Self-Consciousness and consequently no opposition of subject to object, of I to non-I, of the human to the natural.

Hegel studies the most elementary form of Consciousness, of knowledge of Being, and of its revelation by Speech, in Chapter I, given the name "Sensual Certainty" (*sinnliche Gewissheit*). I shall not repeat what he says there. What interests us for the moment is that, starting from *this* Consciousness, from *this* knowledge, there is no way to reach *Self*-Consciousness. To reach it, one must start from something *other* than *contemplative* knowledge of Being, other than its *passive* revelation, which leaves Being as it is in itself, independent of the knowledge that reveals it.

Indeed, we all know that the man who attentively *contemplates* a thing, who wants to see it as it is without changing anything, is "*absorbed*," so to speak, by this contemplation—that is, by this *thing*. He *forgets himself*, he thinks only about the *thing* being contemplated; he thinks neither about his *contemplation*, nor—and even less—about himself, his "I," his *Selbst*. The more he is conscious of the *thing*, the less he is conscious of *himself*. He may perhaps talk about the thing, but he will never talk about himself; in his discourse, the word "I" will not occur.

For this word to appear, something other than purely passive contemplation, which only *reveals* Being, must also be present. And this other thing, according to Hegel, is *Desire, Begierde*, of which he speaks in the beginning of Chapter IV.

Indeed, when man experiences a desire, when he is hungry, for example, and wants to eat, and when he becomes aware of it, he necessarily becomes aware of *himself*. Desire is always revealed as *my* desire, and to reveal desire, one must use the word "I." Man is *absorbed* by his contemplation of the thing in vain; as soon as *desire* for that thing is born, he will immediately be "brought back to *himself*." Suddenly, he will see that, in addition to the thing, there is his contemplation, there is *himself*, which is *not* that thing. And the thing appears to him as an *object* (*Gegen-stand*), as an *external* reality, which is not in him, which is not *he* but a *non*-I.

Hence, it is not purely cognitive and passive contemplation that is at the base of *Self*-Consciousness—i.e., of truly *human* existence (and therefore—in the end—of philosophical existence), but *Desire*. (And, in parenthesis, that is why human existence is possible only where there is something called *Leben*, biological, *animal* life. For there is no Desire without Life.)

Now, what is Desire—one need only think of the desire called "hunger"—but the desire to *transform* the contemplated thing by an action, to overcome it in its being that is unrelated to mine

37

and independent of me, to *negate* it in its independence, and to assimilate it to myself, to make it *mine*, to absorb it in and by my *I*? For Self-Consciousness, and hence philosophy, to exist, then, there must be in Man not only *positive*, passive contemplation, which merely *reveals* being, but also *negating* Desire, and hence *Action* that *transforms* the given being. The human I must be an I of *Desire*—that is, an *active* I, a *negating* I, an I that *transforms* Being and creates a new being by destroying the given being.

Now, what is the I of Desire—the I of a hungry man, for example—but an *emptiness* greedy for content; an emptiness that wants to be filled by what is full, to be filled by *emptying* this fullness, to put itself—once it is filled—in the place of this fullness, to occupy with *its* fullness the emptiness caused by overcoming the fullness that was *not* its own? Therefore, to speak generally: if the true (absolute) philosophy, unlike Kantian and pre-Kantian philosophy, is not a philosophy of *Consciousness*, but rather a philosophy of *Self*-Consciousness, a philosophy *conscious* of itself, taking account of itself, justifying itself, *knowing* itself to be absolute and revealed by itself to itself as such, then the Philosopher must—Man must—in the very foundation of his being not only be passive and positive *contemplation*, but also be active and negating Desire. Now, if he is to be so, he cannot be a *Being* that *is*, that is eternally *identical* to itself, that is self-*sufficient*. Man must be an emptiness, a nothingness, which is not a pure nothingness (*reines Nichts*), but something that *is* to the extent that it *annihilates* Being, in order to realize itself at the expense of Being and to nihilate *in* being. Man is negating *Action*, which transforms given Being and, by transforming it, transforms itself. Man *is* what he is only to the extent that he *becomes* what he is; his true *Being* (*Sein*) is *Becoming* (*Werden*), *Time*, *History*; and he *becomes*, he *is* History only in and by *Action* that negates the given, the Action of Fighting and of Work—of the Work that finally produces the table on which Hegel writes his *Phenomenology*, and of the Fight that is finally that Battle of Jena whose sounds he hears while writing the *Phenomenology*. And that is why, in answering the "What am I?" Hegel had to take account of both that table and those sounds.

There is no human existence without Consciousness or without Self-Consciousness—that is, without revelation of Being by Speech or without Desire that reveals and creates the I. That is why, in the *Phenomenology*—i.e., in phenomenological *anthropology*—the elementary possibility of *revelation* of given Being by Speech (implied in the Chapter "Sensual Certainty") on the one hand, and on the other, *Action* that destroys or negates given Being (Action that arises from and because of Desire), are two irreducible givens, which the *Phenomenology* presupposes as its *premises*. But these premises are not sufficient.

The analysis that uncovers the constituent role of Desire enables us to understand why human existence is possible only with an animal existence as its basis: a stone or a plant (having no Desire) never attains Self-Consciousness and consequently philosophy. But animals do not attain it either. *Animal* Desire, therefore, is a necessary, but not a sufficient, condition of human and philosophical existence. And here is why.

Animal Desire—hunger, for example—and the action that flows from it, negate, destroy the natural given. By negating it, modifying it, making it its own, the animal raises itself above this given. According to Hegel, the animal realizes and reveals its *superiority* to plants by eating them. But by feeding on plants, the animal *depends* on them and hence does not manage truly to go beyond them. Generally speaking, the greedy emptiness—or the I—that is revealed by *biological* Desire is filled—by the *biological* action that flows from it—only with a *natural*, biological content. Therefore, the I, or the pseudo-I, realized by the active satisfaction of this Desire, is just as *natural*, biological, material, as that toward which the Desire and the Action are directed. The Animal raises itself above the Nature that is negated in its animal Desire only to fall back into it immediately by the satisfaction of this Desire. Accordingly, the Animal attains only Selbst-*gefühl*, *Sentiment* of self, but not Selbst-*bewusstsein*, Self-*Consciousness*—that is, it cannot *speak* of itself, it cannot *say* "I. . . ." And this is so because the Animal does not really transcend itself as *given*—i.e., as body; it does not rise *above* itself in order to *come back* toward itself; it has no *distance* with respect to itself in order to *contemplate* itself.

For Self-Consciousness to exist, for philosophy to exist, there must be *transcendence* of self with respect to self as *given*. And this is possible, according to Hegel, only if Desire is directed not toward a *given* being, but toward a *non*being. To desire Being is to fill oneself with this given Being, to enslave oneself to it. To desire non-Being is to liberate oneself from Being, to realize one's autonomy, one's Freedom. To be anthropogenetic, then, Desire must be directed toward a nonbeing—that is, toward another *Desire*, another greedy emptiness, another *I*. For Desire is *absence* of Being, (to be hungry is to be *deprived* of food); it is a Nothingness that *nihilates* in Being, and not a Being that *is*. In other words, Action that is destined to satisfy an animal Desire, which is directed toward a given, existing *thing*, never succeeds in realizing a *human*, self-*conscious* I. Desire is human—or, more exactly, "humanizing," "anthropogenetic"—only provided that it is directed toward another *Desire* and an *other* Desire. To be *human*, man must act not for the sake of subjugating a *thing*, but for the sake of subjugating another *Desire* (for the thing). The man who desires a thing humanly acts not so much to possess the *thing* as to make another *recognize* his *right*—as will be said later—to that thing, to make another recognize him as the *owner* of the thing. And he does this—in the final analysis—in order to make the other recognize his *superiority* over the other. It is only Desire of such a *Recognition* (*Anerkennung*), it is only Action that flows from such a Desire, that creates, realizes, and reveals a *human*, non-biological I.

Therefore, the *Phenomenology* must accept a third irreducible premise: the existence of *several* Desires that can desire one another mutually, each of which wants to negate, to assimilate, to make its own, to subjugate, the other Desire as Desire. This *multiplicity* of Desires is just as "undeducible" as the fact of Desire itself. By accepting it, one can already foresee, or understand ("deduce"), what human existence will be.

If, on the one hand—as Hegel says—Self-Consciousness and Man in general are, finally, nothing but Desire that tries to be satisfied by being recognized by another Desire in its *exclusive* right to satisfaction, it is obvious that Man can be fully realized and revealed—that is, be definitively *satisfied*—only by realizing a universal Recognition. Now if—on the other hand—there is a *multiplicity* of these Desires for universal Recognition, it is obvious that the Action that is born of these Desires can—at least in the beginning—be nothing but a life and death *Fight* (*Kampf auf*

Leben und Tod). A *Fight*, since each will want to subjugate the other, *all* the others, by a negating, destroying *action*. A life and *death* Fight because Desire that is directed toward a Desire directed toward a Desire *goes beyond* the biological given, so that Action carried out for the sake of this Desire is not limited by this given. In other words, Man will risk his biological *life* to satisfy his *nonbiological* Desire. And Hegel says that the being that is incapable of putting its life in danger in order to attain ends that are not immediately vital—i.e. the being that cannot risk its life in a Fight for *Recognition*, in a fight for pure *prestige*—is *not* a truly *human* being.

Therefore, human, historical, self-conscious existence is possible only where there are, or—at least—where there have been, bloody fights, wars for prestige. And thus it was the sounds of one of these Fights that Hegel heard while finishing his *Phenomenology*, in which he became conscious of himself by answering his question "What am I?"

But it is obvious that the three already-mentioned premises in the *Phenomenology* are not sufficient to explain the possibility of the Battle of Jena. Indeed, if *all* men were as I have just said, every Fight for prestige would end in the death of at least one of the adversaries. That is to say, finally, there would remain *only one* man in the world, and—according to Hegel—he would no longer be, he would not be, a *human* being, since the human *reality* is nothing but the fact of the *recognition* of one man by *another* man.

To explain the fact of the Battle of Jena, the fact of the *History* that that battle completes, one must therefore posit a fourth and last irreducible premise in the *Phenomenology*. One must suppose that the Fight ends in such a way that *both* adversaries remain alive. Now, if this is to occur, one must suppose that one of the adversaries *gives in* to the other and submits to him, recognizing him without being recognized by him. One must suppose that the Fight ends in the victory of the one who is ready to go *all the way* over the one who—faced with death—does not manage to raise himself above his biological instinct of preservation (identity). To use Hegel's terminology, one must suppose that there is a victor who becomes the *Master* of the vanquished; or, if one prefers, a vanquished who becomes the *Slave* of the victor. The existence of a difference between Master and Slave or, more exactly, the *possibility* of a difference between *future* Master and *future* Slave is the fourth and last premise of the *Phenomenology*.

The vanquished has subordinated his *human* desire for *Recognition* to the *biological* desire to preserve his *life*: this is what determines and reveals—to him and to the victor—his inferiority. The victor has risked his *life* for a *non*vital end: and this is what determines and reveals—to him and to the vanquished—his superiority over biological life and, consequently, over the vanquished. Thus, the difference between Master and Slave is *realized* in the existence of the victor and of the vanquished, and it is *recognized* by both of them.

The Master's superiority over Nature, founded on the risk of his life in the Fight for prestige, is realized by the fact of the Slave's *Work*. This Work is placed between the Master and Nature. The Slave transforms the *given* conditions of existence so as to make them *conform* to the Master's demands. Nature, transformed by the Slave's Work, *serves* the Master, without his needing to serve it in turn. The enslaving side of the interaction with Nature falls to the lot of the Slave: by enslaving the Slave and forcing him to work, the Master enslaves Nature and thus *realizes* his freedom in Nature. Thus the Master's existence can remain exclusively *war-like*: he fights, but does not work. As for the Slave, his existence is reduced to *Work* (*Arbeit*) which he executes in the Master's *Service* (*Dienst*). He works, but does not fight. And according to Hegel, only action carried out in another's service is *Work* (*Arbeit*) in the proper sense of the word: an essentially human and humanizing action. The being that acts to satisfy its *own* instincts, which—as such—are always *natural*, does not rise above Nature: it remains a *natural* being, an animal. But by acting to satisfy an instinct that is *not* my own, I am acting in relation to what is not—for me—instinct. I am acting in relation to an *idea*, a *non*biological end. And it is this transformation of Nature in relation to a *non*material *idea* that is *Work* in the proper sense of the word: Work that creates a nonnatural, technical, humanized World adapted to the *human* Desire of a being that has *demonstrated* and realized its superiority to Nature by risking its life for the *non*biological end of Recognition. And it is only this Work that could finally produce the *table* on which Hegel wrote his *Phenomenology* and which was a part of the content of the I that he analyzed in answering his question, "What am I?"

Generally speaking, by accepting the four premises mentioned above, namely: (1) the existence of the revelation of given Being by Speech, (2) the existence of a Desire engendering an Action that *negates*, transforms, given Being, (3) the existence of *several* Desires, which can desire one another mutually, and (4) the existence of a *possibility* of difference between the Desires of (future) Masters and the Desires of (future) Slaves—by accepting these four premises, we understand the possibility of a *historical* process, of a *History*, which is, in its totality, the history of the Fights and the Work that finally ended in the wars of Napoleon and the table on which Hegel wrote the *Phenomenology* in order to *understand* both those wars and that table. Inversely, in order to explain the possibility of the *Phenomenology*, which is written on a *table* and which explains the wars of Napoleon, we must suppose the four premises mentioned.[1]

In fine, then, we can say this: Man was born and History began with the first Fight that ended in the appearance of a Master and a Slave. That is to say that Man—at his origin—is always either Master or Slave; and that true Man can exist only where there is a Master *and* a Slave. (If they are to be *human*, they must be at least *two* in number.) And universal history, the history of the interaction between men and of their interaction with Nature, is the history of the interaction between warlike Masters and working Slaves. Consequently, History stops at the moment when the difference, the opposition, between Master and Slave disappears: at the moment when the Master will cease to be Master, because

---

[1] We could try to deduce the first premise from the other three: Speech (*Logos*) that reveals Being is born in and from the Slave's Self-Consciousness (through Work). As for the fourth premise, it postulates the act of *freedom*. For nothing *predisposes* the future Master to Mastery, just as nothing *predisposes* the future Slave to Slavery; each can (freely) *create* himself as Master or Slave. What is *given*, therefore, is not the *difference* between Master and Slave, but the free act that *creates* it. Now, the *free* act is by definition "undeducible." Here, then, we have what is indeed an absolute *premise*. All we can say is that without the primordial free act that creates Mastery and Slavery, history and philosophy could not exist. Now, this act in turn presupposes a multiplicity of Desires that *desire one another mutually*.

he will no longer have a Slave; and the Slave will cease to be Slave, because he will no longer have a Master (although the Slave will not become Master in turn, since he will have no Slave).

Now, according to Hegel, it is in and by the wars of Napoleon, and, in particular, the Battle of Jena, that this completion of History is realized through the dialectical overcoming (*Aufheben*) of both the Master and the Slave. Consequently, the presence of the Battle of Jena in Hegel's consciousness is of capital importance. It is because Hegel hears the sounds of that battle that he can know that History is being completed or has been completed, that—consequently—*his* conception of the World is a *total* conception, that *his* knowledge is an *absolute* knowledge.

However, to *know* this, to know that he is the thinker who can realize the absolute Science, he must *know* that the Napoleonic Wars realize the dialectical synthesis of the Master and the Slave. And to know this, he must know: on the one hand, what the *essence* (*Wesen*) of the Master and the Slave is; and—on the other —how and why History, which began with the "first" Fight for prestige, ended in the wars of Napoleon.

The analysis of the essential character of the Master-Slave opposition—that is, of the motive principle of the historical process— is found in Chapter IV. And as for the analysis of the historical process itself, it is given in Chapter VI.

History, that universal human process that conditioned the coming of Hegel, of the thinker endowed with an *absolute* Knowledge, a process that that thinker must *understand* in and by a *Phenomenology* before he can realize this absolute Knowledge in the "System of Science"—universal history, therefore, is nothing but the history of the *dialectical*—i.e., *active*—relation between Mastery and Slavery. Hence, History will be completed at the moment when the synthesis of the Master and the Slave is realized, that synthesis that is the whole Man, the Citizen of the universal and homogeneous State created by Napoleon.

This conception, according to which History is a dialectic or an inter*action* of Mastery and Slavery, permits us to understand the *meaning* of the division of the historical process into three great periods (of very unequal lengths, incidentally). If History begins with the Fight after which a Master *dominates* a Slave, the first historical period must certainly be the one in which human existence is entirely determined by the existence of the *Master*. Throughout this period, then, it is *Mastery* that will reveal its essence by realizing its existential possibilities through Action. But if History is only a dialectic of Mastery *and* Slavery, this latter too must be entirely revealed by being completely realized through Action. Therefore, the first period must be completed by a second, in which human existence will be determined by *slavish* existence. Finally, if the end of History is the *synthesis* of Mastery and Slavery, and the *understanding* of that synthesis, these two periods must be followed by a third, during which human existence, in some sense neutralized, synthetic, reveals itself to itself by actively realizing its own *possibilities*. But this time, these possibilities also imply the possibility of understanding oneself fully and definitively —that is, perfectly.

But of course, in order to write Chapter VI, in order to understand what History is, it is not sufficient to know that History has three periods. One must also know what each of them is, one must understand the why and the how of each of them and of the transition from one to another. Now, to understand this, one must know what is the *Wesen*, the essential-reality, of Mastery and Slavery, what is the essence of the two principles which, in their interaction, are going to realize the process being studied. And this analysis of the Master as such and of the Slave as such is made in Section B of Chapter IV.

Let us begin with the Master.

The Master is the man who went all the way in a Fight for prestige, who risked his *life* in order to be *recognized* in his absolute superiority by *another* man. That is, to his *real*, natural biological life he preferred something *ideal*, spiritual, *non*biological: the fact of being *anerkannt*, of being *recognized* in and by a *consciousness*, of bearing the *name* of "Master," of being *called* "Master." Thus, he "brought to light," proved (*bewährt*), realized, and revealed his *superiority* over biological existence, over *his* biological existence, over the natural World in general and over everything that knows itself and that he knows to be *bound* to this World, in particular, over the Slave. This superiority, at first purely *ideal*, which consists in the mental fact of being recognized and of knowing that he is recognized as Master by the Slave, is *realized* and materialized through the Slave's *Work*. The Master, who was able to force the Slave to *recognize* him as Master, can also force the Slave to *work* for him, to yield the result of his *Action* to him. Thus, the Master no longer needs to make any effort to satisfy his (natural) desires. The *enslaving* side of this satisfaction has passed to the Slave: the Master, by dominating the working Slave, dominates Nature and lives in it as *Master*. Now, to preserve oneself in Nature without fighting against it is to live in *Genuss*, in Enjoyment. And the enjoyment that one obtains without making any effort is *Lust*, Pleasure. The life of the Masters, to the extent that it is not bloody Fighting, Fighting for prestige with human beings, is a life of pleasure.

At first glance, it seems that the Master realizes the peak of human existence, being the man who is fully satisfied (*befriedigt*), in and by his real existence, by what he is. Now in fact, this is not at all the case.

What is this man, what does he *want* to be, if not a Master? It was to become *Master*, to be *Master* that he risked his life, and not to live a life of pleasure. Now, what he wanted by engaging in the fight was to be recognized by *another*—that is, by someone *other* than himself but who is *like him*, by *another man*. But in fact, at the end of the Fight, he is recognized only by a *Slave*. To be a *man*, he wanted to be recognized by another man. But if to be a man is to be *Master*, the Slave is not a man, and to be recognized by a Slave is not to be recognized by a *man*. He would have to be recognized by another Master. But this is impossible, since— by definition—the Master prefers death to slavish recognition of another's superiority. In short, the Master never succeeds in realizing his end, the end for which he risks his very life. The Master can be satisfied only in and by death, *his* death or the death of his adversary. But one cannot be *befriedigt* (fully satisfied) by what *is*, by what one *is*, in and by *death*. For death *is* not, the dead man *is* not. And what *is*, what lives, is only a Slave. Now, is it worthwhile to risk one's life in order to know that one is recognized by a *Slave*? Obviously not. And that is why, to the extent that the Master is not made brutish by his pleasure and enjoyment, when he takes account of what his *true* end and the motive of his *actions* —i.e., his warlike actions—are, he will *not*, he will *never* be *befriedigt*, satisfied by what *is*, by what *he* is.

In other words, Mastery is an existential impasse. The Master can either make himself *brutish* in pleasure or *die* on the field of battle as Master, but he cannot *live consciously* with the knowledge that he is *satisfied* by what he *is*. Now, it is only conscious satisfaction, *Befriedigung*, that can complete History, for only the Man who *knows* he is *satisfied* by what he is no longer strives to go beyond himself, to go beyond what he is and what is, through Action that transforms Nature, through Action that creates History. If History must be *completed*, if absolute Knowledge must be possible, it is only the Slave who can do it, by attaining Satisfaction. And that is why Hegel says that the "truth" (= revealed reality) of the Master is the Slave. The human ideal, born in the Master, can be *realized* and revealed, can become *Wahrheit* (truth), only in and by Slavery.

To be able to stop and understand himself, a man must be *satisfied*. And for this, of course, he must *cease* to be a Slave. But to be able to cease being *Slave*, he must have *been* a Slave. And since there are Slaves only where there is a Master, Mastery, while itself an *impasse*, is "justified" as a *necessary* stage of the historical existence that leads to the absolute Science of Hegel. The Master appears only for the sake of engendering the Slave who "overcomes" (*aufhebt*) him as Master, while thereby "overcoming" himself as Slave. And this Slave who has been "overcome" is the one who will be satisfied by what he *is* and will understand that he is satisfied in and by Hegel's philosophy, in and by the *Phenomenology*. The Master is only the "catalyst" of the History that will be realized, completed, and "revealed" by the Slave or the ex-Slave who has become a Citizen.

But let us first see what the Slave is in the *beginning*, the Slave of the *Master*, the Slave not yet satisfied by the Citizenship that realizes and reveals his Freedom.

Man became a Slave because he feared death. To be sure, on the one hand this fear (*Furcht*) reveals his dependence with respect to Nature and thus justifies his dependence with respect to the Master, who *dominates* Nature. But on the other hand, this same fear—according to Hegel—has a positive value, which conditions the Slave's *superiority* to the Master. Through animal fear of death (*Angst*) the Slave experienced the dread or the Terror (*Furcht*) of Nothingness, of his nothingness. He caught a glimpse of himself as nothingness, he understood that his whole existence was but a "surpassed," "overcome" (*aufgehoben*) death—a Nothingness maintained in Being. Now—we have seen it and shall see it again—the profound basis of Hegelian anthropology is formed by this idea that Man is not a Being that *is* in an eternal identity to itself in Space, but a Nothingness that *nihilates* as Time in spatial Being, through the *negation* of this Being—through the negation or transformation of the given, starting from an idea or an ideal that does *not* yet *exist*, that is still nothingness (a "project")—through negation that is called the *Action* (*Tat*) of Fighting and of Work (*Kampf und Arbeit*). Hence the Slave, who—through fear of death—grasps the (human) Nothingness that is at the foundation of his (natural) Being, understands himself, understands Man, better than the Master does. From the "first" Fight, the Slave has an intuition of the human reality, and that is the profound reason that it is finally he, and not the Master, who will complete History by revealing the truth of Man, by revealing his reality through Hegelian Science.

But—still thanks to the Master—the Slave has another advantage, conditioned by the fact that he *works* and that he works in the *service* (*Dienst*) of *another*, that he *serves* another by *working*. To work for *another* is to act contrary to the *instincts* that drive man to satisfy his *own* needs. There is no *instinct* that forces the Slave to work for the Master. If he does it, it is from *fear* of the Master. But *this* fear is not the same as the fear he experienced at the moment of the Fight: the danger is no longer *immediate*; the Slave only *knows* that the Master can kill him; he does not *see* him in a murderous posture. In other words, the Slave who *works* for the Master represses his *instincts* in relation to an *idea*, a *concept*.[2] And that is precisely what makes his activity a specifically *human* activity, a *Work*, an *Arbeit*. By acting, he negates, he transforms the given, Nature, *his* Nature; and he does it in relation to an *idea*, to what does not *exist* in the biological sense of the word, in relation to the idea of a *Master*—i.e., to an essentially *social*, human, historical notion. Now, to be able to transform the natural given in relation to a *non*natural idea is to possess a *technique*. And the

[2] According to Hegel, Concept (*Begriff*) and Understanding (*Verstand*) are born of the Slave's Work, whereas sensual Knowledge (*sinnliche Gewissheit*) is an irreducible given. But one could try to deduce *all* human understanding from Work.

idea that engenders a technique is a *scientific* idea, a scientific concept. Finally, to possess scientific concepts is to be endowed with Understanding, *Verstand*, the faculty of *abstract* notions.

Understanding, abstract thought, science, technique, the arts—all these, then, have their origin in the forced work of the Slave. Therefore, the Slave, and not the Master, is the one who realizes all that has to do with these things; in particular Newtonian physics (which so impressed Kant), that physics of Force and of Law, which—according to Hegel—are in the final analysis the force of the victor in the Fight for prestige and the law of the Master who is recognized by the Slave.

But these are not the only advantages procured by Work; Work will also open the way to Freedom or—more exactly—to liberation.

Indeed, the Master realized his freedom by surmounting his *instinct* to live in the Fight. Now, by working for *another*, the Slave too surmounts his *instincts*, and—by thereby raising himself to thought, to science, to technique, by transforming Nature in relation to an idea—he too succeeds in dominating Nature and his "Nature"—that is, the same Nature that dominated him at the moment of the Fight and made him the Slave of the Master. Through his Work, therefore, the Slave comes to the same result to which the Master comes by risking his life in the Fight: he no longer depends on the given, natural conditions of existence; he *modifies* them, starting from the idea he has of himself. In becoming *conscious* of this fact, therefore, he becomes conscious of his *freedom* (*Freiheit*), his autonomy (*Selbständigkeit*). And, by using the *thought* that arises from his Work, he forms the abstract *notion* of the Freedom that has been realized in him by this same Work.

To be sure, in the Slave properly so-called this *notion* of Freedom does not yet correspond to a true *reality*. He frees himself mentally only thanks to *forced* work, only because he is the Slave of a Master. And he *remains* in fact this Slave. Thus he frees himself, so to speak, only to be a Slave freely, to be still more a Slave than he was before having formed the *idea* of Freedom. However, the insufficiency of the Slave is at the same time his perfection: this is because he *is* not actually free, because he has an *idea* of Freedom, an idea that is *not* realized but that can be realized by the conscious and voluntary transformation of given existence, by the active abolition of Slavery. The Master, on the other hand, *is* free; his idea of Freedom is not *abstract*. That is why it is not an *idea* in the proper sense of the word: an *ideal* to realize. And that is why the Master never succeeds in going beyond the freedom that is realized in *himself* and the insufficiency of *that* freedom. Progress in the realization of Freedom can be carried out only by the Slave, who begins with a *non*realized ideal of Freedom. And it is because he has an *ideal*, an *abstract* idea, that progress in the *realization* of Freedom can be completed by an *understanding* of Freedom, by the birth of the *absolute Idea* (*absolute Idee*) of human Freedom, revealed in and by absolute Knowledge.

Generally speaking, it is the Slave, and only he, who can realize a *progress*, who can go beyond the *given* and—in particular—the given that he himself is. On the one hand, as I just said, possessing the *idea* of Freedom and *not being* free, he is led to transform the given (social) conditions of his existence—that is, to realize a historical progress. Furthermore—and this is the important point—this progress has a meaning for him which it does not and cannot have for the Master. The Master's freedom, engendered in and by the Fight, is an impasse. To realize it, he must make it recognized by a *Slave*, he must transform whoever is to recognize it into a *Slave*. Now, my freedom ceases to be a dream, an illusion, an abstract idea, only to the extent that it is *universally recognized* by those whom I recognize as worthy of recognizing it. And this is precisely what the Master can *never* obtain. His freedom, to be sure, is recognized. Therefore, it is *real*. But it is recognized only by Slaves. Therefore, it is insufficient in its reality, it cannot *satisfy* him who realizes it. And yet, as long as it remains a Master's freedom, the situation cannot be otherwise. On the other hand, if—at the start—the Slave's freedom is recognized by no one but himself, if, consequently, it is purely *abstract*, it can end in being *realized* and in being realized in its *perfection*. For the Slave *recognizes* the human reality and dignity of the Master. Therefore, it is sufficient for him to impose his liberty on the Master in order to attain the definitive Satisfaction that *mutual* Recognition gives and thus to stop the historical process.

Of course, in order to do this, he must fight against the Master, that is to say—precisely—he must cease to be a Slave, surmount his fear of death. He must become *other* than what he *is*. Now, in contrast to the warlike Master who will always remain what he already *is*—i.e., Master—the working Slave can change, and he actually does change, thanks to his work.

The human Action of the Master reduces to risking his life. Now, the risk of life is the same at all times and in all places. The risk itself is what counts, and it does not matter whether a stone ax or a machine gun is being used. Accordingly, it is not the Fight as such, the risk of life, but *Work* that one day produces a machine gun, and no longer an ax. The purely warlike attitude of the Master does not vary throughout the centuries, and therefore it cannot engender a historical change. Without the Slave's Work, the "first" Fight would be reproduced indefinitely: nothing would change in it; it would change nothing in the Master; hence nothing would change in Man, through Man, for Man; the World would remain identical to itself, it would be Nature and not a human, historical World.

Quite different is the situation created by Work. Man who works *transforms* given Nature. Hence, if he repeats his act, he repeats it in *different* conditions, and thus his act itself will be different. After making the first ax, man can use it to make a second one, which, by that very fact, will be another, a better ax. Production transforms the means of production; the modification of means simplifies production; and so on. Where there is Work, then, there is necessarily change, progress, historical evolution.[3]

Historical evolution. For what changes as a result of Work is not only the natural World; it is also—and even especially—Man himself. Man, in the beginning, depends on the given, natural conditions of his existence. To be sure, he can rise above these conditions by risking his life in a Fight for prestige. But in this risk he somehow negates the *totality* of these conditions, which are still the same; he negates them *en masse*, without modifying them, and this negation is always the same. Accordingly, the freedom that he creates in and by this act of negation does not depend on the particular forms of the given. It is only by rising above the given conditions through negation brought about in and by *Work*

---

[3] A manufactured object incarnates an idea (a "project") which is independent of the material *hic et nunc*; that is why these objects can be "exchanged." Hence the birth of an "economic," specifically human World, in which money, capital, interest, salary, and so on appear.

that Man remains in contact with the concrete, which varies with space and time. That is why he changes himself by transforming the World.

The scheme of historical evolution, therefore, is as follows:

At the start, the future Master and the future Slave are both determined by a given, natural World independent of them: hence they are not yet truly human, historical beings. Then, by risking his life, the Master raises himself above given Nature, above his given (animal) "nature," and becomes a human being, a being that creates itself in and by its conscious negating Action. Then, he forces the Slave to work. The latter changes the real given World. Hence he too raises himself above Nature, above his (animal) "nature," since he succeeds in making it other than it was. To be sure, the Slave, like the Master, like Man in general, is determined by the real World. But since this World has been *changed*, he changes as well.[4] And since it was *he* who changed the World, it is *he* who changes himself, whereas the Master changes only through the Slave. Therefore, the historical process, the historical becoming of the human being, is the product of the working Slave and not of the warlike Master. To be sure, without the Master, there would have been no History; but only because without him there would have been no Slave and hence no Work.

Therefore—once more—thanks to his Work, the Slave *can* change and become other than he is, that is, he can—finally—cease to be a Slave. Work is *Bildung*, in the double meaning of the word: on the one hand, it forms, transforms the World, humanizes it by making it more adapted to Man; on the other, it transforms, forms, educates man, it humanizes him by bringing him into greater conformity with the *idea* that he has of himself, an idea that—in the beginning—is only an *abstract* idea, an *ideal*. If then, at the start, in the given World the Slave had a fearful "*nature*" and *had* to submit to the Master, to the strong man, it does not mean that this will *always* be the case. Thanks to his work, *he* can become other; and, thanks to his work, the *World* can become other. And

---

[4] Animals also have (pseudo) techniques: the first spider changed the World by weaving the first web. Hence it would be better to say: the World changes essentially (and becomes human) through "exchange," which is possible only as a result of Work that realizes a "project."

this is what actually took place, as universal history and, finally, the French Revolution and Napoleon show.

This creative education of Man by work (*Bildung*) creates History—i.e., human *Time*. Work *is* Time, and that is why it necessarily exists *in* time: it requires time. The transformation of the Slave, which will allow him to surmount his dread, his fear of the Master, by surmounting the terror of death—this transformation is long and painful. In the beginning, the Slave who—by his Work—raised himself to the abstract *idea* of his Freedom, does not succeed in *realizing* it, because he does not yet dare to *act* with a view to this realization, that is to say, he does not dare to fight against the Master and to risk his life in a Fight for Freedom.

Thus it is that, before *realizing* Freedom, the Slave imagines a series of ideologies, by which he seeks to justify himself, to justify his slavery, to reconcile the *ideal* of Freedom with the *fact* of Slavery.

The first of these Slave's ideologies is Stoicism. The Slave tries to persuade himself that he is *actually* free simply by *knowing* that he is free—that is, by having the abstract *idea* of Freedom. The *real* conditions of existence would have no importance at all: no matter whether one be a Roman emperor or a Slave, rich or poor, sick or healthy; it is sufficient to have the *idea* of freedom, or more precisely, of autonomy, of absolute independence of all *given* conditions of existence. (Whence—in parentheses—the modern variant of Stoicism, of which Hegel speaks in Chapter V: freedom is identified with freedom of *thought*; the State is called free when one can *speak* freely in it; so long as *this* freedom is safeguarded, nothing need be changed in that State.)

Hegel's criticism, or, more exactly, his explanation of the fact that Man did not stop at this Stoic solution which is so satisfying at first sight, can appear unconvincing and bizarre. Hegel says that Man abandons Stoicism because, as a Stoic, he is *bored*. The Stoic ideology was invented to justify the Slave's inaction, his refusal to *fight* to *realize* his libertarian ideal. Thus this ideology prevents Man from acting: it obliges him to be content with *talking*. Now, says Hegel, all discourse that remains discourse ends in *boring* Man.

This objection—or explanation—is simplistic only at first sight. In fact, it has a profound metaphysical basis. Man is not a Being that *is*: he is a Nothingness that *nihilates* through the negation of Being. Now, the negation of Being is Action. That is why Hegel says, "the *true* being of man is his *action*." Not to act, therefore, is not to be as a truly *human* being; it is to be as *Sein*, as given, natural being. Hence, it is to fall into decay, to become brutish; and this metaphysical truth is revealed to Man through the phenomenon of boredom: the Man who—like a thing, like an animal, like an angel—remains identical to himself, does not negate, does not negate himself—i.e., does not act, is *bored*. And only Man can be bored.

However that may be, it was the *boredom* caused by Stoic chatter that forced Man to seek something else. In fact, Man can be satisfied only by *action*. Now, to act is to transform what is real. And to transform what is real is to *negate* the given. In the Slave's case, to act effectively would be to negate Slavery—that is, to negate the Master, and hence to risk his life in a Fight against the Master. The Slave does not yet dare to do this. And with boredom driving him to action, he is content to activate his thought in some sense. He makes it *negate* the given. The Stoic Slave becomes the *skeptic-nihilist* Slave.

This new attitude culminates in Solipsism: the value, the very reality of all that is not I is denied, and the universality and radicalism of this negation makes up for its purely *abstract*, verbal character.

Nevertheless, Man does not succeed in remaining in this skeptical-nihilistic attitude. He does not succeed because in fact he contradicts himself through his very existence: how and why is one to live when one denies the value and the being of the World and of other men? Thus, to take nihilism seriously is to commit suicide, to cease completely to act and—consequently—to live. But the *radical* Skeptic does not interest Hegel, because, by definition, he disappears by committing suicide, he ceases to be, and consequently he ceases to be a human being, an agent of historical evolution. Only the Nihilist who *remains alive* is interesting.

Now, this latter must eventually perceive the contradiction implied in his existence. And, generally speaking, the awareness of a *contradiction* is what moves human, historical evolution. To become aware of a contradiction is necessarily to want to remove it. Now, one can in fact overcome the contradiction of a given existence only by *modifying* the, given existence, by transforming it through Action. But in the Slave's case, to transform existence is, again, to fight against the Master. Now, he does not want to do this. He tries, therefore, to justify by a new ideology this contradiction in skeptical existence, which is, all things considered, the Stoic—i.e., slavish—contradiction, between the *idea* or the *ideal* of Freedom and the *reality* of Slavery. And this third and last Slave's ideology is the *Christian* ideology.

At this point, the Slave does not deny the contradictory character of his existence. But he tries to justify it by saying that *all* existence necessarily, inevitably, implies a contradiction. To this end he imagines an "other world," which is "beyond" (*Jenseits*) the natural World of the senses. Here below he is a Slave, and he does nothing to free himself. But he is right, for in *this* World *everything* is Slavery, and the Master is as much a Slave here as he is. But freedom is not an empty word, a simple abstract *idea*, an unrealizable ideal, as in Stoicism and Skepticism. Freedom is *real*, real in the *Beyond*. Hence no need to fight against the Master, since one already *is* free to the extent that one participates in the Beyond, since one is freed by that Beyond, by the intervention of the Beyond in the World of the senses. No need to fight to be recognized by the Master, since one is recognized by a God. No need to fight to become free in this world, which is just as vain and stripped of value for the Christian as for the Skeptic. No need to fight, to act, since—in the Beyond, in the only World that truly counts—one *is* already freed and *equal* to the Master (in the Service of God). Hence one can maintain the Stoic attitude, but with good reason this time. And without being bored, too, for now one does not eternally remain the *same*: one changes and one *must* change, one must always go beyond oneself in order to rise above oneself as something given in the real empirical World, in order to attain the transcendental World, the Beyond which remains inaccessible.

Without Fighting, without effort, therefore, the Christian realizes the Slave's ideal: he obtains—in and through (or for) God—equality with the Master: inequality is but a mirage, like everything in this World of the senses in which Slavery and Mastery hold sway.

Certainly an ingenious solution, Hegel will say. And not at all astonishing that Man through the centuries could believe himself "satisfied" by this pious reward for his Work. But, Hegel adds, all this is too good—too simple, too easy—to be true. In fact, what made Man a Slave was his refusal to risk his life. Hence he will not cease to be a Slave, as long as he is not ready to risk his life in a *Fight* against the Master, as long as he does not accept the idea of his *death*. A liberation without a bloody Fight, therefore, is metaphysically impossible. And this metaphysical impossibility is also revealed in the Christian ideology itself.

Indeed, the Christian Slave can affirm his equality with the Master only by accepting the existence of an "other world" and a transcendent God. Now, this God is necessarily a *Master*, and an *absolute* Master. Thus the Christian frees himself from the human Master only to be enslaved to the divine Master. He does free himself—at least in his idea—from the human Master. But although he no longer has a Master, he does not cease to be a Slave. He is a Slave without a Master, he is a Slave in *himself*, he is the pure essence of Slavery. And this "absolute" Slavery engenders an equally absolute Master. It is before *God* that he is the equal of the Master. Hence he is the Master's equal only in absolute *slavery*. Therefore he remains a *Servant*, the servant of a Master for whose glory and pleasure he works. And this new Master is such that the new Christian Slave is even more a Slave than the pagan Slave.

And if the Slave accepts this new divine Master, he does it for the same reason that he accepted the human Master: through fear of death. He accepted—or produced—his first Slavery because it was the price of his biological *life*. He accepts—or produces—the second, because it is the price of his *eternal* life. For the fundamental motive of the ideology of the "two worlds" and the duality of human existence is the slavish desire for life at any price, sublimated in the desire for an *eternal* life. In the final analysis, Christianity is born from the Slave's terror in the face of Nothingness, his nothingness; that is, for Hegel, from the impossibility of bearing the necessary condition of Man's existence—the condition of death, of finiteness.[5]

[5] There is no human (conscious, articulate, free) existence without Fighting that implies the risk of life—i.e., without death, without finiteness. "Immortal man" is a "squared circle."

Consequently, to overcome the insufficiency of the Christian ideology, to become free from the absolute Master and the Beyond, to *realize* Freedom and to *live* in the World as a human being, autonomous and free—all this is possible only on the condition that one accept the idea of death and, consequently, atheism. And the whole evolution of the Christian World is nothing but a progress toward the atheistic awareness of the essential finiteness of human existence. Only thus, only by "overcoming" Christian *theology*, will Man definitively cease to be a Slave and *realize* this idea of Freedom which, while it remained an abstract idea—i.e., an ideal, engendered Christianity.

This is what is effected in and by the French Revolution, which completes the evolution of the Christian World and inaugurates the third historical World, in which *realized* freedom will finally be conceived (*begriffen*) by philosophy: by German philosophy, and *finally* by Hegel. Now, for a Revolution to succeed in overcoming Christianity *really*, the Christian ideal must first be *realized* in the form of a *World*. For, in order that an ideology may be surpassed, "overcome" by Man, Man must first experience the *realization* of this ideology in the real World in which he lives. The problem, therefore, is to know how the pagan World of Mastery can become a Christian World of Slavery, when there has been no Fight between Masters and Slaves, when there has been no Revolution properly so-called. For if these had taken place, the Slave would have become the free Worker who fights and risks his life; hence he would cease to be a Slave and consequently could not realize a *Christian*, essentially slavish, World.

Hegel resolves this problem in Section A of Chapter VI. Let us see what he says there. Since Hegel does not talk about the *genesis* of the pagan State in the *Phenomenology*, let us study it as a State already formed.

The essential character of this State, of pagan Society, is determined by the fact that it is a State, a Society, of *Masters*. The pagan State recognized only the Masters as citizens. Only he who makes war is a citizen, and it is only the citizen who makes war. The work is assigned to the Slaves, who are on the fringe of the Society and the State. And thus the State, in its totality, is a Master-State, which sees the meaning of its existence not in its work, but in its prestige, in the wars for prestige that it wages in order to make other States, *all* other States, recognize its autonomy and its supremacy.

Now, according to Hegel, it follows from all this that the pagan State of warlike and idle Masters can recognize, can make recognized or realize, only the *universal* element of human existence, while the *particular* element remains on the fringe of the Society and State proper.

This opposition of Particularity and Universality, of *Einzelheit* and *Allgemeinheit*, is fundamental for Hegel. And if History, according to him, can be interpreted as a dialectic of Mastery and Slavery, it can also be understood as a dialectic of the Particular and the Universal in human existence. Moreover, these two interpretations mutually complete one another, since Mastery corresponds to Universality and Slavery to Particularity.

Here is what this means:

Man from the start seeks *Anerkennung*, Recognition. He is not content with attributing a value to himself. He wants this *particular* value, *his own*, to be recognized by *all* men, *universally*.

In other words: Man can be truly "satisfied," History can end, only in and by the formation of a Society, of a State, in which the strictly particular, personal, individual value of each is recognized as such, in its very particularity, by *all*, by Universality incarnated in the State as such; and in which the universal value of the State is recognized and realized by the Particular as such, by *all* the Particulars.[6] Now such a State, such a synthesis of Particularity and Universality, is possible only after the "overcoming" of the opposition between the Master and the Slave, since the synthesis of the Particular and the Universal is also a synthesis of Mastery and Slavery.

As long as the Master is opposed to the Slave, as long as Mastery and Slavery exist, the synthesis of the Particular and the Universal cannot be realized, and human existence will never be "*satisfied*." This is true not only because the *Slave* is not universally recog-

[6] The Particular who realizes a universal value, moreover, is no longer a Particular: he is an Individual (= Citizen of the universal and homogeneous State), a synthesis of the Particular and the Universal. Likewise, the Universal (the State) realized by the Particular is individualized. It is the Individual-State or the State-Individual, incarnated in the person of the universal Head of State (Napoleon) and revealed by the Wise Man (Hegel).

nized; and not only because the Master himself does not achieve *truly* universal recognition, since he does not recognize a part of those who recognize him—the Slaves. This synthesis is impossible because the Master manages to realize and to make recognized only the *universal* element in Man, while the Slave reduces his existence to a purely *particular* value.

The Master constitutes his human value in and by the risk of his life. Now, this risk is everywhere and always—and in *all* men—the same. The Man who risks his life is in no way different, by the sole act of having risked his life, from all the others who have done as much. The human value constituted by the Fight is essentially *universal*, "impersonal." And that is why the Masters' State, which recognizes a man only to the extent that this man risks his life for the State in a war for prestige, recognizes only the purely *universal* element in man, in the citizen: the citizen of this State is just another citizen; as a citizen recognized by the State, he is no different from the others; he is *an* anonymous warrior, he is not Mr. *So-and-So.* And even the Head of State is just another representative of the State, of the Universal, and not an *Individual* properly so-called: in his activity he is a function of the State; the State is not a function of his personal, particular will. In short, the Head of the Greek City-State is not a "dictator" in the modern, Christian, romantic sense of the word. He is not a Napoleon, who *creates* a State through his *personal* will, with a view to realizing and making recognized his *Individuality*. The pagan Head of State accepts a *given* State, and his own value, his very reality, is but a function of this State, of this *universal* element of existence. And that is why the Master, the Pagan, is never "satisfied." Only the Individual can be "satisfied."

As for the Slave's existence, it is limited to the purely *particular* element. The human value constituted by *Work* is essentially *particular*, "personal." *Bildung*, the educative formation of the Worker by Work, depends on the concrete conditions in which the work is carried out, conditions that vary in space and are modified in time as a function of this very work. Therefore it is by Work, finally, that the differences between men are established, that the "particularities," the "personalities," are formed. And thus it is the working Slave, and not the warlike Master, who becomes *conscious* of his "personality" and who imagines "individualistic" ideologies, in which absolute value is attributed to Particularity, to "personality," and not to "Universality," to the State as such and to the Citizen taken as Citizen.

However, what is recognized *universally*, by the *others*, by the State, by Mastery as such, is not Work, nor the worker's "personality," but at best the impersonal *product* of work. As long as the Slave works while remaining a Slave, that is to say, as long as he does not risk his life, as long as he does not fight to impose his personal value on the State, as long as he does not actively intervene in the social life, his particular value remains purely *subjective*: he is the *only* one to recognize it. Hence his value is *uniquely* particular; the *synthesis* of the Particular and the Universal—i.e., Individuality—is no more realized in the Slave than in the Master. And that is why—once more—the synthesis of Particularity and Universality in Individuality, which alone can truly "satisfy" Man, can be realized only in and by a synthetic "overcoming" of Mastery and Slavery.

But let us return to the pagan State, to the City-State of the nonworking warlike Masters.

This State, like every State, is interested in and recognizes only the *Action* of the citizens, which—here—is reduced to warlike action. Hence the pagan State recognizes in the Citizen only the *universal* aspect of human existence. However, the particular element is not, and cannot be, absolutely excluded.

In point of fact, the Master is not only a Master of slaves and a warlike citizen of a State. He is also, of necessity, a member of a Family. And it is to the Family that the *particular* aspect of the pagan Master's existence belongs.

In the bosom of his Family, Man is not just another Master, just another Citizen, just another warrior. He is father, husband, son; and he is *this* father, *this* husband: *such a one*, a "particular." However, his particularity recognized in and by the Family is not truly human. In effect, for the pagan Master who does not work, human, humanizing action reduces to the warlike Action of Fighting. Now, there is no Fighting, no risk of life, within the Family. Therefore it is not human *Action* (*Tat*) that is recognized in and by the Family as such, but solely the *Sein*, the *given static Being*, the biological existence of man, of father, of husband, of son, of brother, and so on.

Now, to attribute an absolute value to a being not in relation to what he *does*, to his acts, but simply because he *is*, because of the simple fact of his *Sein*, his *Being*—is to love him. Hence we can also say that Love is what is realized in and by the ancient Family. And since Love does not depend on the *acts*, on the *activity* of the loved one, it cannot be ended by his very *death*. By loving man in his *inaction*, one considers him *as if* he were dead. Hence death can change nothing in the Love, in the value attributed in and by the Family. And that is why Love and the worship of the dead have their place within the pagan *Family*.

The *particular* and particularist Family, therefore, is a necessary complement of the *universal* and universalist pagan State. However, the pagan Master is as little *befriedigt*, "satisfied," by his family life as he is by his existence as a citizen. His *human* existence is what is realized and recognized in and by the State. But this existence is not truly *his*: it is not *he* who is recognized. As for the Family, it recognizes his personal, particular existence. But this essentially inactive existence is not truly *human*.

Wherever the human Actions of Fighting and of Work are not synthesized in a *single* human being, Man is never fully "satisfied." The realization and the recognition of solely universal *Action* in the State "satisfies" Man as little as the realization and the recognition of his personal, particular *Being* in the Family.

To be sure—in principle—a synthesis of the familial Particular and the political Universal could satisfy Man. But such a synthesis is absolutely impossible in the pagan World. For the Family and the State are mutually exclusive, and yet Man cannot do without the one or the other.

In effect, for the Family, the supreme value is the *Sein*, the natural *Being*, the biological *life* of its member. Now, what the State demands of this member of the Family is precisely the risk of his life, his *death* for the universal cause. To fulfill the duty of the Citizen, therefore, is necessarily to break the law of the Family; and inversely.

In the pagan World this conflict is inevitable and has no solution: Man cannot renounce his Family, since he cannot renounce the Particularity of his Being; nor can he renounce the State, since he cannot renounce the Universality of his Action. And thus he is always and necessarily *criminal*, either toward the State or toward the Family. And this is what constitutes the *tragic* character of pagan life.

Like the hero of ancient tragedy, then, the pagan World of the warlike Masters is in an inevitable conflict without a solution, which necessarily ends in the death, the complete ruin, of this World. And here is how Hegel represents the development of that tragedy in the *Phenomenology*:

In the final analysis, the pagan World perishes because it excludes Work. But the immediate agent of its ruin is, curiously, Woman. For it is the Woman who represents the family principle —i.e., that principle of *Particularity* which is hostile to Society as such and whose victory signifies the ruin of the State, of the Universal properly so-called.

Now on the one hand, the Woman acts on the *young* man, who is not yet completely detached from the Family, who has not yet completely subordinated his Particularity to the Universality of the State. On the other hand, and precisely because the State is a *warlike* State, it is the *young* man—the young military hero—who must finally come to power in the State. And once he has come to power, this young hero (= Alexander the Great) makes the most of his familial, even feminine, Particularity. He tends to transform the State into his *private* property, into a family patrimony, and to make the *citizens* of the State his own *subjects*. And he succeeds.

Why? Well, again because the pagan State excludes Work. Since the only *human* value is the one that is realized in and by Fighting and the risk of life, the life of the State must necessarily be a warlike life: the pagan State is a *human* State only to the extent that it wages perpetual wars for prestige. Now the laws of war, of brute force, are such that the strongest State must little by little swallow up the weaker ones. And the *victorious City* is thus transformed, little by little, into an *Empire*—into the Roman Empire.

Now the inhabitants of the mother City, the Masters properly so-called, are too few to defend the Empire. The Emperor must resort to mercenaries. The result is that the citizens of the City are no longer *obliged* to make war. And little by little, at the end of a certain time, they no longer make war. Thereby they can no longer make any resistance to the particularism of the Emperor, who "overcomes" them as *Citizens* and transforms them into *particulars* belonging to his *patrimony*, into "private persons."

When all is said and done, the former citizens become *slaves* of the sovereign. And they become slaves because they already *are* slaves. In effect, to be a Master is to fight, to risk one's life. Hence the citizens who no longer wage war cease to be Masters, and that is why they become Slaves of the Roman Emperor. And that is also why they accept the *ideology* of their Slaves: first Stoicism, then Skepticism, and—finally—Christianity.

Here we have found the solution to the problem that interests us: the Masters have accepted the ideology of their Slaves; the pagan Man of Mastery has become the Christian Man of Slavery; and all this without a Fight, without a Revolution properly so-called—because the Masters *themselves* have become Slaves. Or more precisely: *pseudo*-Slaves, or—if you will—pseudo-Masters. For they are no longer real *Masters*, since they no longer risk their lives; but they are not real Slaves either, because they do not work in the service of another. They are, so to speak, Slaves without Masters, pseudo-Slaves. And by ceasing to be true Masters, they end in no longer having real Slaves: they free them, and thus the Slaves themselves become Slaves without Masters, pseudo-Masters. Therefore, the opposition of Mastery and Slavery is "overcome." Not, however, because the Slaves have become true Masters. The unification is effected in *pseudo*-Mastery, which is—in fact—a pseudo-*Slavery*, a Slavery without Masters.

This Slave without a Master, this Master without a Slave, is what Hegel calls the *Bourgeois*, the private property-owner. It is by becoming a private property-owner that the Greek Master, a *citizen* of the City, becomes the peaceful Roman Bourgeois, a *subject* of the Emperor, who himself is but a Bourgeois, a private property-owner, whose Empire is his patrimony. And it is also in relation to private property that the freeing of the Slaves is carried out; they become property-owners, Bourgeois, like their ex-masters.

In contrast to the Greek City, then, the Roman Empire is a bourgeois World. And it is as such that it finally becomes a *Christian* World.

The bourgeois World elaborates civil *Law*—the only original creation of Rome, according to Hegel. And the fundamental notion of Roman legal thought, that of the "legal person" (*recht-liche Persönlichkeit*), corresponds to the *Stoic* conception of human existence, as well as to the principle of family particularism. Just like the Family, civil Law attaches an absolute value to the pure and simple *Being* of Man, independently of his Actions. And just as in the Stoic conception, the value attributed to the "person" does not depend on the concrete condition of his existence: a man, and every man equally, is everywhere and always a "legal person." And we can say that the bourgeois State founded on the idea of *civil* Law is the *real* basis of Stoicism, of Stoicism taken not as an abstract *idea*, but as a social, historical *reality*.

And the same is true for nihilistic Skepticism: private *property* (*Eigentum*) is its real basis and its social, historical reality. The nihilistic Skepticism of the solipsistic Slave, who attributes a true value and a true being only to himself, is found again in the private property-owner, who subordinates everything, the State itself, to the absolute value of *his* own property. Thus, if the only *reality* of the particularistic ideologies, the so-called "individualistic" ideologies, is private Property, it is only in a bourgeois World, dominated by the idea of this property, that these ideologies can become real social forces.

Finally, this same bourgeois essence of the Roman Empire is what explains its transformation into a Christian World, makes the reality of Christianity possible, transforms the Christian *idea* and the Christian *ideal* into a social and historical *reality*. And this is why:

To be a truly human being, the Bourgeois (who, in principle, does not fight, does not risk his life) must *work*, just like the Slave. But in contrast to the Slave, since the Bourgeois has no Master, he does not have to work in *another's* service. Therefore, he believes that he works for himself. Now in the Hegelian conception, work can truly be Work, a specifically *human* Action, only on the condition that it be carried out in relation to an *idea* (a "project")—that is, in relation to something other than the *given*, and, in particular, other than the given that the worker himself is. It was thus that the Slave could *work* by being supported by the idea of the *Master*, of Mastery, of *Service* (*Dienst*). A man can also work (and that is the *Hegelian*, definitive solution of the problem) by being supported by the idea of the *Community*, of the State: one can—and one must—work for the State. But the Bourgeois can do neither the one nor the other. He no longer has a Master whom he could have served by working. And he does not yet have a State, for the bourgeois World is but an agglomeration of *private* Property-owners, isolated from each other, without true community.

Hence the Bourgeois' problem seems insoluble: he must work for *another* and can work only for *himself*. Now in fact, Man manages to resolve this problem, and he resolves it once more by the bourgeois principle of private *Property*. The Bourgeois does not work for another. But he does not work for himself, taken as a biological entity, either. He works for himself taken as a "legal *person*," as a private *Property-owner*: he works for Property taken as such—i.e., Property that has now become *money*; he works for Capital.

In other words, the bourgeois Worker presupposes—and conditions—an *Entsagung*, an *Abnegation* of human existence. Man transcends himself, surpasses himself, projects himself far away from himself by projecting himself onto the idea of private Property, of Capital, which—while being the Property-owner's own product—becomes independent of him and enslaves him just as the Master enslaved the Slave; with this difference, however, that the enslavement is now conscious and freely accepted by the Worker. (We see, by the way, that for Hegel, as for Marx, the central phenomenon of the bourgeois World is not the enslavement of the working man, of the *poor* bourgeois, by the rich bourgeois, but the enslavement of *both* by Capital.) However that may be, bourgeois existence presupposes, engenders, and nourishes Abnegation. Now it is precisely this Abnegation that reflects itself in the dualistic Christian ideology, while providing it with a new, specific, nonpagan content. It is the same Christian dualism that is found again in bourgeois existence: the opposition between the "legal Person," the private Property-owner, and the man of flesh and blood; the existence of an ideal, transcendent World, represented in reality by Money, Capital, to which Man is supposed to devote his Actions, to sacrifice his sensual, biological Desires.

And as for the structure of the Christian Beyond, it is formed in the image of the relations realized in the Roman Empire between the Emperor and his subjects, relations which—as we have seen—have the same origin as the Christian ideology: the refusal of death, the desire for animal life, for *Sein*, which in Christianity is sublimated in a desire for immortality, for "eternal life." And if the pagan Master accepts the Christian ideology of his Slave, an ideology that makes him a Servant of the absolute Master, of the King of heaven, of God, it is because—having ceased to risk his life and becoming a peaceful Bourgeois—he sees that he is no longer a *Citizen* who can satisfy himself through a political activity. He sees that he is the passive subject of a despotic Emperor. Just like the Slave, therefore, he has nothing to lose and everything to gain by imagining a transcendent World, in which all men are *equal* before an omnipotent, truly *universal* Master, who recognizes, moreover, the absolute value of each *Particular* as such.

Here, then, is how and why the pagan World of Masters became a Christian bourgeois World:

In opposition to Paganism, to the religion of the Masters, of the warlike Citizens who attribute true value only to Universality, to what is valuable for all men and at all times, Christianity, the religion of the Slaves, or—more exactly—of the Bourgeois-Subjects, attributes an absolute value to Particularity, to the here and now. This change of attitude is clearly manifested in the myth of the incarnation of God in Jesus Christ, as well as in the idea that God has a direct, immediate relation with each man taken separately, without passing through the universal—i.e., social and political—element of Man's existence.

Hence Christianity is first of all a particularistic, family, and slavish reaction against the pagan universalism of the Citizen-Masters. But it is more than that. It also implies the idea of a synthesis of the Particular and the Universal—that is, of Mastery and Slavery too: the idea of Individuality—i.e., of that realization of universal values and realities in and by the Particular and of that universal recognition of the value of the Particular, which alone can give Man *Befriedigung*, the supreme and definitive "Satisfaction."

In other words, Christianity finds the solution to the pagan tragedy. And that is why, since the coming of Christ, there is no longer any true tragedy—that is, inevitable conflict with truly no way out.

The whole problem, now, is to *realize* the Christian idea of Individuality. And the history of the Christian World is nothing but the history of this realization.

Now, according to Hegel, one can realize the Christian *anthropological* ideal (which he accepts in full) only by "overcoming" the Christian *theology*: Christian Man can really become what he would like to be only by becoming a man without God—or, if you will, a God-Man. He must realize *in himself* what at first he thought was realized in his God. To be *really* Christian, he *himself* must become Christ.

According to the Christian *Religion*, Individuality, the synthesis of the Particular and the Universal, is effected only in and by the Beyond, after man's death.

This conception is meaningful only if Man is presupposed to be immortal. Now, according to Hegel, immortality is incompatible with the very essence of human being and, consequently, with Christian anthropology itself.

Therefore, the human ideal can be realized only if it is such that it can be realized by a *mortal* Man who knows he is such. In other words, the Christian synthesis must be effected not in the Beyond, after death, but on earth, during man's life. And this means that the *transcendent* Universal (God), who recognizes the Particular, must be replaced by a Universal that is immanent in the World. And for Hegel this immanent Universal can only be the State. What is supposed to be realized by God in the Kingdom of Heaven must be realized in and by the State, in the earthly kingdom. And that is why Hegel says that the "absolute" State that he has in mind (Napoleon's Empire) is the *realization* of the Christian Kingdom of heaven.

The history of the Christian World, therefore, is the history of the progressive realization of that ideal State, in which Man will finally be "satisfied" by realizing himself as Individuality—a synthesis of the Universal and the Particular, of the Master and the Slave, of Fighting and Work. But in order to realize this State, Man must look away from the Beyond, look toward this earth and act only with a view to this earth. In other words, he must eliminate the Christian idea of transcendence. And that is why the evolution of the Christian World is dual: on the one hand there is the *real* evolution, which prepares the social and political conditions for the coming of the "absolute" State; and on the other, an *ideal* evolution, which eliminates the *transcendent* idea, which brings Heaven back to Earth, as Hegel says.

This ideal evolution, which destroys Christian *Theology*, is the work of the Intellectual. Hegel takes a great interest in the phenomenon of the Christian or bourgeois Intellectual. He talks about it in Section B of Chapter VI, and devotes all of Chapter V to it.[7]

This Intellectual can subsist only in the Christian bourgeois World, in which a man is able not to be a Master—that is, not to have Slaves and not to fight—without thereby becoming a Slave himself. But the bourgeois Intellectual is nonetheless something different from the Bourgeois properly so-called. For if, just like the Bourgeois, the non-Master, he is essentially peaceful and does not *fight*, he differs from the Bourgeois in that he does not *work* either. Hence he is as stripped of the essential character of the Slave as he is of that of the Master.

Not being a Slave, the Intellectual can liberate himself from the essentially slavish aspect of Christianity, namely from its theological, transcendent element. But not being a Master, he can preserve the element of the Particular, the "individualistic" ideology of Christian anthropology. In short, being neither Master nor Slave, he is able—in this *nothingness*, in this absence of all given *determination*—to "realize" in some way the desired synthesis of Mastery and Slavery: he can *conceive* it. However, being *neither Master nor Slave*—that is, abstaining from all Work and from all Fighting—he cannot truly *realize* the synthesis that he discovers: without Fighting and without Work, this synthesis conceived by the Intellectual remains purely *verbal*.

Now, the problem at hand is this *realization*, for only the *reality* of the synthesis can "satisfy" Man, complete History, and establish the absolute Science. Therefore, the ideal process must rejoin the real process; the social and historical conditions must be such that the ideology of the Intellectual can be realized. Now, this is what took place at the moment of the French Revolution, during which the immanent idea of Individuality, elaborated by the Intellectuals of the Enlightenment, was realized in and by the Fight of the working Bourgeois, who were first revolutionaries and then

[7] In fact, the Intellectual of Chapter V (the Man who lives in society and in a State while believing he is, or pretending to be, "alone in the world") is found at every stage of the bourgeois World. But in describing him, Hegel has his contemporaries especially in mind.

citizens of the universal and homogeneous State (the Napoleonic Empire).

The *realization* of the Christian idea, which was secularized by the Intellectual and thus made realizable, is not possible without a Fight, without a social war, without the risk of life. This is true for reasons that are in some sense "metaphysical." Since the idea to be realized is the idea of a synthesis of Mastery and Slavery, it can be realized only if the slavish element of Work is associated with the element of Fighting for life and death, which characterizes the Master: the working-Bourgeois, to become a—"satisfied"— Citizen of the "absolute" State, *must* become a Warrior—that is, he must introduce death into his existence, by consciously and voluntarily risking his life, while knowing that he is mortal. Now we have seen that in the bourgeois World there were no Masters. The Fight in question, therefore, cannot be a class fight properly so-called, a war between the Masters and the Slaves. The Bourgeois is neither Slave nor Master; he is—being the Slave of Capital —his *own* Slave. It is from himself, therefore, that he must free himself. And that is why the liberating risk of life takes the form not of risk on the field of battle, but of the risk created by Robespierre's Terror. The working Bourgeois, turned Revolutionary, himself creates the situation that introduces into him the element of death. And it is only thanks to the Terror that the idea of the final Synthesis, which definitively "satisfies" Man, is realized.

It is in the Terror that the State is born in which this "satisfaction" is attained. This State, for the author of the *Phenomenology*, is Napoleon's Empire. And Napoleon himself *is* the wholly "satisfied" Man, who, in and by his definitive Satisfaction, completes the course of the historical evolution of humanity. He is the human *Individual* in the proper and full sense of the word; because it is through *him*, through *this* particular man, that the "common cause," the truly universal cause, is realized; and because this particular man is recognized, in his very particularity, by all men, universally. The only thing that he lacks is *Self*-Consciousness; he *is* the perfect Man, but he does not yet *know* it, and that is why Man is not fully "satisfied" in him alone. He cannot *say* of himself all that I have just said.

Now, I have said it because I read it in the *Phenomenology*. Therefore it is Hegel, the author of the *Phenomenology*, who is somehow Napoleon's Self-Consciousness. And since the perfect Man, the Man fully "satisfied" by what he *is*, can only be a Man who *knows* what he is, who is fully *self-conscious*, it is Napoleon's existence as *revealed* to all men in and by the *Phenomenology* that is the realized ideal of human existence.

That is why the Christian period (Chapter VI, Section B), which culminates in Napoleon, must be completed by a third historical period, a short one (Chapter VI, Section C), which is the period of German philosophy, culminating in Hegel—the author of the *Phenomenology*.

The phenomenon that completes the historical evolution and thus makes the absolute Science possible, therefore, is the "conception" (*Begreifen*) of Napoleon by Hegel. This dyad, formed by Napoleon and Hegel, is the perfect Man, fully and definitively "satisfied" by what he *is* and by what he *knows* himself to be. *This* is the realization of the ideal revealed by the myth of Jesus Christ, of the God-Man. And that is why Hegel completes Chapter VI with these words: "*Es ist* der erscheinende Gott . . ."; "*This* is the revealed God," the *real*, true Christ.

Now, having said this, Hegel considers himself obliged to come to terms with the Christian, theological interpretation of the idea of Christ. He must speak of the relation between his philosophy, between the *Phenomenology*, and Christian theology. He must say what this theology *is* in reality.

That is the central theme of Chapter VII.

3

SUMMARY OF THE COURSE IN 1937–1938

*Excerpt from the 1938–1939 Annuaire
of the École Pratique des Hautes Études,
Section des Sciences religieuses*

The lectures of this year were dedicated to explaining Chapter VII of the *Phenomenology*, entitled *Die Religion*, in which Hegel studies the structure and evolution of the theological doctrines elaborated in the course of history.

For Hegel, the real object of religious thought is Man himself: every *theology* is necessarily an *anthropology*. The suprasensible entity, transcendent with respect to Nature—i.e., the *Spirit*—is in reality nothing but the negating (i.e., creative) Action realized by Man in the given World. But as long as Man is religious, he is not aware of this: he thinks as a theologian, he substantializes and externalizes the *concept* (*Begriff*) of Spirit by *re-presenting* (*Vorstellen*) it to himself in the form of a Being (*Sein*) existing *outside* of Man and *independently* of his Action. While in fact talking about himself, religious Man believes that he is talking about a God.

This lack of self-consciousness, this imaginative *projection* of the spiritual or human content into the *beyond* (*Vor-stellung*), distinguishes religious (*theo*logical) thought from philosophical (*anthropo*logical) thought. Furthermore, these two types of thought necessarily coexist: while opposing one another, they engender and mutually complete one another. (Pre-Hegelian) Philosophy consciously deals with Man: in it, Man becomes conscious *of himself*. But it reveals Man to himself by *isolating* him from his natural and social World; and it is only *particular* (*Einzelner*) Man, isolated from the World (from the Universal) by being shut up in himself, who can elaborate a "philosophical" anthropology. On the other hand, Theology, unawares, reveals the *universal* aspect of human existence: the State, Society, the People; and Man taken as member of Society, the People, and the

State. As long as History continues, or as long as the perfect State is not realized—that is, as long as the *Particular* is in conflict with the *Universal* of the given natural and social World—the opposition of these two points of view (the "philosophical" and the religious or theological) is inevitable. Man who does not manage to *satisfy* himself through Action in and for the World in which he lives *flees* from this World and takes refuge in his *abstract* intelligence: and this "Intellectual" shut up in himself is the one who becomes conscious of himself in a "philosophical" anthropology, which reflects the *particularist* tendency of human existence. Taken, on the other hand, in his *universalist* tendency, this same Man, turning toward the World, cannot recognize and accept it as his work: (universal) reality appears to him as existing *outside* of him and *independently* of his Action, and the universal ideal seems to him to be situated *beyond* him and his real World. Thus, it is in the form of a *theo*logical myth that he will become conscious of the reality and ideal of the World—and of himself as being a part of the World. And the *particularist* subjectivism of "philosophical" *anthro*pology will always be completed, and embattled, by the *universalist* objectivism of religious *theo*logy.

Theology, therefore, is the—unconscious—reflection of the given historical social World in which the theologian lives, and of the ideal that takes form in it. Consequently, on the one hand, the study of a Religion will allow us to understand the essential character of the World in which this Religion is accepted; and on the other hand, since Theology likewise reflects the social and political ideal that tends to realize itself through transformation of the given, the study of it will also allow us to understand the evolution of this World, an evolution that is carried out according to the ideal, and consequently according to the Theology which reveals this ideal. And that is why the study of real historical evolution (found in Chapter VI) must be completed by the study of the ideal evolution of theological thought (found in Chapter VII).

The existential ideal is elaborated and realized progressively: each step in its elaboration is marked by a determinate Theology, and each step in its realization is represented by the historical World that accepts that Theology and lives according to it. In its perfection, the ideal reveals itself through the idea of *Individuality*—

that is, of satisfaction by the real or active synthesis of the *particularist* and *universalist* tendencies of human existence. This idea first reveals itself to Man in the form of the (Christian) theological notion of the (divine) individuality of the Christ or the man-*God*. And this ideal-idea *realizes* itself in and by the French Revolution, which completes the evolution of the Christian World in the real (and at the same time symbolic) person of the god-*Man* Napoleon, who is both Creator-Head of the perfect State and Citizen actively contributing to the indefinite maintenance of that State. When the *real* opposition between the *Particular* and the *Universal* is thus overcome, the *ideal* conflict between "philosophical" *anthropology* and religious *theology* disappears too. Hence the Philosopher, and this philosopher is Hegel, who *reveals* Man to himself by speaking about his Napoleonic *realization*, reveals him both in his *particularist* aspect and in his *universalist* aspect. Thus his doctrine is both "philosophical" and "theological" at the same time. But, being both the one *and* the other, it is *neither* the one *nor* the other. It is not a "Philosophy" in the pre-Hegelian sense of the word, because it does not work with the notion of an ideal or *abstract* Spirit— i.e., a Spirit *distinct* from natural and social reality and action. And it is not a "Theology," either; for if Theology speaks of a real and *concrete* Spirit, it situates it outside of Man and the World. Hegel's doctrine is *absolute Knowledge (absolutes Wissen)*, which completes and *overcomes (aufhebt)* both "philosophical" evolution and religious or theological evolution, by *revealing* the perfect Man who is realized at the end of History and by presupposing the real *existence* of this Man.

Perfect Man—that is, Man fully and definitively satisfied by what he *is*—being the realization of the *Christian* idea of Individuality, the revelation of this Man by absolute Knowledge has *the same* content as Christian Theology, minus the notion of *transcendence*: it is sufficient to say of Man everything that the Christian says of his God in order to move from the absolute or Christian Theology to Hegel's absolute philosophy or *Science*. And this movement from the one to the other can be carried out thanks to Napoleon, as Hegel showed in Chapter VI.

In Chapter VII, Hegel shows us why and how the most primitive theological doctrine was progressively transformed into this

Christian doctrine which differs from his own doctrine only in its form: Christian theology in reality reveals to us nothing other than the Hegelian *concept* of Individuality, but in the form of the *representation* (*Vorstellung*) of god-manhood.

4

PHILOSOPHY AND WISDOM

*Complete Text of the First Two Lectures
of the Academic Year 1938–1939*

FIRST LECTURE

In the first seven chapters of the *Phenomenology*, Hegel talked about Philosophy. In Chapter VIII he is going to be concerned with something *else*.

When I say this, I use the term "philosophy" in the precise, proper, narrow sense. I am talking about "philo-sophy," the *love* of Wisdom, the *aspiration* to Wisdom, as opposed to "Sophia," to Wisdom itself. Now in Chapter VIII, Hegel is no longer talking about the Philosopher, but about the Wise Man, about Wisdom; for the "absolute Knowledge" (*Das absolute Wissen*) with which this Chapter is concerned is nothing other than "Wisdom" opposed to "Philo-sophy" (and to Theology, as well as vulgar Science).

Before beginning the interpretation of Chapter VIII, then, I would like to say a few words about Wisdom in relation to Philosophy.

All philosophers are in agreement about the *definition* of the Wise Man. Moreover, it is very simple and can be stated in a single sentence: that man is Wise who is capable of answering in a *comprehensible* or satisfactory manner *all* questions that can be asked him concerning his acts, and capable of answering in such fashion that the *entirety* of his answers forms a *coherent* discourse.

75

Or else, what amounts to the same thing: that man is Wise who is *fully* and *perfectly self-conscious.*

Now, an awareness of the meaning of this definition is sufficient to make us understand why Plato, for example, denied the possibility of *realizing* this ideal of Wisdom.

It is the case that one can ask any question at all about any of our acts—that of washing, for example, or of paying taxes—with the result that, after several answers that call forth each time a new "why," one comes to the problems of the relationship between the soul and the body, between the individual and the State; to questions relating to the finite and the infinite, to death and immortality, to God and the World; and finally to the problem of *knowledge* itself, of this coherent and meaningful language that permits us to ask questions and to answer them. In short, by proceeding, so to speak, in the vertical plane, one will quickly come face to face with the *entire body* of the so-called philosophical or "metaphysical" questions.

On the other hand, by setting forth from the same banal act and proceeding in the "horizontal" plane, one will end up—less quickly, of course—surveying all the Sciences taught in modern Universities. And perhaps one will discover still others, not yet in existence.

In a word, to be able to answer *all* questions relating to any *one* of our acts is, in the final analysis, to be able to answer all possible questions *in general.* Therefore: "to answer all questions . . . and so on" is to realize the *encyclopaedia* of possible kinds of knowledge. To be perfectly and completely *self*-conscious is to have at one's disposal—at least virtually—an *encyclopaedic* knowledge in the full sense of the word.

In defining the Wise Man, the Man of absolute Knowledge, as *perfectly* self-conscious—i.e., *omniscient,* at least potentially— Hegel nevertheless had the unheard-of audacity to assert that he *realized* Wisdom in his own person.

When the Wise Man is discussed, he is usually presented in another guise, which seems more easily attainable than omniscience. Thus the Stoics, for example, for whom the idea of the Wise Man plays a central role and who, in contrast to Plato, asserted the possibility and even the reality of such a man, define him as that man who is perfectly *satisfied* by what he *is.* The Wise Man, then, would be the man who *wants* nothing, who *desires* nothing: he wants to *change* nothing, either in himself or outside of himself; therefore he does not *act*. He simply *is* and does not *become*; he maintains himself in *identity* to himself and he is *satisfied* in and by this identity.

Now, for Hegel, this *second* definition of the Wise Man in terms of satisfaction is but a paraphrase of the *first*, the one in terms of perfect self-knowledge. And he accepts both definitions precisely because he identifies them.

Of course, our object is not to *prove* this thesis here. For the proof of it is given by the *entirety* of the *Phenomenology*, or more exactly, by its first seven chapters. I shall only indicate that the assertion that perfect satisfaction implies and presupposes full self-*consciousness* is more acceptable than the inverse assertion, that the man who is perfectly self-conscious is necessarily *satisfied* by what he is, by that of which he becomes conscious. Fundamentally, to prove the first assertion, it suffices to say this: given that one can be satisfied only by knowing that one is satisfied, only by becoming *conscious* of one's satisfaction, it follows that *perfect* satisfaction implies an *absolute* self-consciousness. But I do not insist on this reasoning, for I know that we "moderns" are much too "romantic" to let ourselves be convinced by so-called "easy"— that is, *obvious*—arguments. I shall, then, merely appeal to our psychological experience: we believe in vain that we are satisfied; if someone comes and asks us the question "why" concerning our satisfaction, and we cannot answer, this is enough to make the *satisfaction* disappear as if by enchantment (even if the sensation of *pleasure*, or of *happiness*, or of joy, or of simple well-being resists the test for a while). Anyone can make this experiment for himself. But one can also simply read Plato's dialogue, the *Ion*, in which just such a man appears, one who believes he is *satisfied* by what he *is* and who ceases to be satisfied, solely because he cannot *justify* this satisfaction in answering Socrates' questions. The scene is completely convincing.[1]

[1] However, a very important restriction must be made here. I believe that Plato actually succeeds in convincing all those who *read* and *understand* his dialogue. But here is the difficulty: the number of people who read Plato is limited; and the number of those who understand him is still more limited. It makes no sense, therefore, to say that the scene in question is "convincing" in general: it can convince, so to speak, only those who are *willing* to be convinced.

Generally speaking, there is a tendency to underestimate the difficulties of satisfaction and to overestimate those of omniscience. Accordingly, the thinkers who, on the one hand, believe in the myth of *easy* satisfaction (a myth invented by moralists) and, on the other hand, preserve the ideal of the Wise Man and know that it is extremely difficult to realize, have in mind neither omniscience, which they believe to be unattainable, nor satisfaction, which they believe too easy, but a *third* definition: they identify Wisdom with *moral* perfection. Hence the Wise Man would be the *morally* perfect man.

Hegel believes he can show that this third definition equals the second and, consequently, the first.

I do not believe that anyone can seriously contest the assertion that the *perfect* man is *satisfied* by what he is. Even Christians are obliged to make this assertion once they identify holiness with *perfection*, and not, as they usually do, either with a minimal *imperfection*, a minimum of sin, or, on the contrary, with the maximum *consciousness* of imperfection, of sin. Therefore: whoever speaks of moral *perfection* necessarily also speaks of *satisfaction* by what one is.

To understand why this is so, one need only reflect on the very *concept* of moral perfection, abstracting from its *content*. With regard to this content, opinions can diverge: there has been much discussion of the *content* of the morality that the Wise Man is supposed to realize perfectly. But this does not interest us for the moment. It is sufficient to note this: either the concept of moral

---

And the same remark can be made concerning my "easy" argument. It is, without doubt, "obvious." But it is convincing only for those who are *ready* to trust in the obvious. Now, as I said, we ourselves are sufficiently "romantic" to know that a distinction can be made between (theoretical) *evidence* and (existential) *conviction*. Generally speaking, all that I have said is truly convincing only for those who put the supreme existential value in *Self-Consciousness*. Now, in truth, these people are convinced beforehand. If, for them, Self-Consciousness is the *supreme* value, it is obvious that they can be *fully* satisfied only by a self-*conscious* satisfaction. Inversely, should they attain full self-consciousness, they will thereby be perfectly *satisfied*, even if they do not live in positive pleasure, and even if—from time to time—they are unhappy. For them, satisfaction and self-consciousness are but two aspects of one and the same thing. But for the common mortal, this identification is not at all automatic. On the contrary, they tend to separate the two things, and in preferring *satisfaction*, they believe it to be much more attainable than fullness of *self-consciousness*—that is, omniscience. I shall return to this question later. For the moment, I must go on.

perfection has no meaning, or else it must be understood as a human existence that serves as the model for *all* men, the final end and motive of their actions being conformity to this model. If, then, the Wise Man realizes moral perfection in his person, we must say that his existence serves as the model both for *himself* and for *others*: he wants to resemble himself indefinitely, and the others want to resemble him. Now, this is equivalent to saying that the Wise Man is *satisfied* by what he *is*. He is satisfied subjectively in himself, since there is nothing in him that urges him to go beyond himself, to change—that is, to negate, not to accept what he already is. And he is objectively satisfied, by universal "recognition," for no one would want to force him to change the state that satisfies him.

I said that the concept of moral *perfection* is meaningful only provided that it is *universally* valid—i.e., accepted as the model by *all* men. This may appear debatable, given that we have got into the habit of talking about *several* irreducible existential types— that is, several essentially different moralities. And, of course, I have no intention of disputing this pluralism—i.e., this ethical relativism. I only wanted to say that in these conditions it is no longer meaningful to speak of *perfection*. For in this case the concept of "perfection" is *strictly* identical to that of "subjective *satisfaction*." In effect, to assert the *plurality* of existential or moral types is to assert that recognition by *all* men is not implied in the ideal of the perfection realizable within each one of these types: therefore, one need only *believe oneself* perfect in order to *be* perfect; now, to believe that one is *perfect* is obviously to be *satisfied* by what one is. Inversely, to be satisfied by what one is is obviously to *believe* that one is perfect—that is, in the case which we are considering, to *be* perfect. Hence it is solely by asserting that there is only *one* type of moral perfection that one *completes* the concept of satisfaction when one speaks of the perfection of the satisfied man: namely, one completes the concept of *subjective* satisfaction by that of *objective* satisfaction—i.e., of satisfaction by universal *recognition*. But as I said, even in this case one must say that the truly *perfect* man is *satisfied* by what he is. It is only the inverse assertion that appears debatable: it seems possible to be satisfied without being willing and able to serve as the model for *all* others.

I have already said that I cannot reproduce the Hegelian proof of the theory that the *satisfied* man is morally *perfect*—i.e., that he serves as the model to *all* others. I shall only mention that Hegel succeeds in proving this by showing that man can be *satisfied* only by being *universally recognized*—that is, he shows that man can be satisfied only by being perfect (and that he is perfect, moreover, only by being satisfied). And he manages to do this by identifying man with Self-Consciousness. This is to say that here again the argument is convincing only for those who are *willing* to be convinced (who are *open* to conviction by reasoning). In other words, Hegel only shows that the first definition of the Wise Man (by Self-Consciousness) coincides with the definitions by satisfaction and by ("moral") perfection. But he proves nothing at all to the man who denies the first definition—that is, who denies that the Wise Man must be self-conscious. (The only thing that Hegel can say is that to those who deny it nothing at all can be proved.) To put it otherwise, he does not succeed in showing that the satisfied man is actually taken as the model by *all* men. He only proves what is obvious from the start: that the fully satisfied and perfectly self-conscious man serves as the "morally perfect" model for all those who put the supreme existential value in self-consciousness—that is, for those who, by definition, accept the ideal that this man realizes.

At first glance, then, Hegel's argument is a simple tautology. And it seems that for him, too, there is an irreducible pluralism, which deprives the concept of perfection of its meaning. But Hegel would not accept this interpretation. He would say that his *concept* of perfection is valid, since it is *universally* valid (as is every *concept*). Those who reject it have no *concept* at all.

While discussing the second definition of the Wise Man, we already found ourselves in an analogous situation, and I said that we would have to discuss it (see note 1, Ed.). The moment has come for this.

We have seen that for Hegel the three definitions of Wisdom are rigorously equivalent. The Wise Man is the perfectly self-conscious man—that is, the man who is fully satisfied by what he is—that is, the man who realizes moral perfection by his existence, or in other words, who serves as the model for himself and for *all* others. This means—and this restriction is important: for all those *for* whom he exists—i.e., for those who *understand* him, who know that he *exists*, and who know *what* he is. For the moment let us set aside this restriction. The Wise Man, then, is *universally* recognized. This is to say that there is only one possible type of Wisdom. In making this assertion, we run into the contrary thesis of pluralism or existential relativism. How does Hegel manage to *prove* his thesis? In point of fact, he can prove it only by starting from the first definition of Wisdom, put as an axiom. As for the proof, it is very simple. Let us admit that the Wise Man is *perfectly* self-conscious. We have seen that perfect self-consciousness equals omniscience. In other words, the Wise Man's knowledge is *total*, the Wise Man reveals the *totality* of Being through the *entirety* of his thought. Now, since Being obeys the principle of *identity* to itself, there is only one unique *totality* of Being, and consequently only one unique knowledge that reveals it entirely. Therefore there is only one unique possible type of (conscious) Wisdom.

Now, if the ideal of self-conscious Wisdom is *unique*, we must say that the Wise Man who realizes it also realizes moral *perfection*, and consequently that he is *satisfied* by what he is. Therefore it is sufficient to suppose that the Wise Man is fully *self-conscious* in order to be able to assert that self-consciousness, subjective satisfaction, and objective perfection completely coincide in Wisdom (which is necessarily unique). In other words, to arrive at this three-fold Hegelian definition it is sufficient to suppose that man *is* Self-Consciousness in his very "essence" and being, that it is through Self-Consciousness and only through Self-Consciousness that he differs from animals and things. Starting from this supposition, one can actually *deduce* the threefold definition that we were talking about.

Once more, I am not concerned with reproducing this deduction here, which is given in the *entirety* of the first seven chapters of the *Phenomenology*. But I shall say that it is irrefutable.

Therefore: a reading of the first seven chapters of the *Phenomenology* shows that the definition of man by Self-Consciousness is sufficient grounds for the necessary conclusion that there *must* be an ideal of the Wise Man, that there *can* be only *one* type of Wise Man, and that the Wise Man answers to the threefold Hegelian definition. At least, this is what Hegel himself would have said. But a closer examination shows that Hegel presupposes a bit more than the simple fact of the existence of Self-Consciousness. He supposes that this Self-Consciousness naturally, spontaneously, tends to *extend* itself, to *expand*, to spread through the *whole* domain of the reality given to man and in man. As a matter of fact, the dialectical movement of the *Phenomenology* always takes place according to the following schema: a situation A has been constituted, and Hegel describes it; then he says that, once this situation is given, the man who realizes it must himself *necessarily* become *conscious* of it; finally he shows how the situation A changes *as a result of this coming to consciousness* and is transformed into a new situation B; and so on. Now, it is possible that the coming to consciousness in question is much less necessary, less natural, less universal, than Hegel thinks. It is possible that in the normal case man, even self-*conscious* man, opposes an *extension* of this consciousness, tends to *enclose* himself in it, to reject into the unconscious (the automatic, and so on) everything that goes beyond the already-conscious range. Now, if this is truly the case, the dialectical movement that ends in the ideal (and the reality) of Wisdom ceases to be *necessary*. In order that this movement may come to its end, at each dialectical turning point there must actually be a Self-Consciousness that tends to extend itself to the new reality. And nothing proves that such a Self-Consciousness must *necessarily* be there at the moment when it is needed.

Therefore, for the deductions of the *Phenomenology* to be valid, it is necessary to suppose not only a Self-Consciousness, but also a Self-Consciousness that always has a tendency to *extend* itself as much as possible. This supplementary condition is, in my opinion, very important. I shall come back to it shortly. For the moment, I would simply like to say that, in my opinion, the discussion can only turn on the *premises* of the *Phenomenology*, and not on the *deductions* found in it. Personally, I believe that if the *premises* of the *Phenomenology* are accepted, no objection can be made to the *conclusions* that Hegel draws from them. In any case, up to now I have heard of no serious objection of this kind. To accept the starting point *necessarily* leads to the final result, that is, to the concept of the Wise Man in his threefold definition.

But we must not forget that the final result of the *Phenomenology* has a *double* aspect. On the one hand, Hegel deduces the threefold *ideal* of the Wise Man; on the other hand, he asserts that this ideal is *realized*, namely, by himself, that is, by the author of the deduction in question. Now, it is obvious that the *deductions* of the *Phenomenology* can only prove the *ideal* possibility, so to speak, of the Wise Man. But the *Phenomenology* cannot prove the *real possibility* of the Wise Man; and still less his very *reality*. In fact Plato, who starts with the same supposition as Hegel (Man = Self-Consciousness), recognizes, to be sure, that the Wise Man whom we have in view is the necessary *ideal* of *thought*, or better, of discourse; but he denies that this ideal can be *realized* by man. (This means: by *real* man, living in a *real* World, during the length of time limited by his birth and his death).

Now, since we have here a question of *reality*—that is, of *fact*—Hegel can refute Platonic skepticism only by pointing to a *fact*.

I shall return to the question of the *reality* of the Wise Man. For the moment, I want to talk only about "theoretical" difficulties, so to speak, by developing the remarks that I already made above and promised to come back to.

We have seen that one can ask not only the question of *fact*, but also the question of *right*: one can cast doubt on Plato-Hegel's starting point, that is, on the identification of man and Self-Consciousness and on the assertion that Self-Consciousness always tends to extend itself as much as possible. To be sure, the deduction of the *Phenomenology* is not *hypothetical*. For, without a doubt, Self-Consciousness is not an arbitrary "axiom" that can be denied, but an undebatable *fact*. However, it can be interpreted differently. One can deny that Self-Consciousness reveals man's "essence." Or else, in simpler language, one can say: *either* that Self-Consciousness is a sort of sickness that man must, and can, surmount; *or* that, alongside of conscious men, there are *unconscious* men, who are nevertheless just as *human*—although in a different way. Now, by doing this, one denies the *universality* of Wisdom. Which means: one challenges the *identity* of the three definitions of the Wise Man.

Now the denial of the Hegelian identification of satisfaction-perfection with Self-Consciousness was by no means invented by me. It has actually been made. One need only call to mind the Hindu thinkers, who say that man approaches satisfaction-perfection in dreamless sleep, that satisfaction-perfection is realized in the absolute night of the "fourth state" (*tûria*) of the Brahmins, or in Nirvana, in the extinction of all consciousness, of the Buddhists. Generally speaking, one need only think of all those who seek satisfaction-perfection in *absolute silence*, who exclude even monologue or dialogue with God. One can think, too, of the ideal that Nietzsche called "Chinese," the ideal of the "citizen" (in the non-Hegelian sense of the term) who is made completely "brutish" in and by the *security* of his *well-being* (Cf. *Joyful Science*, Book I, § 24). Finally, one can think of the ideal of "salvation" through erotic or esthetic (unconscious) "ecstasy"—for example, musical "ecstasy."

Now, there is no doubt that men have been *satisfied* in unconsciousness, since they have voluntarily remained in *identity* to themselves until their death. And, if you like, one can say that they have realized "moral *perfection*" (or a moral perfection), since there have been men who took them as the model. [The word "perfection" is then used improperly, since the *universality* of the ideal of the Wise Man no longer plays any role. Incidentally, Nietzsche seriously envisaged the possibility that the ideal that he called "Chinese" might become *universal*. And this does not seem to be absurd: it is possible, if it is not opposed. And then one could speak of a satisfied *perfection* in the proper sense of the word.]

Well, these are *facts* that are brought in opposition to Hegel. And, obviously, he can make no answer. He can at best oppose the *fact* of the conscious Wise Man to the *facts* of unconscious "Wise Men." And if this fact did not exist . . . ? In any case, by definition, Hegel cannot refute, "convert," the unconscious "Wise Man." He can refute him, "convert" him, only with *speech*. Now, by beginning to *speak* or to listen to a *discourse*, this "Wise Man" already accepts the Hegelian ideal. If he truly is what he is—an unconscious "Wise Man"—he will refuse all *discussion*. And then one could refute him only as one "refutes" a fact, a thing, or a beast: by physically destroying him.

To be sure, Hegel could say that the unconscious "Wise Man" is not a truly human being. But that would be only an arbitrary definition. This is to say: Hegelian Wisdom is a necessary ideal only for a definite type of human being, namely, for the man who puts the supreme value in Self-Consciousness; and only this man can realize this ideal.

In other words: the Platonic-Hegelian ideal of Wisdom is valid only for the *Philosopher*.

Now we understand better the significance of the more precise statement that I made, namely, that in the *Phenomenology* Hegel presupposes not only the fact that man is *essentially* self-conscious, but also the fact that man's self-consciousness naturally and necessarily tends to *extend* itself as much as possible. This more precise statement means, quite simply, that Hegel presupposes the existence of the *Philosopher*: for the dialectical movement of the *Phenomenology* to come to its end, marked by the idea—and the realization—of Wisdom, of absolute Knowledge, at each dialectical turning point there must be a *Philosopher* who is ready to become *conscious* of the newly constituted reality. Indeed, it is the Philosopher, and only he, who wants to *know* at all costs where he is, to *become aware* of what he is, and who does not go on any further before he has become aware of it. The others, although self-conscious, close themselves up within the range of things of which they have already become conscious and remain impervious to new facts in themselves and outside of themselves. For them: "the more things change, the more they stay the same." Or, in other words: "they stick to their principles." (Also, for them: "a war is always a war"; and "all dictatorships are alike.") In short, it is not by *themselves*, but through the *Philosopher* that they become aware—and even so, reluctantly—of an *essential* change in the "situation" —that is, in the World in which they live and, consequently, in themselves.

Therefore, the man whom the *Phenomenology* has in view— that is, the man who necessarily comes to the Platonic-Hegelian ideal of the Wise Man and is supposed some day to be able to realize this ideal—is not man simply. It is solely the *Philosopher*.

We can now state the notion of "Philosophy" precisely. If Philosophy is Love of Wisdom, if to be a Philosopher means to want to become a Wise Man, the Wise Man that the Philosopher wants to become is *necessarily* the Platonic-Hegelian Wise Man— that is, the perfect and satisfied man who is essentially and completely *conscious* of his perfection and satisfaction. Indeed, it is obvious that Philosophy can be nothing other than a form of self-consciousness. If the Sciences, for example, Mathematics, relate to the real which gives them a content (i.e., a meaning) through the intermediary of space-time, Philosophy relates to the real only through Self-Consciousness. Without this pivot of Self-Consciousness, so-called "metaphysical" philosophical speculations are just as "formal," empty of content—that is, deprived of every kind of *meaning*—as the speculations of pure mathematics. Therefore, Philosophy that is something other than a simple "mental game" comparable to a card game implies and presupposes the ideal of Wisdom understood as full and perfect Self-Consciousness.

Now we can bring the Philosopher and the Wise Man face to face.

FIRST: If Wisdom is the art of *answering* all questions that can be asked concerning human existence, Philosophy is the art of *asking* them; the Philosopher is the man who always ends up asking a question that he can no longer answer (and that he can answer, when he wants to answer it at all costs, only by ceasing to be a Philosopher, without thereby becoming a Wise Man: that is, by answering either with something that is in *contradiction* with the rest of his discourse, or with an appeal to an *incomprehensible* and ineffable "unconscious").

SECOND: If the Wise Man is the man who is *satisfied* by what he *is*—i.e., by that of which he becomes *conscious* in himself, the Philosopher becomes conscious of his state of *non*satisfaction; the Philosopher is essentially a *discontented* man (which does not necessarily mean an unhappy man); and he is discontented, as Philosopher, by the sole fact of not *knowing* that he is satisfied. If we want to be nasty, we can say that the Philosopher is discontented because he does not know what he *wants*. But if we want to be just, we must say that he is discontented because he does not *know* what he wants. He has desires, like everyone. But the satisfaction of his desires does not satisfy him, as Philosopher, as long as he does not *understand* them, that is, as long as he does not fit them into the coherent *whole* of his discourse that reveals his existence—that is, as long as he does not *justify* them (generally, but not necessarily, this justification takes the form of a so-called "moral" justification). And that is why the ideal of unconscious "Wisdom" or "satisfaction" does not exist for the Philosopher: the simple fact of not *understanding* his well-being, his pleasure, his joy, or his happiness, or even his "ecstasy," would suffice to make him discontented, unsatisfied. Now, if conscious satisfaction

86

finds expression in *identity* to self, consciousness of nonsatisfaction provokes and reveals a *change*: the Philosopher is the man who *changes*, essentially; and who changes *consciously*, who *wants* to change, who wants to become and to be *other* than he is, and wants all this solely because he does not *know* that he is satisfied by what he is. Now, since self-consciousness finds expression in a *discourse* (*Logos*) and since a discourse that reveals a *change* is called a dialectical discourse, we can say that every Philosopher is necessarily a dialectician.[2]

THIRD: If the Wise Man serves as the model for himself and for others (which means: for Philosophers, that is, for those who tend toward the ideal realized by the Wise Man), the Philosopher is, so to speak, a negative model: he reveals his existence only in order to show that one must not be like him, to show that man wants to be not Philosopher, but Wise Man. Hence the Philosopher changes because he *knows* what he ought *not* to be and what he *ought* to become. In other words, he realizes a *progress* in his changes.[3]

Therefore, the Philosopher's dialectical discourse, which reveals his change, reveals a progress. And since every *revealed* progress has a *pedagogical* value, it can be said, in summary, that every Philosophy is necessarily (as Plato saw very well) a pedagogical dialectic or a dialectical pedagogy, which starts with the first question relative to the existence of the one who asks it and finally ends, at least in principle, in Wisdom, that is, in the answer (if only virtual) to *all* possible questions.

The fact that a man has decided to *read* the *Phenomenology* proves that he loves Philosophy. The fact that he *understands* the *Phenomenology* proves that he is a Philosopher, since, by reading and understanding it, he actually makes the consciousness he had of himself *grow*. As a Philosopher, he is interested in himself and not

---

[2] His dialectic, according to the first definition of Wisdom, can be reduced in the final analysis to a series of questions (relating to his existence) and answers.

[3] It is obvious, by the way, that if the term "progress" is meaningful only in relation to a *conscious* change, *every* conscious change is necessarily a progress. Indeed, given that Self-Consciousness implies and presupposes *memory*, it can be said that every change in the domain of Self-Consciousness means an *extension* of Self-Consciousness. Now, I do not believe that progress can be defined otherwise than in the following manner: there is progress from A to B, if A can be understood from B but B cannot be understood from A.

87

interested in all those who are not Philosophers—i.e., those who, from *principle*, refuse to read the *Phenomenology* and hence to extend their self-consciousness. Leaving them to their own fate and returning to himself, the Philosopher learns through the *Phenomenology* that, being a Philosopher, he is a "lover of *Wisdom*," as it is defined in and by this book. This is to say that he learns that he wants to be a *Wise Man*: namely, a perfectly self-*conscious* man, fully *satisfied* by this coming to consciousness, and thus serving as the model for all his "colleagues." And, by seeing in the Wise Man the human *ideal* in general, the Philosopher attributes to himself as Philosopher a human value without equal (since, according to him, only the Philosopher can become a Wise Man).

The whole question reduces to knowing if the Philosopher can truly hope to become a Wise Man. Hegel tells him that he can: he claims to have attained Wisdom (in and by the *Phenomenology*). But Plato says no: man will never attain Wisdom.

In order to come to a decision, one must know what both of these attitudes mean. One must understand the significance of: (1) the acceptance of the *ideal* of Wisdom and the denial of its *realization* (Plato's case); (2) the assertion of a man who says he *is* a Wise Man (Hegel's case).

SECOND LECTURE

We have come to the following result:

Philosophy is meaningful and has a reason for existing only in the event that it presents itself as the road leading to Wisdom, or at least to the extent that it is guided by the ideal of the Wise Man. Inversely, acceptance of the ideal of the Wise Man necessarily leads to Philosophy conceived as a means of attaining this ideal, or at least of directing oneself by it and toward it.

With respect to the *definition* of the Wise Man and the Philosopher, Plato, who marks the beginning of classical philosophy, agrees with Hegel, who marks its end. About the Wise Man, the only possible fundamental divergence is that which exists between Hegel and Plato—i.e., while accepting the ideal of the Wise Man and the Platonic-Hegelian definition of him, one can either assert or deny the possibility of *realizing* Wisdom, of *actually* becoming a Wise Man after being a Philosopher.

Let us now see what this divergence means. Certainly one can, like Plato, deny the possibility of realizing Wisdom. But then, one of two things: either the ideal of the Wise Man is never realized anywhere; and then the Philosopher is simply a madman, who claims or wants to be what one can *not* be and (what is worse) what he *knows* to be impossible. Or else he is not a madman; and then his ideal of Wisdom is or will be realized, and his definition of the Wise Man is or will be a truth. But since it cannot, by definition, be realized by *man* in *time*, it is or will be realized by a being *other* than man, *outside* of time. We all know that such a being is called God. Therefore, if with Plato one denies the possibility of the human Wise Man, one must either deny Philosophy, or assert the existence of God.

Let us make this assertion and see what it means. On the one hand, truth reveals what *is*. On the other hand, it remains eternally *identical* to itself. Therefore, it reveals a being that remains in identity to itself. Now by definition, the man who eternally remains a Philosopher always *changes*. (And since the World *implies* changing man, this World in its entirety also changes). Human discourse contains truth, then, only to the extent that it reveals being *other* than man (and the World); it is true only to the extent that it reveals *God*, who is the only being that is *perfect*, *satisfied*, and *conscious* of itself and of its perfect satisfaction. Hence all philosophical progress is, in fact, not an *anthropo-*logical, but a *theo-*logical progress. Wisdom for man means, not perfect coming to consciousness of *self*, but perfect knowledge of *God*.

The opposition between Plato and Hegel, then, is not an opposition *within* Philosophy. It is an opposition between Philosophy and Theology—that is, in the final analysis, between Wisdom and Religion. From the *subjective* point of view this opposition can be presented in the following manner: the Philosopher hopes to attain Wisdom (which, for him, is *self*-consciousness) through a *continuous* process of dialectical pedagogy, in which each step is conditioned and determined only by all the preceding steps; the Religious man, on the other hand, can hope to attain Wisdom (which, for him, is knowledge of *God*) only by an abrupt jump, by what is called a "conversion," which is conditioned, at least in part, by an element *external* to the process that leads to it and which is called "revelation" or "grace." From the *objective* point of view, the same opposition can be presented in the following manner: the knowledge that the Philosopher is supposed to end with can be revealed as absolute or total—i.e., as entirely and definitively true, only by being revealed as *circular* (which means that in developing it, one ends at the point from which one started); the knowledge that the Religious man ends up with, on the contrary, is absolute or total without being circular. Or else, if you prefer: the circle of religious or theological knowledge is closed only by a "single point," which interrupts the continuity of the line, this point being God. God is a *particular* being (because essentially *different* from the World and from man) that is nevertheless absolute and *total*. Hence knowledge is *total* as soon as it implies a perfect understanding of *God*. Thus, the remainder of absolute knowledge, which deals with man and the World, can be partial—that is, open, noncircular. For the atheistic Philosopher, on the other hand, circularity is the one and only guarantee of totality—that is, of the absolute *truth* of knowledge. Moving from *knowledge* to *empirical* reality, we can express the same opposition thus: given that the Wise Man's knowledge reveals nothing other than Man in the World, the reality that transforms this *total* and *circular* knowledge into truth is the *universal* and *homogeneous* State ("homogeneous" here means free from internal contradictions: from class strife, and so on); therefore, the Philosopher can attain absolute knowledge only *after* the realization of this State, that is to say, after the completion of History; for the Religious man, on the other hand, the *universal* and *homogeneous* reality that proves his total knowledge to be true is not the State, but God, who is supposed to be universal and homogeneous at *any* moment *whatsoever* of the historical evolution of the World and Man; hence the Religious man can attain his absolute knowledge at *any* historical moment *whatsoever*, in any real conditions; for this to take place, it is sufficient that *God* reveal himself to (or in and by) a man.[4]

In the final analysis, and speaking very generally, there are *three*, and only three, possible types of existential attitudes:

First, one can deny the Platonic-Hegelian *ideal* of the Wise Man. In other words, one can deny that the supreme value is contained in *Self*-Consciousness. By deciding for this attitude, one decides against *every* kind of Philosophy. But there is more. It must be said that, all things considered, this decision takes away the meaning of *all* human discourse whatsoever. In its radical form, this attitude ends in absolute *silence*.

Therefore: *First*, by rejecting the ideal of Wisdom, one decides against all meaningful discourse in favor of an absolute silence or a "language" deprived of every kind of meaning (mathematical, musical "languages," and so on). *Second*, in accepting this ideal but denying that *man* can realize it, one opts for a discourse which is, to be sure, *meaningful* but which relates to a reality that is *essentially* other than mine: one opts against Philosophy for

---

[4] I do not dwell on these questions at greater length because I shall have to talk about them in my commentary on Chapter VIII. I should only like to mention that the history of philosophy does indeed confirm this way of looking at things—namely, that to deny the possibility of the Wise Man is to transform Philosophy into Theology, and to deny God is necessarily to assert the possibility of man's realizing Wisdom (some day).

Plato, who denied this possibility, saw very well that his dialectical, pedagogical, philosophical discourse could be meaningful only provided that it was theological, always being related in the final analysis to the ἐν ἀγαθόν, to the *transcendent* perfect One. And the Wisdom to which his philosophy is supposed to lead is (according to the seventh "Letter") a "conversion," which ends in a contemplation of God in *silence*. Aristotle, who wanted to eliminate the *transcendent* ἀγαθόν from Platonism and to maintain the *absolute* value of discourse, immediately proceeded to assert the possibility of realizing Wisdom on earth. Descartes' case is even more significant (because less conscious). He denies the possibility of Wisdom, since he defines man by *error* (whereas Hegel defines him as the being that *overcomes* error through action). And to be able to develop his system, he must introduce from the beginning a transcendent God: the *totality*—i.e., the *circularity*—of the *system* is not what guarantees its truth in each of its parts, but the direct relation of its parts to the *single* total being—that is, to God, who is thus the only guarantee of all truth. Spinoza, on the other hand, who wants to eliminate the transcendent element of Cartesianism, develops his system

Theology. Finally, *third*, one can opt for Philosophy. But then one is *forced* to accept the possibility of some day *realizing* the ideal of Wisdom.

With full knowledge of the problem, Hegel opts for this third attitude. And he does not merely opt for it. In the *Phenomenology* he tries to *prove* that it is the only one possible.

Actually, he does not succeed in doing so. He cannot refute those who aspire to an existential ideal that excludes Self-Consciousness, or at the very least the indefinite extension of Self-Consciousness. And as for Theology, he only succeeds in showing that the Religious man's existence is necessarily an existence in unhappiness. But since he himself says that the Religious man is *satisfied* by his unhappiness, he cannot refute him either, unless he appeals once more to the extension of *self*-consciousness. Now, this extension no longer interests the Religious man, once he believes he has attained perfect understanding of *God*.

In short, the *Phenomenology* only shows that the ideal of the Wise Man, as it is defined therein, is the necessary ideal of *Philosophy*, and of *every* philosophy—that is, of every man who puts the supreme value on Self-*Consciousness*, which is precisely a consciousness of *self* and not of something *else*.

This restriction is by no means an *objection* to the *Phenomenology*. Indeed, Hegel writes the *Phenomenology* to answer the question, "What am I?" Now, the man who *asks* this question—that is, the man who, before continuing to live and act, wants to become *conscious* of himself—is by definition a *Philosopher*. To answer the question, "What am I?" therefore, is necessarily to talk about the Philosopher. In other words, the man with whom the

in a book entitled *Ethics*, which treats of *human* Wisdom. Finally Kant, in discovering the transcendental, believes he can do without the transcendent; or else, what is the same thing: he believes he can avoid the alternative of asserting or denying Wisdom by supposing an *infinite* or *indefinite* philosophical progress. But we know that this was but an illusion: to be sure, he does not need God in each of the two parts of his 'System," but he *cannot* do without God if he wants to make a *system* out of these two parts,—i.e., to *unite* them; actually, he abandons the "System" and merely attaches the two "*critiques*" together by means of a third "*Critique*"; and he knows full well that this union has the value, not of a truth, but of a simple "as if"; in order to make this System become *theological*, it suffices to transform the third "*Critique*" into a third part of the "*System*."

Phenomenology is concerned is not man simply, but the Philosopher (or more exactly, the *Phenomenology* is concerned with the various human types only to the extent that these types are integrated in the person of the Philosopher who analyzes himself in it—that is, in the person of Hegel, who wonders, "What am I?"). No wonder, then, that Hegel manages to prove to the man who *reads* the *Phenomenology* (and who is consequently himself a Philosopher) that man as he is described in the *Phenomenology* tends (ever more consciously) toward the ideal of Wisdom and at last realizes it. Indeed, the man who gives a *complete* answer to the question "What am I?" is by definition a Wise Man. That is to say that in *answering* (in the strict sense of the word) the question "What am I?" one necessarily answers, not "I am a Philosopher," but "I am a Wise Man." [5]

Therefore: the answer to the question asked in the *Phenomenology* is at the same time the proof of the *reality* of Wisdom, and hence a refutation of Plato and of Theology in general *by fact*. The whole question, therefore, is to know if the answer given at the end of the *Phenomenology*, or more exactly by the *entirety* of this work (or by its first seven chapters), is truly a *total* answer, an answer to *all* possible questions relating to human existence, and consequently to the existence of him who asks them. Now, Hegel believes that he proves the *totality* of the answer by its *circularity*.

This idea of circularity is, if you will, the *only* original element introduced by Hegel. The definition of Philosophy and Wisdom that he gives or presupposes is that of *all* philosophers. The assertion that Wisdom is *realizable* had already been made by Aristotle. The Stoics even asserted that Wisdom was already *realized*. And it is more than likely that certain Epicureans spoke of the Wise Man in the first person. However, none of these thinkers indicated a sufficient *criterion* for the determination of the Wise Man. In practice, they always settled for the fact of *satisfaction*: either in its subjective aspect ("immobility," absence of desires, and so on); or in its objective aspect of identity to oneself, of conscious agreement with oneself (which is usually presented from the ethical

---

[5] And the Discourse of the man who *knows* that he is Wise is no longer the *Phenomenology*, which is still a philosophy (i.e., the discourse of one who *aspires* to Wisdom), but the finished *Science*—i.e., the *Encyclopaedia*.

point of view). But no one ever succeeded in proving that the pretender to Wisdom actually realized fullness of *Self-Conscious-ness*. Now, we have seen that without *this* aspect of Wisdom, the ideal itself is no longer meaningful.

Hegel, I believe, is the first one to find *an* answer (I do not say "*the* answer") to the question of knowing whether the understanding that one has of *oneself*, and consequently the understanding that one has in *general*, is, or is not, *total, unable to be sur-passed, unable to be modified*—that is, *universally* and *definitively* valid or *absolutely* true. According to him, this answer is given by the circularity of the understanding or knowledge. The Wise Man's "absolute Knowledge" is *circular*, and *all* circular knowl-edge (only *one* such knowledge is possible) is the "absolute Knowledge" of the Wise Man.

To ask any question whatsoever leads sooner or later, after a longer or shorter series of answers-questions, to one of the questions found within the circular Knowledge that the Wise Man possesses. To start with this question and to proceed logically *necessarily* leads to the starting point. Thus it is clear that *all* possible ques-tions-answers have been exhausted; or, in other words, a *total* answer has been obtained: each part of the circular Knowledge has for its answer the *whole* of this knowledge, which—being circular—is the entirety of *all* Knowledge.

It is known that Hegel asserted that his knowledge is circular, and that circularity is the *necessary* and *sufficient* condition of *absolute* truth—that is, of *complete, universal*, and *definitive* (or "eternal") truth. But people generally forget (and only in the *Phenomenology* do they learn) that the conception of circularity, like every Hegelian conception, has a double aspect: an *ideal* or, if you will, abstract aspect; and a *real* or, if you will, concrete or "existential" aspect. And it is only the entirety of both aspects that constitutes what Hegel calls the *Begriff* (the concrete concept).

The *real* aspect of the "circularity" of Wisdom is the "circular" *existence* of the Wise Man. In the Wise Man's absolute Knowl-edge, each question is its own answer, but is so only because he goes through the *totality* of questions-answers that forms the en-tirety of the System. Likewise, in his existence, the Wise Man remains in *identity* with himself, he is closed up in himself; but he remains in *identity* with *himself* because he passes through the *totality* of *others*, and he is *closed up* in himself because he closes up the *totality* of others in himself. Which (according to the *Phenomenology*) means, quite simply, that the only man who can be Wise is a Citizen of the *universal* and *homogeneous* State—that is to say, the State of the *Tun Aller und Jeder*, in which each man exists only through and for the whole, and the whole exists through and for each man.

The absolute Knowledge of the Wise Man who realizes perfect self-consciousness is an answer to the question, "What am I?" The Wise Man's real existence must therefore be "circular" (that is to say, for Hegel, he must be a Citizen of the universal and homogeneous State) in order that the knowledge that reveals this existence may itself be *circular*—i.e., an absolute truth. Therefore: only the Citizen of the perfect State can realize absolute Knowledge. Inversely, since Hegel supposes that every man is a Philosopher—that is, made so as to become *conscious* of what he is (at least, it is only in these men that Hegel is interested, and only of them that he speaks)—a Citizen of the perfect State always eventually understands himself in and by a circular—i.e., absolute—knowledge.

This conception entails a very important consequence: Wisdom can be realized, according to Hegel, only at the end of History.[6]

This too is universally understood. It was always known that for Hegel, not only does the coming of Wisdom complete History,[7] but also that this coming is possible only at the end of History. This is known, but why this is true is not always very well understood. And one cannot understand this as long as one does not know that the Wise Man must necessarily be Citizen of the *universal* (i.e., nonexpandible) and *homogeneous* (i.e., nontransformable) State. And one cannot know this until one has understood that this State is nothing other than the real basis (the "substructure") of the circularity of the absolute System: the

---

[6] For according to the analyses of the *Phenomenology*, the State in question necessarily marks the end of the history of humanity (that is, of humanity that is self-*conscious* or aspires to this consciousness).

[7] Which is trivial, for *if everything* is known, there is actually no longer any means of *making progress* or of changing (that is, for the *Philosopher*; but only for him does this problem exist).

Citizen of this State, as active Citizen, *realizes* the circularity that he *reveals*, as contemplative Wise Man, through his System.[8]

Therefore, for Hegel there is a double criterion for the *realization* of Wisdom: on the one hand, the universality and homogeneity of the State in which the Wise Man lives; and on the other hand, the *circularity* of his Knowledge. On the one hand, IN the *Phenomenology*, Hegel has described the perfect State: the reader need only observe the historical reality in order to see that this State is real, or at least to be convinced of its imminent realization. On the other hand, BY the *Phenomenology*, Hegel has shown that his knowledge is circular. And that is why he believed he could assert that he actually realized in his person the ideal of all Philosophy—that is, the ideal of Wisdom.

What is our attitude with respect to all this?

I said that we are faced with three, and only three, possibilities. I believe we can eliminate the first without *discussion*. First, because strictly speaking, it *cannot be discussed*; and next, because the very fact of our study of the *Phenomenology* proves that *silent* satisfaction (to which this first possibility finally reduces)

[8] Starting from this conception, we understand Hegel's attitude toward Plato. According to Hegel, Plato was right in denying the possibility of the Wise Man. For Plato's "Ideal" State (which according to Hegel, moreover, merely reflects the real State of his time) is not the universal and homogeneous State; the Citizen of this State, therefore, is not *"circular,"* and hence the knowledge of this Citizen, which reveals his Citizen's reality, is not circular either. Accordingly, the attempt to assert the possibility of the Wise Man within this *imperfect* State made it necessary to transform the very ideal of Wisdom into the caricature of the Stoic and Skeptic "Wise Man." Hegel has shown in the *Phenomenology* that these would-be "Wise Men" are not at all conscious of themselves. And as soon as such a "Wise Man" becomes self-conscious, he immediately sees that he does not realize perfection. He even sees that he cannot realize it. And thus it is that, becoming a Christian, he thinks that perfection has been realized outside of the World and Man, by God. Thus, the would-be "Wise Man," having become a Christian, rediscovers the Platonic, or better, theological, conception. But he *re-discovers* Plato; therefore he is more *conscious* than Plato. That is to say, he knows *why* he cannot be a Wise Man; he knows that he cannot be a Wise Man because the State in which he exists is not perfect. He can then have the idea of a perfect State and try to *realize* it. And at the moment he does this, he will become (by ceasing to be a Platonist and a Christian) a Hegelian; more exactly—he *will be* Hegel, the *real* Wise Man, the *successful* Aristotelian, Stoic, and Skeptic. If you please, this is Plato again: Hegelian philosophy is a *theo-logy*; however, its God is the Wise Man.

does not tempt us overmuch. Therefore only one serious dilemma remains for us, the dilemma: Plato or Hegel—that is, in the final analysis, the dilemma: *Theo*-logy or Philo-*sophy*.

Now, we are faced with a fact. A man who is clearly not mad, named Hegel, claims to have realized Wisdom. Therefore, before deciding for or against Philosophy or Theology—that is, for or against the assertion of the impossibility of realizing Wisdom— we must see whether or not Hegel was right in asserting that he is a Wise Man, whether through his very being he has not already settled once for all the question that interests us.

And in order to resolve this question we must see: (1) if the current state of things actually corresponds to what for Hegel is the perfect State and the end of History; and (2) if Hegel's Knowledge is truly circular.

The answer to the first question seems very easy at first sight— the perfect State? Possible, of course, but we are indeed far from it. However, at the time of writing the *Phenomenology* in 1806, Hegel, too, knew full well that the State was not yet realized in deed in all its perfection. He only asserted that the *germ* of this State was present in the World and that the necessary and sufficient conditions for its growth were in existence. Now, can we with certainty deny the presence of such a germ and such conditions in our World? And even if we wanted to deny it, we would not succeed in settling once for all the question of Hegelian Wisdom. For we certainly cannot assert, on the basis of attempts already made, that the State in question is impossible *in principle*. Now if this State is possible, Wisdom is also possible. And then no need to abandon Philosophy and take flight into some Religion or other; hence no need to subordinate the consciousness that I have of myself to a coming to consciousness of what I am not: of God, or of some inhuman perfection (esthetic or other), or of race, people, or nation.

What, then, does the fact that the perfect State foreseen by Hegel is not yet realized mean for us? In these conditions Hegel's philosophy, especially the anthropology of the *Phenomenology*, ceases to be a *truth*, since it does not reveal a *reality*. But it is not thereby necessarily an error. It would be an error only if it could be proved that the universal and homogeneous State that he has in view is *impossible*. But this *cannot* be proved. Now, what is neither an error nor a truth is an idea, or, if you prefer, an ideal. This idea can be transformed into *truth* only by negating *action*, which will destroy the World that does not correspond to the idea and will create by this very destruction the World in conformity with the ideal. In other words, one can accept the anthropology of the *Phenomenology*, even with the knowledge that the perfect man (the Wise Man) with whom it is finally concerned is not yet realized, only on the condition that one wants to *act* with a view to the realization of the Hegelian State that is indispensable to the existence of this man—to act, or at least to *accept* and "justify" such an action, if it is done by someone, somewhere.

However, this by no means exempts us from studying the second Hegelian criterion, that of *circularity*.

Still less, given that it is infinitely more important than the first. In the first case—end of History, perfect State—what is involved is a verification of *fact*, that is to say, of something essentially *uncertain*. In the second—circularity—what is involved is a logical, rational analysis, in which no divergence of opinion is possible. Accordingly, if we see that Hegel's system actually is circular, we must conclude in spite of appearances (and perhaps even in spite of common sense) that History is completed and consequently that the State in which this system could be realized is the perfect State. This, by the way, is what Hegel himself did, as we know. After the fall of Napoleon, he declared that the Prussian State (which, in other respects, he detests) was the definitive or perfect State. And he could not do otherwise, given that he was convinced of the circularity of his system.

Therefore, the whole question for us reduces to this: if the *Phenomenology* is actually circular, we must accept it outright, along with everything that follows from it; if it is not, we must consider it as a hypothetical-deductive whole, and verify all the hypotheses and deductions one by one.[9]

One must begin, therefore, by studying the *Phenomenology*

[9] Moreover, it is not sufficient that the *Phenomenology* be circular: the Logic (or the *Encyclopaedia*) must be so, too; and, what is much more important, the System in its *entirety*, that is to say, the entirety of the *Phenomenology* and the *Encyclopaedia*, must also be circular. Now, it is precisely there that the non-circularity of Hegel's system is perfectly obvious. But here I can say so only in passing and without proof.

from the point of view of its circularity. However, before doing this, one must: (1) know what this requirement of circularity means; and (2) understand why the truly true, absolute truth can only be circular.

5

A NOTE ON ETERNITY, TIME,
AND THE CONCEPT

*Complete Text of the Sixth through Eighth Lectures
of the Academic Year 1398–1939*

SIXTH LECTURE

To speak of the appearance of Science in the concrete reality of the historical World makes it necessary to speak of a before and an after—that is, of a becoming, and consequently of *Time*. In asking the question of the relation between Science and objective Reality, therefore, one must ask the question of the relation between Science and Time. And this is what Hegel does in the Second Stage of the Second Section of the Second Part of Chapter VIII.

The problem that we are tackling here is far from new. One can even say that it has been asked as long as philosophy has existed. Indeed, all philosophies have sought, and generally claim to have found, the truth, or at least some truths. Now, truth in the strict sense of the term is supposed to be a thing that cannot be either modified or denied: it is, as we say, "universally and necessarily" valid—i.e., it is not subject to changes; it is, as we also say, *eternal* or nontemporal. On the other hand, there is no doubt that it is *found* at a certain moment of time and that it exists *in* time, because it exists through and for Man who lives in the World. Therefore, to pose the problem of truth, even partial truth, is necessarily to pose the problem of time, or more particularly, the problem of the relation between time and the eternal or between time and the intemporal. And this is the problem that Hegel poses and resolves in the "Second Stage" in question.

To use Hegel's terms, we can call the coherent whole of conceptual understanding that lays claim to the truth—*Begriff*, Concept. And, indeed, the truth is always a "concept" in the broad sense, that is to say, a coherent whole of *words* having a meaning. Then we can pose the problem by asking what the relations are between the Concept and Time.

Hegel answers this question in the very first words of the Second Stage; and one must say that he answers it in quite an unexpected manner. This is what he says (page 558, lines 10–11): "*Die* Zeit *ist der* Begriff *selbst, der* da ist" ("*Time* is the *Concept* itself, which *is there* [in empirical existence]"). And it must be underlined that in writing this strange sentence, Hegel weighed his words carefully. For he already said exactly the same thing in the Preface to the *Phenomenology*, where we read (page 38, lines 33–37): "*Was die* Zeit *betrifft, . . . so ist sie der daseiende Begriff selbst*" ("In what concerns *Time*, [it must be said that] it is the Concept itself which exists empirically").

It is very clear: "*Die Zeit ist der daseiende Begriff selbst.*" And at the same time, it is quite incomprehensible. In order to understand better what Hegel means, it is useful briefly to review the solutions to the problem that Plato and Aristotle, Spinoza and Kant proposed before him. This is what I am going to do in the sixth through eighth lectures.

The problem is to establish a positive or negative relation between the Concept and Time. Now, it is obvious that there is only a very limited number of possibilities here, as the following formulas show:

$$
\begin{aligned}
&\text{I.} \quad C = E \\
&\text{II.} \quad C = E'/ \text{ and relates to} \begin{cases} 1.\ E\text{-----} \\ 2.\ T \end{cases} \begin{cases} a.\ \text{outside of T} \\ b.\ \text{in T} \end{cases} \\
&\text{III.} \quad C = T \\
&[\text{IV.} \quad C = T']
\end{aligned}
$$

C symbolizes the Concept. Not some determined concept or other, but *the* Concept—that is, the integration of all concepts, the complete system of concepts, the "idea of ideas," or the *Idea* in the Hegelian (Cf. *Logik*) and Kantian sense of the word. *T* designates Time or temporal reality. *E* represents the opposite of Time—that is, Eternity, nontemporal reality in the *positive* sense.

101

E' signifies "eternal," as opposed to "Eternity." (Just as this table *is*, without being Being, the Concept can be conceived as *eternal* without being Eternity: it "participates" in Eternity, it is an eternal function of Eternity, and so on; but Eternity itself is something other than the Concept.) Finally, *T'* is the "temporal," distinguished from Time itself as the "eternal" is distinguished from Eternity.

The formulas, then, can be read as follows. *First possibility*: the Concept *is* Eternity. Hence it is *related* to nothing: it is obviously not related to *Time*; and it is not *related* to Eternity either, since it *is* Eternity. This is Parmenides' position. (But since the fully developed and truly understood Parmenidean point of view is known to us only through Spinoza, it is of him that I shall speak in discussing this possibility). *Third possibility*: the Concept *is* Time, and hence is *related* neither to Eternity nor to Time; this is Hegel's position. Possibilities I and III, being identifications, cannot be subdivided. On the other hand, *possibility II* is subdivided into two possibilities, the first of which has in turn two variants; thus three possible types of philosophy are obtained, and all philosophies other than those of Parmenides-Spinoza and Hegel can actually be divided up among these three types.[1]

There is still *possibility IV*: the Concept is temporal. But this is no longer a *philosophical* possibility. For this (skeptical) type of thought makes all philosophy impossible by denying the very idea of truth: being *temporal*, the concept *essentially* changes; that is to say that there is no *definitive* knowledge, hence no *true* knowledge in the proper sense of the word. *Possibility III*, on the other hand, is compatible with the idea of truth; for if everything that is *in* Time (i.e., everything that is *temporal*) always *changes*, Time itself does not change.

Once again, then, the *second possibility* divides into two. Since it is *eternal*, and not *Eternity*, the Concept is *related* to something

---

[1] At least with regard to the problem that interests us. This problem, moreover, expresses the *essential* content of every philosophy, so that it can be said that in general there are only five *irreducible*—i.e., *essentially* different—philosophical types: an impossible type (possibility I: Parmenides-Spinoza); three relatively possible, but insufficient types (possibility II: Plato, Aristotle, Kant); and a true type, which, by the way, needs to be *developed*, to be *realized*; for I personally believe that this has not yet been done (Hegel and Heidegger represent this third possibility).

other than itself. Whence two variants: (1) the ancient or pagan variant, according to which the *eternal* Concept is related to *Eternity*; a variant clearly formulated by Plato and Aristotle (who agree on this point); and (2) the modern or Judaeo-Christian variant, clearly formulated by Kant: the *eternal* Concept is related to *Time*. The first variant in turn implies two possible types: (1) the eternal Concept related to Eternity which is *outside* of Time (Plato); and (2) the eternal Concept related to Eternity *in* Time (Aristotle).[2]

The universe of ideas, the idea of ideas—this in Plato is what in Hegel is called *Begriff*, Concept (or in the *Logik*, Idea). The World of phenomena is what Hegel calls *Dasein*, empirical Existence. To simplify, then, let us speak of "Concept" and of "Existence." Existence is essentially *change*—that is, a *temporal* entity. On the other hand, there is change *only* in Existence— that is, Existence is not only *temporal*, but Time itself. The Concept, on the other hand, does not—*essentially*—change. Therefore it is essentially something *other* than temporal, and other than *Time*. Hence it would be tempting to say with Parmenides (and Spinoza) that it *is* Eternity. But Plato does not say so; for he believes he has discovered that the Concept (i.e., the Logos, the *word*—or discourse endowed with a *meaning*) is *related* to something that is *other* than the Concept (or the word) itself. (Here is the point where Plato, and Platonizing philosophers from Plato to Kant, must be attacked, if one wants to avoid the disagreeable anthropological consequences implied by their philosophies). Therefore the Concept *is* not *Eternity*. It is merely *eternal*. Consequently one must pose the problem of the *relations* between the eternal Concept on the one hand, and Time and Eternity on the other.

Let us first state a fact of which Plato is not ignorant: real, empirically existing man utters discourses that have a meaning. Therefore: *concepts*, and consequently *the* integral Concept, sub-

---

[2] It is obvious that the second (the modern) variant cannot be subdivided in the same way as the first (the ancient), because there can be no Time *in* Eternity. However, there have been Christian philosophers who—explicitly or implicitly— made this assertion; but either they made meaningless plays on words, or else— unawares—they realized the Hegelian (or atheistic) type of philosophy.

sist in *time*, while being by definition *eternal*—i.e., something essentially other than time. (They exist *in* change; but, since they do not change, they are necessarily something other than change). If we symbolize temporal existence (Man in the World) by a line, we must represent the Concept by a *singular* point *on* this line: this point is essentially *other* than the other points of the line (see Figure 1). Now for Plato, the Concept is *related* to something *other* than itself. (It is on this point that Plato criticized Parmenides-Spinoza; it is on this point that Hegel criticizes Plato and all other philosophers: for him, as for Parmenides-Spinoza, the Concept is *related* to nothing, except to itself). Now, being eternal, the Concept must be related to *Eternity*, says Plato. (Aristotle follows him in this; but Kant opposes it and says that the eternal Concept is related to Time). But, Plato says, Eternity can only be *outside* of Time (which is denied by Aristotle, who discovers Eternity *in* Time). Therefore, we must complete our schema in the manner indicated by Figure 2.

Let us go further. The appearance of concepts, and even of *the* Concept, in existence is not a unique phenomenon. In any case, the Concept can appear at any moment of time whatsoever. Hence the line that symbolizes existence implies *several* eternal singular points (Figure 3). Now by definition, *Eternity*—i.e., the entity to which the Concept is related—is always the *same*; and the *relation* of the Concept to this entity is also always the *same*. Therefore: at *every* instant of time (of the existence of Man in the World) the *same* relation to one and the *same* extratemporal entity is possible. If we want to symbolize Plato's conception, we must therefore modify our schema in the manner indicated by Figure 4.

Thus we find the schema of the metaphysics of the *Timaeus*: a circular time, the circularity of which (and the circularity of what, being temporal, is *in* time) is determined by the *relation* of what is *in* Time to what is *outside* of Time. And at the same time we find the famous "central point" that a Christian theology (i.e., in my view, a variant of Platonism) must necessarily introduce into the Hegelian circle that symbolizes absolute or circular knowledge. The circle thus drawn can obviously symbolize the *totality* of *Knowledge*: both of Knowledge relating to Man in the (temporal) World; and of Knowledge relating to what is outside of

Figure 1

Figure 2

Figure 3

Figure 4

Figure 5

Figure 6

"Theology"
(Plato)

Figure 7

"Pessimistic Skepticism"
or "Relativism"

Figure 8

Silence

"Mysticism"

Figure 9

"Optimistic Skepticism"
or "Criticism"
(Kant)

Figure 10

"Absolute Knowledge"
(Hegel)

Figure 11

this Knowledge—that is, outside of *Man* who exists in the World and outside of the World that implies existing (i.e., temporal) Man. This "central point" (which necessarily appears once the Concept is interpreted as a *relationship* with something *other* than the Concept—that is, once the element of *transcendence* is introduced into Knowledge) has been called God. Furthermore, we have seen that this theistic schema has no specifically Christian aspect, since we derived it from the Platonic conception.[3]

Let us say, then, that the "central point" is God. We can do so since for Plato the ἓν ἀγαθόν, symbolized by this point, is also θεός.

But the name makes no difference. Let us rather see what the thing means. And to this end, let us transform the drawing, that is to say, make it more precise.

First, let us simplify. The Concept *can* be repeated in time. But its repetition does not change it, nor does it change its relation to Eternity; in a word, it changes nothing. Hence we can do away with all the radii of the circle, except for one (Figure 5). (Except for one, for the fact of the Concept's presence in Time is of capital importance; now, the point on the circumference symbolizes *human* knowledge which is accomplished in Time). And now let us see what is symbolized by this radius.

The radius symbolizes the *relation* between the eternal Concept and Eternity or the eternal Entity. Therefore this relation too is nontemporal or eternal. Nevertheless, it is clearly a *relation* in the strict sense—i.e., a relation between two *different* things. Therefore the radius has, if you will, *extension* (in Space, since there is no Time in it). Therefore we did well to symbolize it by a line (a dotted line, to distinguish it from the solid temporal line). However, the relation in question is undeniably *double* (Figure 6). Indeed, on the one hand the (eternal) Concept situated in Time— i.e., the Word—*rises* up through its *meaning* to the entity revealed by this meaning; and on the other hand, this entity *descends* through the *meaning* toward the Word, which it thus *creates* as *Word* out of its phonetic, sound-giving, changing reality. Without

---

[3] Generally speaking, it is the schema of all *mono-theistic* knowledge—that is, of all Knowledge that recognizes a *transcendence*, and only one transcendent entity. And one can say that every philosophy recognizes a transcendence: except the *acosmism* of Parmenides-Spinoza (possibility I), and the *atheism* of Hegel (possibility III).

the Word, Eternity would not be *represented* in Time, and consequently it would not be accessible to Man. And without Eternity, the Word would have no meaning and would not raise Man above Time and change; there would be no *truth* for Man. (Or, taking *a* concept as an example of *the* Concept: the *word* "Dog" reveals the *essence* of the dog, and without this word this essence would not be revealed to man; but the *essence* of the *dog* is what realizes the meaning of the word; the *dog* is what allows man to develop the *word* "Dog" into a *judgment*, saying: "the dog is an animal with four feet, covered with hair, etc.") Generally speaking, there is a movement from the word to the thing, and a return from the thing to the word. And it is only this *double* relation that constitutes the *truth* or the revelation of reality, that is to say, the *Concept* in the proper sense. And on the other hand, this double relation *exhausts* the truth or the Concept: the (eternal) Concept is related only to Eternity, and Eternity reveals itself exclusively through the Concept. Hence, even though they are in Time, they nonetheless have no relations with Time and the temporal. Therefore the double, or better, *circular*, relation of the (eternal) Concept and Eternity *cuts through* the temporal circle. Change as change remains inaccessible to the Concept. In other words, there is no truth in the temporal, either before or after the Concept. Through the Concept, one can rise from the temporal to Eternity; and then one can fall back to the temporal. But after the fall one is exactly what one was before. In order to live in the Concept— that is, in the truth—it is necessary to live *outside* of Time in the *eternal* circle. In other words: the eternal circle of *absolute* knowledge, even though it is in Time, has no relation to Time; and the *entirety* of Knowledge is *absolute* only to the extent that it implies an *eternal* circle which is related *only* to Eternity. And that is why we must represent the Platonic conception of absolute Knowledge in the manner indicated by Figure 7. In other words, again we find the schema of theo-logical Knowledge. (The circle with a point in the center was but a simple graphical variant of this schema.)

Thus we see that the difference between the theological System and the atheistic Hegelian System is to be traced back to the very beginning point. Speaking in metaphysical terms, we can say that a theistic System properly so-called—that is, a frankly transcendentalist and mono-theistic System—results as soon as the Concept (i.e., absolute Knowledge) is defined as an *eternal* entity that is *related* to Eternity, Eternity being *outside* of Time.

Let us see what this means for the temporal World of phenomena. Understanding of this World (and of Man who lives in it) is symbolized by the large circle. So, let us take away the small circle of the eternal Concept (Figure 8). Then, two interpretations are possible. FIRST, one can say that the arc has fixed, definitive, impassable limits (Figure 9). Thus we find the schema of the Knowledge that I have called "mystical" in the broad sense of the word. Taking God away from a given theological System, then, can lead in the end to a mystical System, in which one can speak of everything except God, who is essentially ineffable. And if one is radical, one will say that it cannot even be said of God that he *is* God; the most that can be said is that he is ineffable. And the ineffable Being can reveal itself through whatever you like: through "ecstasy," through music, and so on; but not through Speech.[4]

But with regard to the other things—i.e., the temporal entities—*everything* can be said. In other words, the Knowledge that relates to them can, in principle, be *total*, definitive; since Time is *limited*, it and its content can be *exhausted* by Discourse. However, in saying *everything* that can be said about the temporal (worldly and human) reality, one attains its *limit*—that is, the limit of what is beyond. But the establishment of the *presence* of the beyond proves that one cannot be content with *Discourse*, even total. One sees that one is obliged to go beyond Discourse through a *silence*—"mystical," "ecstatic," "algorithmic," "sonorous," or otherwise.

SECOND, one can say that after the small circle that symbolizes the eternal Concept has been taken away, the arc of the large circle is without limits (its two "farthest" points being on the small circle that has been removed): Figure 8. In this case, we have the schema of skeptical or relative Knowledge—i.e., the schema of the absence of true Knowledge in the strict sense of the term. Knowledge is related to Time—that is, to change. But since

---

[4] In Plato the "mystical" tendency is very clear: the ἐν ἀγαθόν is "revealed" in and by a *silent* contemplation.

Time is now without limits, change never stops. Hence there is no eternal or definitive Knowledge: there is no *epistēmē*, there is only *doxa*. But in another way, even in this case, one can say that the circle is closed. Then the ideal of Hegelian absolute Knowledge—that is, circular Knowledge—is set up (cf. Figure 11). But this ideal forever remains an ideal: the circle of real Knowledge is never actually closed (Figure 10). It is the optimistic form of skepticism. It is the skepticism of the eternal "why," of humanity "that always learns," that ceaselessly marches on like an individual man toward an end that it will never attain. And the *truth* remains "blank"—according to the definition of the Devil in "*Le Puits de Sainte Claire.*" It is also the "eternal task" (*ewige Aufgabe*) of Kantian Criticism. In the two variants of skeptical knowledge, then, philosophy as a road that actually leads to Wisdom is obviously impossible.

Inversely, through the introduction of the *eternal* Concept—i.e., discursive *truth*—into a given "mystical" or "skeptical" System, a *theo*-logical System is always obtained, even if the term God does not explicitly enter into it. For in this case the truth would necessarily reveal a Being situated *outside* of Time—that is, outside of the World and Man.

Well then, once more, what does the *theological* (not the mystical or skeptical) System mean for understanding of the temporal World?

In principle, *everything* can be said about the World and Man. Knowledge that relates to them is *total*. However, in itself, Knowledge relating to Time and the temporal remains relative: it is a *doxa*. Only by relating it in its entirety to *eternal* Knowledge related to Eternity can one say something *definitive* about the temporal.

LET US CONSIDER THE WORLD. In theological language (in the narrow sense of the term) one must say that events in the World, as well as the World itself, are contingent: hence there is no absolute *Knowledge* relating to them. But if, *per impossible*, God's designs and *His* creative will were known, there could be a true *Science* of the World. Speaking in symbolic theological terms, one can say that there is *Science* relating to the World only to the extent that this World implies *geometrical* elements. Indeed, Kant showed us that if algorithm is to be transformed into *Discourse*, it must be related either to Time or to Space. Here, since its being related to Time is excluded by definition, it can be related only to Space (which, in this conception, is a Space *outside* of Time). And indeed, one can *speak* of geometry: "the circle" is also a *word* that has a meaning (and one can *say* what it is), as opposed to a nonspatialized integral, for example, which can be *expressed* only by an algorithm. Therefore, the theological System can fabricate a real *geometry*, that is to say, a *geometrical* physics, and nothing else. Now, this physics can tell us that the earth is *round*, but it cannot tell us why it attracts heavy objects (because the force of attraction, like every force, is not only a spatial, but also an essentially temporal phenomenon); and consequently, it cannot say what the earth is as *Earth*—a planet on which trees grow and man lives.

AS FOR MAN himself, the case is the same for him. There is true *Science* concerning him only to the extent that he is related to *Eternity*. I can *prove* the existence of *God*: it is an eternal truth. But I cannot prove *my* existence on the same grounds, unless I conceive of myself as an *eternal* idea in God. As for me in my temporal or worldly existence, I can know nothing. Moreover, absolute Knowledge related to *Eternity* is precisely what makes an *absolute* Knowledge relating to the temporal *impossible*. Let us take Christian theology as an example. What truly matters for the Christian is to know whether he is saved or damned in consequence of his worldly or temporal existence. Now, the analysis of the eternal concept that reveals God shows that this cannot be known, that this can never be known. If the Christian does not want to be "mystical," that is, to renounce Discourse completely, he must necessarily be *skeptical* with respect to his temporal existence. Do what he will, he will not be *certain* that he is acting well.[5]

In short, in the theological System there is an *absolute* Knowledge in and through *Bewusstsein*, but there is no absolute Knowledge through and in *Selbst*-bewusstsein.

Finally, we can present the theological System in its anthropological aspect by explaining the significance in it of the idea of

---

[5] But the Christian admits that God's decision is in conformity with human reason.

human *freedom* (that is to say, the idea of Man himself, since man without freedom is but an animal).

We do not need to define freedom here.[6]

We all have "an idea of what it is," as we say; even if we do not know how to *define* freedom. And the "idea" that we have of it is sufficient to enable us to say this:

The free act is situated, so to speak, *outside* of the line of temporal evolution. The *hic et nunc*, represented by a point on this line, is *determined, fixed, defined* by the past which, through it, determines the future as well. The *hic et nunc* of the free act, on the other hand, is *unexplainable*, on the basis of its past; it is not fixed or determined by it. Even while existing in space-time, the being endowed with freedom must be able to *detach* itself from the *hic et nunc*, to rise *above* it, to take up a *position* in relation to it. But the free act is related to the *hic et nunc*: it is effected in given determined conditions. That is to say: the *content* of the *hic et nunc* must be preserved, while being *detached* from the *hic et nunc*. Now, that which preserves the content of a perception while detaching it from the *hic et nunc* of sensation is precisely the Concept or the Word that has a meaning. (This *table* is bound to the *hic et nunc*; but the *meaning* of the *words* "this table" exists everywhere and always). And that is why everyone agrees that only a *speaking* being can be free.[7]

As for Plato, who believes that virtue can be taught, and taught through dialectic—i.e., through Discourse—obviously the free act, for him, has the same nature as the act of conceptual understanding: for him, they are but two complementary aspects of one and the same thing.

Now, for Plato the Concept is (1) *eternal*, and (2) it is *related* to Eternity, which (3) is *outside* of Time. The application of this definition of the Concept to the free act leads to the following results:

Just as the Concept is not related to the temporal reality in which *doxa* reigns, so the free act, too, is impossible in *this* reality. In and

---

[6] In point of fact, either this word has no meaning, or else it is the *Negativity* of which Hegel speaks, and which a Descartes and a Kant had in view without speaking of it explicitly. But no matter.

[7] Hegel, it is true, reverses this assertion and says that only a free being can speak; but he too maintains the close connection between language and freedom.

by the free act, man relates himself to something that is situated *outside* of Time. That is, as Plato says in his well-known myth: the soul *chooses* its destiny *before* its birth. There is *choice*, hence *freedom*. But this choice is made *outside* of temporal existence, which existence is absolutely *determined* in its evolution. In his myth Plato adopts the idea of metempsychosis: the choice can be repeated, and the choices differ among themselves. But in truth, this hypothesis does not fit in well with the entirety of the Platonic system, in which the nontemporal admits of no variations. Accordingly, fairly soon one comes to the (gnostic and Christian) conception of a unique choice, fixed by the relation between the extra-temporal Eternity (or God) and the free agent. It is the idea of the Angel who decides once and for all, and outside of time properly so-called, for or against God, and becomes a "virtuous" Angel or a forever "fallen" Angel or Devil.[8]

Generally speaking, this whole conception does not manage to explain *temporal* existence as *such*, that is, as History. History here is always a comedy, and not a tragedy: the tragic is before or after, and in any case outside of, temporal life; this life itself realizes a program fixed beforehand and therefore, taken in itself, has neither any meaning nor any value.

In conclusion, then, this can be said: every system of *theo*-logical absolute Knowledge sees in the Concept an *eternal* entity, which is *related* to Eternity. And inversely, *this* conception of the Concept necessarily leads in the end, once developed, to a *theo*-logical Knowledge. If, as in Plato, Eternity is situated *outside* of Time, the System is rigorously *mono*-theistic and radically *tran*-scendentalist: the being of God is *essentially* different from the being of him who speaks of God; and this divine Being is abso-lutely one and unique, that is to say, it is eternally identical to itself or it excludes all change.

In relation to the natural World, this System gives a purely

---

[8] This conception also comes to light in the dogma of original sin: in Adam, man, in his entirety, freely decides once and for all. Here the act is in time; but it is not *related* to time; it is related to the *eternal* commandment of *God*, this God being *outside* of time. As for the freedom of man properly so-called—it is the stumbling block of all theology, and particularly of Christian theology. Even if divine election is a cooperation with man (which in itself is quite "heretical"), human acts are judged all at once by God, so that freedom remains a unique act, situated outside of time and related to Eternity.

geometrical theory, which can at most operate with the notion of purely incorporeal "movement" (as Descartes does), but not with the notion of force: this System admits kinematics or phoronomy, but excludes dynamics. Consequently, it does not explain biological phenomena, in which Time is *constituent*. And in relation to the human World, this System at best explains "angelic" existence, but deprives historical life, that is, Man's *temporal* existence, of any meaning and value.

SEVENTH LECTURE

I have discussed at some length the Platonic conception, which corresponds to possibility II, 1, *a*.

Let us now move on to Aristotle—that is, to possibility II, 1, *b*.

Aristotle saw Plato's difficulties. And at the same time he made a great discovery. Just like Plato, Aristotle defines the Concept as eternal. That is, he defines it as a relation to something else. And this something else for him, as for Plato, is not Time but Eternity. (*Epistēmē* exists only in the cosmos in which there are ideas—i.e., eternal entities, having Eternity as their *topos*.) But Aristotle saw what Plato seems not to have seen; namely, that Eternity is not *outside* of Time, but *in* Time. At the very least, there is something eternal in Time.

In fact, Plato reasoned as follows: All real dogs change; the concept "dog," on the other hand, remains identical to itself; therefore it must be related to an Eternity situated outside of real dogs—that is, outside of Time. (This Eternity is the "idea" of dog, and consequently, in the final analysis, the Idea of ideas.) To which Aristotle answered: to be sure, the concept "dog" is related to Eternity; but Eternity subsists *in* Time; for if real *dogs* change, *the* real dog—that is, the *species* "dog"—does not change. Since the species is *eternal*, even though it is placed *in* Time, it is possible to relate the Concept to Eternity *in* Time. Therefore there is an

113

absolute Knowledge relating to the temporal World, to the extent that this World implies Eternity. In other words, Plato forgot that in Heracleitus' river there are permanent eddies. First of all, they are the animals and the plants. The eternal or immutable axis of the "eddies" is the *telos* or the entelechy; and this same entelechy is what appears, in relation to the Concept, as the Idea of the "eddy." But there are also planets, and finally the Cosmos. Hence Aristotle says: Time itself is *eternal*. It is circular,[9] but the circle is gone around again and again, eternally.[10] Therefore the Cosmos has the same structure as does the animal. The Aristotelian System thus gives an explanation of life and a biological conception of the World.

Theologically speaking, the conception that relates the eternal Concept to Eternity *in* Time equals *Polytheism*. To be sure, Aristotle is too far removed from the totemic mentality to assert that animals and plants are gods. But when he says that the planets are gods, he maintains a greater agreement with his system than does Plato with his. But, all things considered, the difference is not very important: mono- or poly-theism—in both cases we are dealing with a *theo*-logical knowledge. The cosmic revolution is eternally repeated; and it is solely because there is an *eternal* repetition that there is an absolute Knowledge relating to the Cosmos. Now, it is one and the same Eternity that manifests itself in and through the eternal return of Time. In other words, there is a supreme god, the God properly so-called, who maintains the Cosmos in its identity and thus makes conceptual Knowledge possible. And, while manifesting itself through the course of Time, this divine Eternity differs essentially from everything that is *in* Time. At most, man can speak of himself too, taken as species, when he speaks of God. It remains nonetheless true that the difference is *essential* between him, taken as historical individual, and the eternal God of whom he speaks. Once more, then, as in Plato, it is an absolute Knowledge of *Bewusstsein*, and not of *Selbst-Bewusstsein*. (For the species has no *Selbst-Bewusstsein*, no *Selbst* or Self; at the most, it says "we," but not "I.")

[9] As in Hegel.
[10] Whereas in Hegel the circuit is made only once.

Therefore, the Aristotelian System explains Man's biological existence but not his truly human—i.e., historical—existence. And we see this even better by turning to the anthropological level—that is, by posing the problem of *freedom*.

To be sure, Aristotle talks about freedom. But everyone talks about freedom. Even Spinoza! But if it is not to be a word-game, if the true notion of freedom (made explicit in the Hegelian conception, as it is formulated in the *Phenomenology*) is sought, it must be admitted that it is not compatible with Aristotle's System. As a matter of fact, we know that this System excludes, by definition, a *creative* God. (By definition, for Eternity in Time signifies: *eternity* of the World, *return*, and *eternal* return.) Now, where there is no place for God's creative action, there is still less place for Man's creative action: Man undergoes History, but does not create it; therefore he is not *free* in Time. On this point, Aristotle does not go beyond Plato. But his System is still less acceptable than the Platonic System, for it excludes even the *transcendent* free act. In fact, since Eternity is *in* Time, and the eternal Concept is related to Eternity *in* Time, all possibility of going outside of Time is excluded. One is *outside* of Time only by being *in* Time. A temporal existence that one could *choose* outside of Time would be conceptually *unknowable*, because it would not be *eternal* in Time, whereas the Concept can be related only to an *Eternity* in Time. In short: to the extent that Man changes, he does not know; and not *knowing*, he is not free (by definition); and to the extent that he *knows*, he does not change and hence is not free either, in the usual sense of the word.

Indeed, for Aristotle as for Plato, one can have an absolute Knowledge of Man only by relating Man to Eternity. The individual soul is too small to be known, Plato says in the *Republic*: to know it, one must see it enlarged—that is, one must contemplate the City. Now for Aristotle, Plato's eternal State is but a utopia; in actual fact, all States sooner or later change and perish; hence there is no absolute political Knowledge relating to *one* of the possible forms of the State. But, happily, there is a closed cycle in the transformation of States, which is *eternally* repeated. Therefore this cycle can be understood *conceptually*; and by speaking of it, one can grasp the different States and Man himself through concepts. To be sure. But if all this is true, History has nothing to do with what is called "History" today; and in this History, Man is anything but free.

Therefore, by replacing geometry with biology, the Aristotelian variant of the Platonic System explains Man as animal, but does not explain him as historical and free individual; it does not even explain him—as Plato did—as fallen Angel.

Alongside the great philosophies there have always been more or less barbaric or barbarized theories. The Platonic-Aristotelian notion of the Concept has also been barbarized: either by a vulgar and absurd denial, or by a distorted acceptance.

The *vulgar denial* consists in saying that the Concept, far from being eternal, is just as temporal as any other thing existing in Time. It is our possibility IV, of which I shall not speak, since it does away with the very idea of a true or genuine Knowledge. It is Skepticism or Relativism, which Plato denounced under the name of "Sophistic"; which Kant criticized, calling it "Empiricism"; and which Husserl quite recently denounced once more under the name of "Psychologism." Let us speak no further about it.

Let us rather say a few words about the *distorted acceptance*, which is no less absurd, although less *obviously* absurd. People who hold this view continue to say that the Concept is eternal. But while being eternal, it is in Time; which means, they say, that it is related to what is in Time—i.e., to the temporal. (Not to Time, but to the temporal—i.e., to what is *in* Time.) And being related to the temporal, it is related to it in Time, existing—in Time—*before* the temporal properly so-called. It is the well-known notion of the *a priori* or the "innate idea" that *precedes* experience.

This "apriorism" (called "Dogmatism" by Kant) is what the famous first sentence of the Introduction to the *Critique of Pure Reason* is directed against: there is no doubt, Kant says (more or less), that experience—i.e., the temporal reality—always precedes in time the concept that appears in time as *my* Knowledge. And indeed there can be no possible doubt on this subject. Vulgar Apriorism begins from a supposed fact and ends in a truly untenable conception: on the gnoseological level as well as on the anthropological level (where the notorious "free will" is discussed).

One need only develop this Apriorism somewhat in order to come either to Skepticism or Relativism, or to Kant; or, finally, to the return to Plato and Aristotle.

Kant, like every philosopher worthy of the name, knows full well that the Concept can neither be defined as temporal, nor be related to the temporal (which, by the way, amounts to the same thing); for him, as for Plato and Aristotle, the Concept is *eternal*. Now, being *eternal* and not *Eternity*, the Concept must be *related* to something, and *related* in the strict sense of the term—that is, related to something *other* than itself. But, seeing the difficulties that Plato and Aristotle encountered by relating the eternal Concept to Eternity, Kant had the unheard-of audacity to relate it to Time (and not, of course, to the temporal—i.e., to what is *in* Time).

The whole Kantian conception is summed up in this celebrated sentence: "without intuition the concept is empty; without the concept intuition is blind."

But before speaking of this Kantian formula, I want to mention in a few words another solution to the problem, namely, Spinoza's.

As I have already said, Spinoza's System is the perfect incarnation of the absurd. (And that is why, when one tries to "realize" his thought, as we say, one experiences the same feeling of dizziness as when one is faced with a paradox of formal logic or set theory.)

Now, a particularly curious thing: *absolute* error or absurdity is, and must be, just as "circular" as the truth. Thus, Spinoza's (and Parmenides') absolute Knowledge must be symbolized by a closed circle (without a central point, of course): Figure 12. Indeed, if Spinoza says that the Concept *is* Eternity, whereas Hegel says that it *is* Time, they have this much in common: the Concept is not a *relationship*. (Or, if you like, it is in relation only to itself.) Being and (conceptual) Thought are one and the same thing, Parmenides said. Thought (or the Concept) is the attribute of Substance, which is not different from its attribute, Spinoza says. Therefore, in both cases—that is, in Parmenides-Spinoza and in Hegel—there is no "reflection" *on* Being. In both cases, Being *itself* is what reflects on itself in and through, or—better yet—as,

Concept. Absolute Knowledge that reflects the totality of Being, therefore, is just as closed in itself, just as "circular," as Being itself in its totality: there is nothing outside of the Knowledge, as there is nothing outside of Being. But there is an essential difference: Parmenides-Spinoza's Concept-Being is *Eternity*, whereas Hegel's Concept-Being is *Time*. Consequently, Spinozist absolute Knowledge, too, must *be* Eternity. That is to say that it must exclude Time. In other words: there is no need of Time to realize it; the *Ethics* must be thought, written, and read "in a trice." And that is the thing's absurdity. [Plotinus, however, accepts this consequence.]

This absurdity was already denounced by Plato in his *Parmenides*. If Being is truly one (or more exactly, the One)—i.e., if it excludes diversity, all diversity—and therefore all change— i.e., if it is Eternity that *annuls* Time—if, I say, Being is the One, a man could not *speak* of it, Plato remarks. Indeed, Discourse would have to be just as *one* as the Being that it reveals, and therefore could not go beyond the single word "one." And even that. . . . For *Time* is still the crucial question. Discourse must be *intemporal*: now, if he has not the time, man cannot even pronounce a *single* word. If Being is *one*, or, what amounts to the same thing, if the Concept *is* Eternity, "absolute Knowledge" reduces for Man to absolute *silence*.[11]

I say: for Man. That is, for the speaking being that lives in Time and needs time in order to live and to speak (i.e., in order to think by means of the Concept). Now, as we have seen, the Concept *as such* is not (or at least does not seem to be) necessarily attached to Time. The universe of Concepts or of Ideas can be conceived of as a universe of *Discourse*: as an eternal Discourse, in which all the elements coexist. [This is what Plotinus says.] And as a matter of fact, there are (it seems) *non*temporal relations, between Concepts: all Euclid's theorems, for example, exist simultaneously within the entirety of his axioms. [And Plotinus insists on this fact.] Hence there would be a nontemporal *Discourse*.[12] The *idea* of the Spinozist System, then, is not absurd: quite simply, it is the idea of *absolute* Knowledge. What is absurd is that this System is

---

[11] Plato accepts this: the One is ineffable.

[12] Just as there are nontemporal movements, as Descartes correctly remarks.

"Absolute Knowledge"
(Spinoza and Hegel)

Figure 12

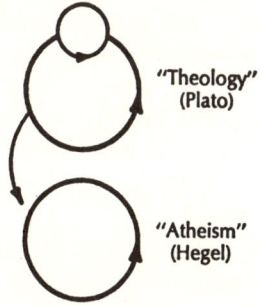
"Theology"
(Plato)

"Atheism"
(Hegel)

Figure 16

"Monotheistic Theology"
(Plato)

Figure 13

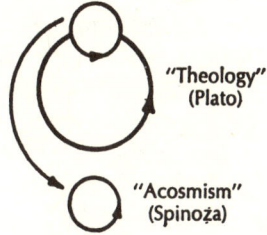
"Polytheistic Theology"
(Aristotle)

Figure 14

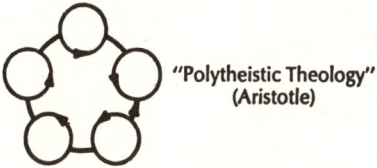
"Theology"
(Plato)

"Acosmism"
(Spinoza)

Figure 17

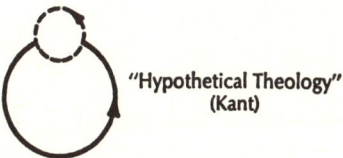
"Hypothetical Theology"
(Kant)

Figure 15

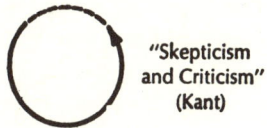
"Skepticism
and Criticism"
(Kant)

Figure 18

119

supposed to have been fabricated by a *man*, who in actual fact needed *time* in order to fabricate it. [Accordingly, in Plotinus, this system belongs to the eternal Intelligence.] Or else, again: the *System* can exist outside of Time; but, starting from temporal existence, there is no *access* to this System. (The Spinozist System is Hegel's *Logik*, for which there would not and could not be a *Phenomenology* that "leads" to it; or else, it is Descartes' System, to which one could not find access through a *Discourse on Method*.)

The *Ethics* is made in accordance with a method of which an account *cannot* be given in *human* language. For the *Ethics* explains everything, except the possibility for a man living in time to write it. And if the *Phenomenology* explains why the *Logik* appears at a certain moment of history and not at another, the *Ethics* proves the impossibility of its own appearance at *any* moment of time whatsoever. In short, the *Ethics* could have been written, *if it is true*, only by God himself; and, let us take care to note—by a nonincarnated God.

Therefore, the difference between Spinoza and Hegel can be formulated in the following way: Hegel *becomes* God by thinking or writing the *Logik*; or, if you like, it is by becoming God that he writes or thinks it. Spinoza, on the other hand, must *be* God from all eternity in order to be able to write or think his *Ethics*. Now, if a being that *becomes* God in time can be called "God" only provided that it uses this term as a metaphor (a correct metaphor, by the way), the being that has always *been* God is God in the proper and strict sense of the word. Therefore, to be a Spinozist is actually to replace God the Father (who has no Son, incidentally) by Spinoza, while maintaining the notion of divine transcendence in all its rigor; it is to say that Spinoza is the transcendent God who speaks, to be sure, to human beings, but who speaks to them as eternal *God*. And this, obviously, is the height of absurdity: to take Spinoza seriously is actually to be—or to become—mad.

Spinoza, like Hegel, identifies Man (that is to say, the Wise Man) and God. It seems, then, that in both cases it could be said indifferently either that there is nothing other than God, or that there is nothing other than Man. Now in point of fact, the two assertions are not identical, and if the first is accepted by Spinoza, only the second expresses Hegel's thought. And that is what Hegel means by saying that Spinoza's System is not a pan-theism, but an a-cosmism: it is the Universe or the totality of Being reduced to God alone, but to a God without World and without men. And to say this is to say that everything that is change, becoming, time, does not exist for Science. For if the *Ethics* is, in fact, concerned with these things, how or why they appear in it is not known.

With the use of our symbolic circles, then, the difference between Hegel's and Spinoza's Systems can be represented in the following manner:

Let us start with the theistic System. In its pure form, it is Plato's System. But in general it symbolizes possibility II (see Figure 13). For Aristotle, several small circles must be inscribed in the large circle to symbolize the relation of Eternity and Time (Figure 14); but these circles ought to have fitted together; in the end, there would again be the Platonic symbol with only one small circle. (That is to say: all truly coherent theism is a mono-theism.) As for Kant, the same symbol can serve; but the small circle must be drawn with a dotted line, to show that Kant's theology has, for him, only the value of an "as if" (Figure 15). In short, the symbol of the theistic System is valid for every System that defines the Concept as an *eternal* entity in relation to *something other* than itself, no matter whether this other thing is Eternity in Time or outside of Time, or Time itself. But let us return to Spinoza. Starting with the theistic system, Hegel does away with the small circle (reduced beforehand, by his predecessors, to a single *point*): see Figure 16. Spinoza, on the other hand, does away with the large circle: see Figure 17.

Hence the symbol is the same in both cases: a homogeneous closed circle. And this is important. For we see that it is sufficient to deny that the Concept is a *relation* with *something other* than itself in order to set up the ideal of *absolute*—that is, *circular*—Knowledge. And indeed, if the Concept is related to *another* reality, an *isolated* concept can be established as true by adequation to this autonomous reality. In this case there are *partial* facts, or even *partial* truths. But if the Concept *is* revealed Being itself, it can be established as true only through itself. The proof itself no longer differs from *that* which has to be proved. And this means that the truth is a "System," as Hegel says. The word "system" is not found in Spinoza. But the thing itself is there. Setting aside Parmenides, Spinoza is the only philosopher who understood that the principle of all or nothing is valid for Knowledge: either one knows *everything*, or else one *knows* nothing; for one sees that one *truly* knows something only by seeing that one knows *everything*. And that is why the study of Spinoza is so instructive, despite the *absurdity* of his point of view. Spinoza sets up the ideal of *total*, or "systematic," or "circular," Knowledge. However, *his* System is *impossible in Time*. And Hegel's whole effort consists in creating a Spinozist System which can be written by a *man* living in a *historical* World. And that is why, while admitting with Spinoza that the Concept is not a *relation*, Hegel identifies it not with Eternity, but with Time. (On this subject see the Preface to the *Phenomenology*, pp. 19ff.)

We shall see later what this means. For the moment, I want to underline once more that the symbols of both systems are identical. They differ only in their *source* (which is not seen in the drawing): doing away with the small or the large circle. And again, this indeed corresponds to the reality. It is understandable that a *temporal* Knowledge could finally embrace the *totality* of becoming. But it is not understandable that an *eternal* Knowledge could absorb everything that is in Time: for the simple reason that it would absorb us ourselves. It would be the absolute Knowledge of *Bewusstsein*, which would have completely absorbed *Selbstbewusstsein*. And this, obviously, is absurd.

I shall stop here. To know what the identification of the Concept with Eternity means, one must read the whole *Ethics*.

Let us proceed, or return, to Kant.

Kant agrees with Plato and Aristotle (in opposition to Parmenides-Spinoza and Hegel) that the Concept is an *eternal* entity, in *relation* with something *other* than itself. However, he relates this eternal Concept not to Eternity, but to Time.

We can say, moreover, that Kant defines the Concept as a *relation* precisely because he sees the impossibility of Spinozism (just as Plato had done to avoid the impossibility of Eleaticism). Perhaps he did not read Spinoza. But in the "Transcendental Deduction of the Categories" and in the "Schematismus" he says why the

Spinozist conception of Knowledge is impossible: it is impossible, because for us—that is, for man—"without intuition the concept is empty."

The Parmenidean-Spinozist (and Hegelian) Concept, which is not *in relation* with a Being *other* than itself, but which *is* Being revealing itself to itself—this Parmenidean-Spinozist Concept is called the "transcendental I" or the *transcendentale Synthesis der Apperception* in Kant.

"Transcendental" in Kant means: that which makes experience *possible*. Now, experience is essentially *temporal*, and *everything* that is temporal belongs to the domain of experience. "Transcendental," therefore, means: that which makes the temporal as temporal possible. Kant says that the transcendental entity is "before" Time or "outside of" Time. Hence the transcendental is "eternal" or, as Kant himself says, *a priori*; this is to say that it precedes "the temporal taken as temporal." To say that there is *epistēmē*, absolute Knowledge, truly true truth, is to say that there are universally and necessarily valid concepts—that is, concepts that on the one hand are valid at *every* moment of time, and on the other hand *exclude* Time from themselves (that is, can never be *modified*); therefore, it is to say that there are *a priori*, or transcendental, or *eternal*, concepts.

Now, the eternal Concept (like every eternal entity) is not eternal in and by itself. It is eternal by its coming from Eternity, by its origin. Now, the origin of the eternal Concept is the "transcendental I" or the "transcendental Synthesis." This I or this Synthesis, therefore, is not *eternal*; it *is* Eternity. Therefore, Kant's transcendental Self-Consciousness is Parmenides' Substance conceived of as spiritual subject—that is, God. It is the real Eternity, which reveals itself to itself in and by the Concept. It is the source of all Being revealed by the Concept, and the source of all conceptual *revelation* of Being; it is the *eternal* source of all temporal Being.

However, Kant says, we men can say of the "transcendental I" that it *is* and that it is *one*; but that is all we can say of it. In other words, Kant accepts the Platonic critique of Parmenides: if the Concept *is* Eternity, then absolute Knowledge reduces to the single word "ἕν" or "ὄν," and there is no possible *Discourse*. (Moreover, strictly speaking, one cannot even say of the "transcendental I" that it *is* and that it is *one*. For, as we shall soon see, the categories of Being and Quantity cannot be applied in this case. Therefore, the most that can be said is that it is "Something" and not Nothingness; but one cannot say that it is a *thing* having such or such qualities; now, this Being, of which one can only say that it *is*, is a *Sein* which, as Hegel will say, does not differ from *Nichts*, from Nothingness.)

The Parmenidean-Spinozist System is therefore impossible, Kant says. The essential self-conscious unity of Eternity has twelve aspects, which are the twelve famous categories-concepts. These twelve aspects of Eternity are obviously eternal; they "precede" everything that is in Time, they are "before" Time; hence they are valid at every moment of Time, and, since they exclude Time, they cannot be modified; they are *a priori*. Now, Parmenides' and Spinoza's error (or illusion) consisted in this: they believed that the eternal which *comes* from Eternity *reveals* this eternity by *determining* it—that is, by qualifying it. For Parmenides and Spinoza, the concepts-categories are attributes of the One which is, and can be *attributed* to it. Now for Kant, none of this holds true.[13]

None of this holds true, because it is impossible. And at the end of § 16 of the second edition of the *Critique of Pure Reason* Kant explains why.

A determination of Eternity by the eternal concepts-categories would be possible only by an Understanding (*Verstand*) "through the *Self*-Consciousness of which," he says, "the whole *Manifold* (*das Mannigfaltige*) would be given at the same time"; or else, again: by an Understanding such that the objects of its representations exist through the sole fact of the existence of these representations themselves; in other words—by a *divine* (or "archetypal") Understanding. For in point of fact, the being which, by thinking of *itself*, thinks of *everything* that can be thought, and which creates the objects thought by the sole act of thinking of them, is God. Hence Spinoza was right to give the name "God" to Parmenides' ἐν-ὄν which *coincides* with the Concept that reveals

---

[13] For Plotinus, they cannot be attributed to the One. But they can be attributed to the One-which-is, which for him is the second Hypostasis: Intelligence or the intelligible Cosmos.

it. But he was wrong to forget that God alone can apply this Concept to himself. For us who are not God, to apply *our* Concept to *God* is to relate the Concept to something other than this Concept itself. Now, the Concept which is a *relation* in the proper sense of the word—that is, a relation to *something else*—is, at most, eternal, but not Eternity. This is to say: either the very basis of Spinozism is false (the Concept *is not* Eternity); or else, if the Concept *is* Eternity, only God can be a Spinozist. To assert that one is not God and to write the *Ethics* is not to know what one is doing; it is to do something of which one cannot give an account, to do something "absurd."

But in principle, according to Kant, God *could* write the *Ethics*. The whole question, then, is to know whether a man (Spinoza) can *be* God. Now, for Kant, this is impossible, because Man can draw nothing from the content of his *Self*-Consciousness: taken in itself, the human I is a point without content, an empty receptacle, and the (manifold) content must be *given* (*gegeben*) to it, it must come from *elsewhere*. Or, what amounts to the same thing: it is not sufficient for Man to *think* in order that there be *true* knowledge; in addition, the object of which Man thinks must *exist*, and exist *independently* of his act of thinking of it. Or else, again, as Kant says: human Consciousness necessarily has *two* constituent elements: the *Begriff* or Concept, and the *Anschauung* or Intuition, the latter presenting a (manifold) content *given* to Man and not *produced* by him, or *from* him, or *in* him.

The Concept possessed by a being that is not God is, therefore, a *relation*: in other words, it can be eternal, but it is not Eternity. And that is why Spinozism is "absurd." It is absurd because Spinoza is not God.

But there is still the conception of Plato-Aristotle, which admits that the (human) Concept is a *relation*, but a relation related to Eternity and not to Time. That is to say: Eternity (or God) implies the manifold in its own unity, and it itself creates the manifold which it reveals by the Concept. Therefore, being the eternal development of Eternity in itself, this manifold *itself* is Eternity: it is the (manifold) Universe of ideas-concepts, which has nothing to do with the World of space-time. But it is Eternity itself that develops itself in this Universe; our merely *eternal* Concept does not produce it. Hence this Universe is *given* to us; and *our* Concept is *related* to it. In other words, *our* absolute Knowledge is not the Knowledge which God has of himself; it is the Knowledge which we have of *God*, of a God essentially different from us, of a *transcendent* God. It is a theo-logical Knowledge in the strict sense of the term, a Knowledge which is the *relation* of the eternal Concept to Eternity (and not to *Time*).

Now according to Kant, this too is impossible. For the simple reason that the relation of the eternal to Eternity must itself be eternal or nontemporal, whereas *our* Knowledge is not only in Time, but, even more important, it itself is temporal: we need time in order to think.

In principle, Kant says, there could be a nonspatial-temporal Intuition (*Anschauung*). In principle, the concepts-categories can be applied to any given manifold whatsoever. Therefore a non-divine being could, in principle, develop an absolute Knowledge revealing the nonspatial-temporal Universe of the Platonic Ideas. But the nondivine being called Man cannot do so. If Spinozism is possible only for God, Platonism is possible only for a nondivine intelligence other than human intelligence, an "angelic" intelligence, for example. For, once more (and this is an irreducible and inexplicable fact, according to Kant; cf. the end of § 21): for us human beings, the given manifold is always a manifold given in spatial-temporal form.

We can think only provided that a manifold is given to us. But this manifold must *exist*: in its whole and in each of its elements. Therefore Parmenides' one and unique *Being* must be differentiated into a manifold Being. Now for us, the identical can be diverse only provided that it is Space or is *in* Space. [As a matter of fact, two identical geometrical points can be different only by their positions in space; and space is nothing other than the infinite whole of points which are rigorously identical with respect to their intrinsic character (which, by the way, is the absence of all "character") and are nonetheless different one from another.] But in order that there be knowledge, the diverse must be *identified*: every act of knowing is a *synthesis*, Kant says, which introduces *unity* into the (given) manifold. Now for us, the diverse can be identical only in Time or as Time.[14]

---

[14] As a matter of fact, to identify the point A with the point B is to cause the point to *pass* from A to B; generally speaking, to identify two different things is

Therefore for us, knowledge—that is, the identification of the diverse—can be accomplished only *in* Time, because the very identification of the diverse *is* Time. It was always known that the human Concept appears at some moment *of* Time; and it was known that Man needs time in order to think. But Kant was the first to see that this is not accidental, but essential to Man. Hence the World in which Man thinks is necessarily a *temporal* World. And if actual human thought is related to what is *in* Time, the Kantian analysis shows that *Time* is what makes the actual exercise of thought possible. In other words, we can use our eternal Concepts only provided that we relate them to Time as such—that is, provided that we "schematize" them—as Kant says.

Therefore: the "transcendental I" which is simply *Self*-Consciousness is Spinoza's God; and *we* can say nothing about it. The "transcendental I," source of the categories-concepts which are related to a nonspatial-temporal manifold—i.e., to an *eternal* manifold—is the I as it was conceived of by Platonic-Aristotelian or pre-Kantian philosophy in general; now, this I is not human, for it is supposed to be able to think *outside* of Time.[15] Therefore, only the "transcendental I" which is the origin of *schematized* categories—that is, of Concepts related to Time—is the *human* "transcendental I," which makes actual *human* thought possible.

Human thought is accomplished in Time, and it is a temporal phenomenon. As such, it is purely empirical: it is a *doxa*. But in order that the (eternal) Concept be applied to the *temporal*, it is first necessary to "schematize" the Concept—that is, to apply it to Time as such. This application is accomplished "before" Time or "outside" of Time. It is *a priori*—that is, unmodifiable and always valid. Therefore, absolute Knowledge is the entirety of the rela-

---

to say that they are one and the same thing which has *changed*; and Time is but the infinite whole of all identifications of the diverse—that is, of all *changes* whatsoever.

[15] It is not sufficient to geometrize physics, as Plato and Descartes do; it would still be necessary to geometrize the thought of the philosopher who performs this geometrization—that is, to exclude Time from this thought itself; now, this is impossible. The ideal of the "universal tensor" in modern relativist physics is the ideal of a nontemporal knowledge: the *whole* content would be given *simultaneously* in this formula; but even if this tensor is possible, it is only an algorithm, and not a Discourse; all *discursive* thought is necessarily developed in Time, because even the attributing of the predicate to the subject is a temporal act.

tions between the (eternal) Concept and Time; it is the entirety of the *synthetischen Grundsätze*; it is Kant's ontology.

Let us now see the result of this Kantian conception for the World and for Man. In the natural World, Time is represented by motion. The temporalized Concept, therefore, is related to real motion. And what makes the temporalized Concept *possible*—i.e., the "schematism" or the relation to Time "anterior" to Time—corresponds to what makes real motion really possible—i.e., *force*. Therefore, to say that the (eternal) Concept is in relation with Time is to set forth, among other things, a *dynamic* conception of matter and the World—that is, a physics of *forces*. Hence Kantian philosophy will necessarily encounter Newtonian physics. And inversely, if the World actually is as Newton's physics describes it, Kant's philosophy must be accepted as a given truth.

But even leaving aside the fact that the Newtonian World is just as uninhabitable for Man as Plato's geometrical World, we can indicate an insufficiency in the Kantian-Newtonian conception of the purely natural World. The impossibility of relating the Concept to Eternity ultimately means the impossibility of having an absolute *geometrical* understanding of the World. In other words, the notion of the Cosmos—that is, of the *eternal* or static structure of the natural Universe—is denied. And, consequently, the existence of eternal structures *in* the World is not explained: in particular, the biological species cannot be explained, as it is by Aristotle. Generally speaking, purely spatial structure is not explained: the motion of the planets, for example, is explained by force, but the structure of the solar system is not explained. And here the impossibility of explaining is absolute: the fact that in the real World laws apply to *stable* entities is, for Kant, a "transcendental *chance*." One can say that that's the way *it is*; and that is all one can say about it.

To be sure, Kant develops a theory of the living being in the third "Critique." But this theory is valid only in the mode of "as if," since the third "Critique" has no equivalent in the "System." [16] And what is valid for the animal in particular is also valid for the animal in general, that is, for the Cosmos: here too the cosmology

---

[16] This is so precisely because knowledge properly so-called starts with the relation between the Concept and Time, and not between the Concept and Eternity.

(in other respects like that of Leibniz) has only a "regulative" value. And the same holds for God: God being Eternity, there is no possible *Knowledge* relating to God.

In fine, if Kantian Knowledge is closed—that is, total and definitive or absolute—we again find the theistic or Platonic schema of two circles (see Figure 13). But since the Concept is not related to Eternity, the small circle remains forever purely hypothetical (Figure 15). However, when it is done away with, what is obtained is not the single closed circle of Hegel (Figure 16), but the open circle without fixed limits of Skepticism (Figure 18). Indeed, since the *eternal* Concept is related to *Time*, no *absolute* adequation is possible. At best it is the *infinite* eternal of Time which can completely fill up the framework of the *eternal* concepts-categories. Thought that is *in* Time, therefore, never attains this end. And that is why Kant says that absolute Knowledge is an *unendliche Aufgabe*, an *infinite* task.

Let us now see what the Kantian conception means on the anthropological level. The Concept is eternal, but it is related to Time. If the Concept is *eternal*, it is because there is something in Man that places him outside of Time: it is *freedom*—that is, the "transcendental I" taken as "practical Reason" or "pure Will." If there is *relation* of Concept to Time, there is also *application* of "pure Will" to the temporal reality. But to the extent that there is *a priori concept* (which means, here: act of freedom), the relation to Time is accomplished "*before*" Time. The act of freedom, while being related to Time, is therefore outside of Time. It is the renowned "choice of the intelligible character." This choice is not temporal, but it *determines* Man's whole temporal existence, in which, therefore, there is no freedom.

Thus we again meet Plato's myth. However, in Plato, the Concept is related to Eternity, while in Kant it is related to Time. And this difference finds expression here in the fact that the "transcendental choice" is effected not, as in Plato, with a view to what Man is (or "has been") *outside* of Time, but with a view to what he is (or "will be") *in* Time. In Plato, it has to do with an *affirmation*, in Kant—with a *negation*; there it has to do with becoming in Time what one *is* eternally; here—with not being eternally what one has become in Time; there—*acceptance* of eternal Nature, here—*negation* of temporal Nature. Or, to restate it: there—

freedom of the Angel who clings to or separates himself from God; here—freedom of fallen Man who repudiates his sin in a single extratemporal act.[17]

Therefore, here, as in the description of the natural World, there is a progress. But, in both cases, there is an irreducible insufficiency. Man, as historical being, remains inexplicable: neither the World of *concrete* things in which he lives, nor the History that he creates by *temporal* free acts, is understood.

In fine, we end with the following result:

Possibility I is excluded, because it cannot be realized by Man. Possibility IV is likewise excluded, because it does away with the very idea of a truth in the proper sense of the term. Possibility II gives partial explanations. But in none of its three variants does it manage to give an account of History—that is, of Man taken as free creator in Time; in any case, even if one can barely manage to speak of an infinite historical evolution in the Kantian or "criticist" variant, it is impossible to attain an absolute Knowledge relating to History, and hence to historical Man.

In consequence, if philosophy is to attain an absolute Knowledge relating to Man, as we currently conceive of him, it must accept possibility III. And this is what Hegel did, in saying that the Concept *is* Time. Our concern is to see what that means.

EIGHT H LECTURE

With Hegel, we move on to the third possibility: namely, the one that identifies the Concept with Time.

At the dawn of philosophy, Parmenides identified the Concept with Eternity. Hence Time had *nothing* to do with the Concept; with absolute Knowledge, *epistēmē*, or truth; nor, finally, with Man, to the extent that, as the bearer of the Concept, he is the

---

[17] The Christian act must indeed be conceived of in such a way: since it must be compatible with eternal divine grace, the Christian act must be "transcendental."

empirical existence of Knowledge in the temporal World. More-over, this *temporal* existence of the Concept in the World is inexplicable from Parmenides' point of view. Man's *temporal* exist-ence is just as inexplicable for him as it is for Spinoza, who also identified the Concept with Eternity.

With Plato, the existence of Man becomes necessary for Knowl-edge. True Knowledge—that is, the Concept—is now a *relation*. Therefore, absolute Knowledge necessarily implies two elements, and one of them can just barely be called "Man." But the Concept is *eternal*, and it is related to Eternity situated outside of Time. The Eternal, to be sure, is not Eternity. The eternal Concept is something other than Eternity; already it is closer to Time, if I may say so, than the Parmenidean-Spinozist Concept. But, although not Eternity, it is nonetheless related to Eternity, and the Eternity to which it is related has nothing to do with Time.

Only with Aristotle does Time make its way into absolute Knowledge. The Eternity to which the (eternal) Concept is related is now situated *in* Time. But Time enters into *absolute* Knowledge only to the extent that Time itself is *eternal* ("eternal return").

Kant is the first to break with this pagan conception and, in metaphysics itself, to take account of the pre-philosophical Judaeo-Christian anthropology of the Bible and the *Epistle to the Romans*, which is the anthropology of *historical* Man endowed with an *immortal* "soul." For Kant, the Concept—while remaining *eternal* —is related to Time taken as Time.

Therefore, there remains only one possibility of going further in the direction of bringing the Concept and Time together. To do this, and to avoid the difficulties of earlier conceptions, one must *identify* the Concept and Time. That is what Hegel does. And that is his great discovery, which makes him a great philoso-pher, a philosopher of the order of Plato, Aristotle, and Kant.

Hegel is the first to identify the Concept and Time. And, curi-ously enough, he himself says it in so many words, whereas one would search in vain in the other philosophers for the explicit formulas that I have used in my schematic exposition. Hegel said it as early as the Preface to the *Phenomenology*, where the para-doxical sentence that I have already cited is found: "*Was die* Zeit *betrifft, . . . so ist sie der daseiende Begriff selbst"* (As for *Time*, it is the empirically existing Concept itself). And he repeats it word for word in Chapter VIII.

This sentence marks an extremely important date in the history of philosophy. Disregarding Parmenides-Spinoza, we can say that there are two great periods in this history: one that goes from Plato to Kant, and one that begins with Hegel. And I have already said (although, of course, I was not able to prove it) that the philosophers who do not identify the Concept and Time cannot give an account of History—that is, of the existence of the man whom each of us believes himself to be—that is, the *free* and *historical individual.*

The principal aim, then, of the reform introduced by Hegel was the desire to give an account of the fact of History. On its *phenomenological* level, Hegel's philosophy (or more exactly, his "Science") describes the existence of Man who sees that he lives in a World in which he *knows* that he is a *free* and *historical individual.* And on its *metaphysical* level, this philosophy tells us what the World in which Man can *appear* thus to himself must *be.* Finally, on the *ontological* level, the problem is to see what Being itself must be in order to *exist* as such a World. And Hegel answers by saying that this is possibly only if the real Concept (that is, Being revealed to itself by an empirically existing Discourse) *is* Time.

Hegel's *whole* philosophy or "Science," therefore, can be summed up in the sentence cited: *"Time* is the Concept itself which is *there* in empirical existence"—that is, in real Space or the World.

But of course, it is not sufficient to have read that sentence in order to know what Hegelian philosophy is; just as it is not sufficient to say that the *eternal* Concept is *related* to Time in order to know what Kant's philosophy is, for example. It is necessary to *develop* these condensed formulas. And to develop the formula *entirely* is to reconstruct the *entirety* of the philosophy in question (with the supposition that its author has made no error in his own development of the fundamental formula).

Of course, we cannot try to reconstruct here the entirety of Hegelian philosophy from the identification of the empirically existing Concept and Time. I must be satisfied with making several quite general remarks, like those that I made in discussing the other conceptions of the relation between the Concept and Time.

The aim of Hegel's philosophy is to give an account of the fact of History. From this it can be concluded that the Time that he identifies with the Concept is *historical* Time, the Time in which human history unfolds, or better still, the Time that realizes itself (not as the motion of the stars, for example, but) as universal History.[18]

In the *Phenomenology*, Hegel is very radical. As a matter of fact (at the end of the next to last paragraph of the book and at the beginning of the last, page 563), he says that Nature is Space, whereas Time *is* History. In other words: there is no natural, cosmic Time; there is Time only to the extent that there is *History*, that is, *human* existence—that is, *speaking existence*. Man who, in the course of History, reveals Being by his Discourse, *is the* "empirically existing Concept" (*der daseiende Begriff*), and Time is nothing other than this Concept. Without Man, Nature would be *Space*, and *only* Space. Only Man is in Time, and Time does not exist outside of Man; therefore, Man *is* Time, and Time *is* Man— that is, the "Concept which is there in the [spatial] empirical existence" of Nature (*der Begriff der da ist*).

But in his other writings, Hegel is less radical. In them, he admits the existence of a cosmic Time.[19] But in so doing, Hegel identifies cosmic Time and historical Time.[20]

But for the moment, no matter. If Hegel identifies both Times, if he admits only one Time, we can apply everything that he says about Time in general to *historical* Time (which is all that interests us here).

Now, curiously enough, the crucial text on Time is found in the "Philosophy of *Nature*" of the *Jenenser Realphilosophie*. Mr. Alexandre Koyré has done a translation and commentary of this

---

[18] Therefore, the identification of Time and the Concept amounts to understanding History as the history of human *Discourse* which reveals Being. And we know that actually, for Hegel, *real* Time—i.e., universal History—is in the final analysis the history of *philosophy*.

[19] It may be that it is actually impossible to do without Time in Nature; for it is probable that (biological) life, at least, is an *essentially* temporal phenomenon.

[20] This, in my opinion, is his basic error; for if life is a temporal phenomenon, biological Time surely has a structure different from that of historical or human Time; the whole question is to know how these two Times coexist; and they probably coexist with a cosmic or physical Time, which is different from both in its structure.

text in an article which resulted from his course on the writings of Hegel's youth: a conclusive article, which is the source and basis of my interpretation of the *Phenomenology*. Here I shall merely reproduce in a few words the principal consequences implied by Mr. Koyré's analysis.

The text in question clearly shows that the Time that Hegel has in view is the Time that, for us, is historical (and not biological or cosmic) Time. In effect, this Time is characterized by the primacy of the Future. In the Time that pre-Hegelian Philosophy considered, the movement went from the Past toward the Future, by way of the Present.[21] In the Time of which Hegel speaks, on the other hand, the movement is engendered in the Future and goes toward the Present by way of the Past: Future → Past → Present (→ Future). And this is indeed the specific structure of properly *human*—that is, *historical*—Time.

In fact, let us consider the *phenomenological* (or better, anthropological) projection of this *metaphysical* analysis of Time.[22] The movement engendered by the Future is the movement that arises from Desire. This means: from specifically human Desire—that is, creative Desire—that is, Desire that is directed toward an entity that does not exist and has not existed in the real natural World. Only then can the movement be said to be engendered by the Future, for the Future is precisely what does not (yet) exist and has not (already) existed. Now, we know that Desire can be directed toward an absolutely *non*existent entity only provided that it is directed toward another Desire taken as Desire. As a matter of fact, Desire is the presence of an *absence*: I am thirsty because there is an *absence* of water in me. It is indeed, then, the presence of a future in the present: of the future act of drinking.

[21] It may be that the Time in which the Present takes primacy is cosmic or physical Time, whereas biological Time would be characterized by the primacy of the Past. It does seem that the physical or cosmic object is but a simple *presence* (*Gegenwart*), whereas the fundamental biological phenomenon is probably *Memory* in the broad sense, and the specifically human phenomenon is without a doubt the *Project*. Moreover, it could be that the cosmic and biological forms of Time exist as Time only in relation to Man—that is, in relation to historical Time.

[22] On the ontological level, the problem would be to study the relations between Thesis = Identity, Antithesis = Negativity, and Synthesis = Totality. But I shall not talk about this.

To desire to drink is to desire something (water) that *is*: hence, it is to act in terms of the present. But to act in terms of the desire for a *desire* is to act in terms of what does not (yet) exist—that is, in terms of the future. The being that acts thus, therefore, is in a Time in which the Future takes primacy. And inversely, the Future can really take primacy only if, in the real (spatial) World, there is a being capable of acting thus.

Now, in Chapter IV of the *Phenomenology*, Hegel shows that the Desire that is directed toward another Desire is necessarily the Desire for *Recognition*, which—by opposing the Master to the Slave—engenders *History* and moves it (as long as it is not definitively overcome by Satisfaction). Therefore: by realizing itself, the Time in which the Future takes primacy engenders History, which lasts as long as *this* Time lasts; and this Time lasts only as long as History lasts—that is, as long as human acts accomplished with a view to social *Recognition* are carried out.

Now, if Desire is the presence of an *absence*, it is not—taken as such—an empirical *reality*: it does not exist in a positive manner in the natural—i.e., spatial—Present. On the contrary, it is like a gap or a "hole" in Space: an emptiness, a nothingness. (And it is into this "hole," so to speak, that the purely temporal Future takes its place, within the spatial Present.) Desire that is related to Desire, therefore, is related to nothing. To "realize" it, therefore, is to realize nothing. In being related only to the Future, one does not come to a reality, and consequently one is not really in motion. On the other hand, if one affirms or accepts the present (or better, spatial) real, one *desires* nothing; hence one is not related to the Future, one does not go beyond the Present, and consequently one does not move either. Therefore: in order to *realize* itself, Desire must be related to a *reality*; but it cannot be related to it in a *positive* manner. Hence it must be related to it *negatively*. Therefore Desire is necessarily the Desire to *negate* the real or present given. And the *reality* of Desire comes from the *negation* of the given *reality*.[23] Now, the *negated* real is the real that has *ceased* to be: it is the *past* real, or the *real* Past. Desire determined by the

---

[23] The *desire* to drink is an *absence* of water, but the quality of this desire (thirst) is determined not by *absence* as such, but by the fact that it is an absence of *water* (and not of something else), and this desire *realizes* itself by the "negation" of *real* water (in the act of drinking).

Future appears, in the *Present*, as a reality (that is, as satisfied Desire) only on the condition that it has negated a real—that is, a *Past*. The manner in which the *Past* has been (negatively) formed in terms of the *Future* is what determines the quality of the real *Present*. And only the Present thus determined by the Future and the Past is a human or historical Present.[24] Therefore, generally speaking: the *historical* movement arises from the Future and passes through the Past in order to *realize* itself in the Present or as temporal Present. The Time that Hegel has in view, then, is human or historical Time: it is the Time of conscious and voluntary action which realizes in the *present* a Project for the future, which Project is formed on the basis of knowledge of the *past*.[25]

Therefore, we are dealing with historical Time, and Hegel says that this "Time is the Concept itself which *exists empirically*." For the moment let us disregard the term "Concept." Hegel says, then, that Time is something, an X, that *exists empirically*. Now, this assertion can be deduced from the very analysis of the Hegelian notion of (historical) Time. Time in which the Future takes primacy can be realized, can *exist*, only provided that it *negates* or annihilates. In order that Time may exist, therefore, there must

---

[24] Indeed, we say that a moment is "historical" when the action that is performed in it is performed in terms of the idea that the agent has of the future (that is, in terms of a *Project*): one decides on a *future* war, and so on; therefore, one acts in terms of the *future*. But if the moment is to be truly "historical," there must be *change*; in other words, the decision must be *negative* with respect to the given: in deciding for the future war, one decides *against* the prevailing peace. And, through the decision for the future war, the peace is transformed into the past. Now, the *present* historical act, *launched* by the idea of the future (by the Project), is *determined* by this past that it creates: if the peace is sure and honorable, the negation that relegates it to the past is the act of a madman or a criminal; if it is humiliating, its negation is an act worthy of a statesman; and so on.

[25] As an example of a "historic moment" let us take the celebrated anecdote of the "Rubicon." What is there in the *present* properly so-called? A man takes a walk at night on the bank of a small river. In other words, something extremely banal, nothing "historic." For even if the man in question was Caesar, the event would in no sense be "historic" if Caesar were taking such a walk solely because of some sort of insomnia. The moment is historic because the man taking a nocturnal walk is thinking about a *coup d'état*, the civil war, the conquest of Rome, and worldwide dominion. And, let us take care to notice: because he has the *project* of doing it, for all this is still in the *future*. The event in question, therefore, would not be historic if there were not a *real presence* (*Gegenwart*) of the *future* in the real World (first of all, in Caesar's brain). Therefore, the present

also be something other than Time. This other thing is first of all Space (as it were, the place where things are stopped). Therefore: no Time without Space; Time is something that is in Space.[26] Time is the *negation* of Space (of diversity); but if it is something and not nothingness, it is because it is the negation of *Space*. Now, only that which really exists—that is, which *resists*—can be really negated. But Space that resists is full: it is extended *matter*, it is *real* Space—that is, the natural *World*. Therefore, Time must exist in a *World*: it is indeed, then, something which *"ist da,"* as Hegel says, which is *there* in a Space, and which is *there* in *empirical* Space—that is, in a sensible Space or a natural World. Time *annihilates* this World by causing it at every instant to sink into the nothingness of the past. But Time *is* nothing but this *nihilation* of the World; and if there were no *real* World that was annihilated, Time would only be pure nothingness: there would be no Time. Hence Time that *is*, therefore, is indeed something that "exists empirically"—i.e., exists in a real Space or a spatial World.

Now, we have seen that the presence of Time (in which the Future takes primacy) in the real World is called Desire (which

---

is "historical" only because there is in it a relation to the *future*, or more exactly, because it is a function of the future (Caesar taking a walk *because* he is thinking of the future). And it is in this sense that one can speak of a *primacy of the future* in historical Time. But this is not sufficient. Suppose that the person taking a walk is a Roman adolescent who is "dreaming" of worldwide dominion, or a "megalomaniac" in the clinical sense of the word who is constructing a "project," otherwise identical to Caesar's. Immediately, the walk ceases to be a "historic event." It is historic solely because it is *Caesar* who, while taking a walk, is thinking about his project (or "making up his mind," that is, transforming a "hypothesis" without any precise relation to real Time into a concrete "project for the future"). Why? Because Caesar has the *possibility* (but not the *certainty*, for then there would be no *future* properly so-called, nor a genuine *project*) of realizing his plans. Now, his whole *past*, and only his past, is what assures him of this possibility. The past—that is, the entirety of the actions of fighting and work effected at various present times in terms of the project—that is, in terms of the future. This *past* is what distinguishes the "project" from a simple "dream" or "utopia." Consequently, there is a "historic moment" only when the *present* is ordered in terms of the *future*, on the condition that the future makes its way into the present not in an *immediate* manner (*unmittelbar*; the case of a utopia), but having been *mediated* (*vermittelt*) by the *past*—that is, by an *already accomplished* action.

[26] I said that Desire—that is, Time—is a "hole"; now, for a "hole" to exist, there must be a space in which the hole exists.

INTRODUCTION TO THE READING OF HEGEL

is directed toward another Desire), and that this Desire is a specifically human Desire, since the Action that realizes it is Man's
very being. The real presence of Time in the World, therefore, is
called *Man*. Time *is* Man, and Man *is* Time.

In the *Phenomenology*, Hegel does not say this in so many words,
because he avoids the word "man." But in the Lectures delivered
at Jena he says: "*Geist ist Zeit*" ("*Spirit is* Time"). Now, "Spirit"
in Hegel (and especially in this context) means "*human* Spirit" or
Man, more particularly, collective Man—that is, the People or
State, and, finally, Man as a whole or humanity in the totality of
its spatial-temporal existence, that is, the totality of universal History.

Therefore, Time (that is, historical Time, with the rhythm:
Future → Past → Present) *is* Man in his empirical—that is, spatial—
integral reality: Time *is* the History of Man in the World. And
indeed, without Man, there would be no Time in the World;
Nature that did not shelter Man would be only a real *Space*.[27] To
be sure, the animal, too, has desires, and it acts in terms of these
desires, by negating the real: it eats and drinks, just like man. But
the animal's desires are *natural*; they are directed toward what *is*,
and hence they are *determined* by what is; the negating action
that is effected in terms of *these* desires, therefore, cannot *essentially* negate, it cannot change the *essence* of what is. Therefore,
in its *entirety*—that is, in its *reality*—Being is not modified by
these "natural" desires; it does not essentially change because of
them; it remains *identical* to itself, and thus it is *Space*, and not
Time. To be sure, an animal transforms the aspect of the natural
World in which it lives. But it dies and gives back to the earth
what it has taken from it. And since the animal is *identically*
repeated by its offspring, the changes that it brings about in the
World are repeated, too. And hence in its entirety, Nature remains
what it is.[28] Man, on the other hand, *essentially* transforms the
World by the negating Action of his Fights and his Work, Action
which arises from *non*natural human Desire directed toward an-

[27] Of four dimensions.
[28] If there is Time, it is biological Time, Aristotle's circular Time; it is
Eternity in Time; it is Time in which everything changes in order to remain
the same thing.

other Desire—that is, toward something that does not exist really in the natural World.[29] Only Man creates and destroys *essentially*. Therefore, the natural reality implies Time only if it implies a human reality. Now, man essentially creates and destroys in terms of the idea that he forms of the Future. And the idea of the Future appears in the real present in the form of a Desire directed toward another Desire—that is, in the form of a Desire for social *Recognition*. Now, Action that arises from *this* Desire engenders History. Hence there is *Time* only where there is *History*.

Therefore: *"die Zeit ist der daseiende Begriff selbst"* means: *Time is* Man in the World and his real History. But Hegel also says: "Geist *ist Zeit.*" That is to say, *Man is* Time. And we have just seen what this means: Man is Desire directed toward another Desire—that is, Desire for Recognition—that is, negating Action performed for the sake of satisfying this Desire for Recognition—that is, bloody Fighting for prestige—that is, the relation between Master and Slave—that is, Work—that is, historical evolution which finally comes to the universal and homogeneous State and to the absolute Knowledge that reveals complete Man realized in and by this State. In short, to say that Man *is* Time is to say all that Hegel says of Man in the *Phenomenology*. And it is also to say that the existing Universe, and Being itself, must be such that Man thus conceived of is *possible* and can be *realized*. Hence the sentence that identifies Spirit and Time sums up Hegel's whole philosophy, just as the other schematic formulas enumerated above sum up the whole philosophy of a Plato, an Aristotle, etc.

But in those schematic formulas, the *Concept* is what was mentioned. Now, Hegel too says not only "Geist *ist Zeit,*" but also *"die Zeit ist der* Begriff *der da ist."*

To be sure, these are two different ways of saying the same thing. If Man *is* Time, and if Time *is* the "empirically existing Concept," it can be said that Man *is* the "empirically existing Concept." And so, indeed, he is: as the only speaking being in the World, he *is* Logos (or Discourse) incarnate, Logos become flesh

---

[29] Thus the olive tree of Pericles' time is "the same" olive tree as that of Venizelos' time; but Pericles' Greece is a past that never again becomes a present; and, with respect to Pericles, Venizelos represents a future that as yet has never been a past.

and thus existing as an empirical reality in the natural World. Man is the *Dasein* of the *Begriff*, and the "empirically existing Concept" is Man. Therefore, to say that Time is the "empirically existing Concept" is indeed to say that Time is Man, provided that Man is conceived of as Hegel conceives of him in the *Phenomenology*. Hence everything that Hegel says of Man in the *Phenomenology* is also valid for Time. And inversely, everything that can be said of the "appearance" (*Erscheinung*) or "*Phänomenologie*" of Time (that is, of Spirit) in the World is said by Hegel in the *Phenomenology*.

Therefore, to understand the paradoxical identification of Time and the Concept, one must know the whole of the *Phenomenology*. On the one hand, one must know that the Time in question is human or historical Time—that is, Time in which the Future that determines the Present by way of the Past takes primacy. And on the other hand, one must know how Hegel defines the Concept.[30]

It remains for me, then, briefly to go over what the Concept, the *Begriff*, is for Hegel.

In Chapter VII of the *Phenomenology*, Hegel said that all *conceptual* understanding (*Begreifen*) is equivalent to a *murder*. Let us, then, recall what he had in view. As long as the Meaning (or Essence, Concept, Logos, Idea, etc.) is embodied in an empirically existing entity, this Meaning or Essence, as well as this entity, *lives*. For example, as long as the Meaning (or Essence) "dog" is embodied in a sensible entity, this Meaning (Essence) *lives*: it is the real dog, the living dog which runs, drinks, and eats. But when the Meaning (Essence) "dog" passes into the *word* "dog"—that is, becomes *abstract* Concept which is *different* from the sensible reality that it reveals by its Meaning—the Meaning (Essence) *dies*: the *word* "dog" does not run, drink, and eat; in it the Meaning (Essence) *ceases* to live—that is, it *dies*. And that is why the *conceptual* understanding of empirical reality is equivalent to a *murder*. To be sure, Hegel knows full well that it is not necessary to kill a dog in order to understand it through its Concept—that is,

[30] The *Hegelian* Concept is identified with *Hegelian* Time. But the *pre*-Hegelian Concept cannot be identified with *pre*-Hegelian Time; nor the *Hegelian* Concept with *pre*-Hegelian Time; nor the *pre*-Hegelian Concept with *Hegelian* Time.

in order to give it a name or define it—nor is it necessary to wait for it actually to die in order to do so.[31] However, Hegel says, if the dog were not *mortal*—that is, essentially *finite* or limited with respect to its duration—one could not *detach* its Concept from it— that is, cause the Meaning (Essence) that is embodied in the *real* dog to pass into the *non*living word—into the *word* (endowed with a meaning)—that is, into the *abstract* Concept—into the Concept that exists not in the dog (which realizes it) but in the man (who thinks it)—that is, in something *other* than the sensible reality which the concept reveals by its Meaning. The Concept "dog" which is *my* Concept (of the dog), the Concept, therefore, which is something *other* than the living dog and is *related* to a living dog as to an *external* reality—this *abstract* Concept is possible only if the dog is *essentially* mortal. That is, if the dog dies or is anni- hilated at *every* instant of its existence. Now, this dog which is annihilated at every instant is precisely the dog which endures in Time, which at every instant ceases to live or exist in the Present so as to be annihilated in the Past, or *as* Past.[32] If the dog were eternal, if it existed outside of Time or without Time, the Concept "dog" would never be *detached* from the dog itself. The empirical existence (*Dasein*) of the Concept "dog" would be the living dog, and not the *word* "dog" (either thought or spoken). Hence, there would be no *Discourse* (Logos) in the World; and since the empirically existing Discourse is solely Man (actually speaking Man), there would be no Man in the World. The Concept-word

---

[31] Let us note, however, that a conceptual or "scientific" understanding of the dog actually leads, sooner or later, to its *dissection.*

[32] Therefore: for Aristotle there is a concept "dog" only because there is an *eternal* real dog, namely, the *species* "dog," which is always in the present; for Hegel, on the other hand, there is a concept "dog" only because the real dog is a *temporal* entity—that is, an essentially finite or "mortal" entity, an entity which is annihilated at every instant: and the Concept *is* the permanent support of this nihilation of the spatial real, which nihilation is itself nothing other than *Time.* For Hegel too, then, the Concept is something that is preserved ("eternally," if you will, but in the sense of: as long as Time lasts). But for him, it is only the *Concept* "dog" that is preserved (the Concept—that is, the temporal *nihilation* of the real dog, which nihilation actually lasts as long as Time lasts, since Time *is* this nihilation as such); whereas for Aristotle, the real *dog* is what is preserved (eternally, in the strict sense, since there is *eternal* return), at least as *species.* That is why Hegel explains what Aristotle cannot explain, namely, the preserva- tion (in and by Man) of the Concept of an animal belonging, for example, to an *extinct* species (even if there are no fossil remains).

INTRODUCTION TO THE READING OF HEGEL

detaches itself from the sensible *hic et nunc*; but it can thus detach itself only because the *hic et nunc*—i.e., spatial being—is temporal, because it *annihilates* itself in the Past. And the real which *disappears* into the Past *preserves* itself (as nonreal) in the Present in the form of the Word-Concept. The Universe of Discourse (the World of Ideas) is the permanent rainbow which forms above a waterfall: and the waterfall is the *temporal real* which is annihilated in the nothingness of the Past.[33]

To be sure, the Real *endures* in Time as *real*. But by the fact of enduring in *Time*, it is its own *remembrance*: at each instant it realizes its Essence or Meaning, and this is to say that it realizes in

---

[33] Kant himself saw that conceptual knowledge implied *Memory*, and Hegel maintains this idea (which is Platonic, in the final analysis). For Hegel too, the Er-*innerung*—that is, the internalization of the objective real effected in and by the Concept which reveals this real but is *in me*—is also *Erinnerung*—that is, remembrance. Now, there is Memory only where there is Time, where the real *present* is annihilated through becoming unreal past. Generally speaking, in his theory of the Concept, Hegel merely makes more precise (and consequently transforms) the Kantian theory of the *Schematismus*. For Kant, the Concepts (= Categories) apply to given Being (*Sein*) because Time serves as their "Schema"—that is, as intermediary or "mediation" (*Vermittlung*, in Hegel). But this "mediation" is purely *passive*: Time is contemplation, intuition, *Anschauung*. In Hegel, on the other hand, the "mediation" is *active*; it is *Tat* or *Tun*, Action negating the given, the activity of Fighting and Work. Now, this Negation of the given (of *Sein*) or of the "present" *is* (historical) Time, and (historical) Time *is* this active Negation. In Hegel as in Kant, therefore, Time is what allows the application of the Concept to Being. But in Hegel, this Time that mediates conceptual thought is "materialized": it is a *movement* (*Bewegung*), and a *dialectical* "movement"—that is, precisely, it is active—hence it negates, hence it transforms (the given), hence it creates (new things). If Man can understand (reveal) Being by the Concept, it is because he *transforms* (given) Being in terms of this Concept (which is then a Project) and makes it conform to it. Now, the transformation of given Being in terms of the Concept-project is, precisely, conscious and voluntary *Action*, *Tun* which is *Arbeit* and *Kampf*. For Kant, Being *is* in conformity with the Concept, and the "mediation" by Time merely allows one to move from one to the other without modifying either the one or the other. And that is why Kant cannot *explain* this conformity of Being and the Concept: for him, it is a given, that is to say, a *chance* (*transcendentale Zufälligkeit*). Hegel, on the other hand, *explains* this conformity (which for him is a *process* of conforming) by his dialectical ontology: Being *becomes* conformable to the Concept (at the end of History) through the completed totality of negating Action which *transforms* Being in terms of this same Concept. Therefore: in Kant, Time is "schema" and passive "intuition"; in Hegel, it is "movement" and conscious and voluntary "action." Consequently, the Concept or the *a priori* in Kant is a "notion," which allows Man to *conform* to given Being; whereas in Hegel, the *a priori* Concept is a "project," which allows Man to *transform* given Being and *make* it conform.

the Present what is left of it after its annihilation in the Past; and this something that is left and that it re-realizes is its *concept*. At the moment when the present Real sinks into the Past, its Meaning (Essence) *detaches itself* from its reality (Existence); and it is here that appears the possibility of retaining this Meaning *outside* of the reality by causing it to pass into the Word. And this Word reveals the Meaning of the Real which *realizes* in the Present its own Past— that is, this same Past that is "eternally" preserved in the Word-Concept. In short, the Concept can have an empirical existence in the World (this existence being nothing other than human existence) only if the World is *temporal*, only if *Time* has an empirical existence in the World. And that is why it can be said that Time *is* the empirically existing Concept.[34]

[34] On the ontological level, this "metaphysical" (or cosmological) statement means: Being must have a *trinitary* structure, as "Synthesis" or "Totality" which unites "Thesis" or "Identity" with "Antithesis" or "Negativity" (this presence of the *negation* of Being in *existing* Being is, precisely, Time). In order better to understand the identification of the Concept with Time, it is useful to proceed as follows: Let us form the concept of Being—that is, of the *totality* of what *is*. What is the difference between this concept "Being" and Being itself? From the point of view of content, they are identical, since we have made no "abstraction." And nonetheless, in spite of what Parmenides thought, the concept "Being" is not Being (otherwise, there would be no Discourse, the Concept would not be Logos). What distinguishes Being from the concept "Being" is solely the *Being* of Being itself; for Being as Being *is*, but it does not *exist* as Being in the concept "Being" (even though it "is" present by its content—i.e., as the *meaning* of the concept "Being"). Therefore the concept "Being" is obtained by *subtracting* being from Being: Being minus being equals the concept "Being" (and does not equal Nothingness or "zero"; for the negation *of A* is not Nothingness, but "non-A"—that is, "something"). Now, this subtraction of being from Being, at first sight paradoxical or even "impossible," is in reality something quite "common": it is literally done "at every instant" and is called "Time." For Time is what, at every instant, takes away from Being—i.e., from the totality of what *is* (in the Present)— its being, by causing it to pass into the Past where Being *is* not (or *no longer* is). But for there to be Time, there must "be" a Past (the pure or "eternal" Present is not Time): therefore, the Past and Being that has sunk into the Past (past Being) are not Nothingness; they are "something." Now, a thing *is* something only in the Present. In order to *be* something, therefore, the Past and past Being must preserve themselves in the Present while ceasing to be present. And the *presence* of *past* Being is the concept "Being"—that is, Being from which one has taken away the being without transforming it into pure Nothingness. If you will, the concept "Being," therefore, is the "remembrance" of Being (in both senses: Being is what "remembers," and it "remembers" its being). But on our present level, one does not generally speak of "memory"; the "memory" that we have in mind is called "Time" (or more exactly "Temporality"—this general "medium" of Being, in which "in addition" to the Present there is something else: the Past—

Therefore: no Concept in the World as long as there is no empirically existing Time in this World. Now, we have seen that the empirical existence of Time in the World is human Desire (i.e., Desire that is directed toward a Desire as Desire). Therefore: no conceptual understanding without Desire. Now, Desire is realized by negating Action: and *human* Desire is realized by the Action of the Fight to the death for pure prestige. And this Fight is realized by the victory of the Master over the Slave, and by the latter's work in the Master's service. This Work of the Slave is what *realizes* the Master's Desire by *satisfying* it. Therefore, and Hegel says so expressly in Chapter IV, no Concept without Work; it is from the Slave's Work that *Denken* and *Verstand*, Understanding and Thought—that is, conceptual understanding of the World—are born.

And now we understand why. It is Work, and only Work, that transforms the World in an *essential* manner, by creating truly *new* realities. If there were only animals on earth, Aristotle would be right: the Concept would be embodied in the eternal species, eternally identical to itself; and it would not exist, as Plato claimed

---

and the Future; but I shall not talk about the Future here). Therefore: if there is a concept "Being," it is because Being is *temporal* (and one can say that the Concept *is* Time—i.e., the coexistence of the Present and the Past). Now, it is obvious that Being is "in conformity" with the concept "Being," since the latter is Being itself minus being. One can say, then, that Being is the *being* of the concept "Being." And that is why Being which *is* (in the Present) can be "conceived of" or revealed by the Concept. Or, more exactly, Being *is* conceived of at "each instant" of its being. Or else, again: Being is not only Being, but also *Truth*—that is, the adequation of the Concept and Being. This is simple. The whole question is to know where *error* comes from. In order that error be possible, the Concept must be *detached* from Being and *opposed* to it. It is Man who does this; and more exactly, Man *is* the Concept detached from Being; or better yet, he is the *act* of detaching the Concept from Being. He does so by negating-Negativity—that is, by Action, and it is here that the Future (the Pro-ject) enters in. This detaching is equivalent to an inadequation (the profound meaning of *errare* humanum *est*), and it is necessary to negate or act again in order to achieve conformity between the Concept (= Project) and Being (made to conform to the Project by Action). For Man, therefore, the adequation of Being and the Concept is a *process* (*Bewegung*), and the truth (*Wahrheit*) is a *result*. And only this "result of the process" merits the name of (discursive) "truth," for only this process is Logos or Discourse. (Before its negation by Man, Being does not *speak*, for the Concept *detached* from Being is what *is* in the Word or Logos, or as Word-logos.) Hegel says all this in a passage in the Preface to the *Phenomenology*, which gives the key to understanding his whole system (p. 29, l. 26–p. 30, l. 15).

it did, *outside* of Time and the World. But then it would not be understandable how the Concept could exist outside of the species, how it could exist in the temporal World in the form of a *word*. Therefore, it would not be understandable how Man could exist— Man—i.e., that being which is not a dog, for example, and in which the Meaning (Essence) "dog" nonetheless exists just as much as in the dog, since there is in it the Word-Concept "dog." For this to be possible, Being revealed by the Concept must be essentially temporal—that is, finite, or possessing a beginning and an ending in Time. Now, not the natural object, nor even the animal or plant, but only the product of human Work is essentially temporal. Human Work is what *temporalizes* the spatial natural World; Work, therefore, is what engenders the Concept which exists in the natural World while being something other than this World: Work, therefore, is what engenders Man in this World, Work is what transforms the purely natural World into a technical World inhabited by Man—that is, into a historical World.

Only the World transformed by human Work reveals itself in and by the Concept which exists empirically in the World without being the World. Therefore, the Concept *is* Work, and Work *is* the Concept. And if, as Marx quite correctly remarks, Work for Hegel is "*das* Wesen *des Menschen*" ("the very essence of Man"), it can also be said that man's essence, for Hegel, is the Concept. And that is why Hegel says not only that Time is the *Begriff*, but also that it is the *Geist*. For if Work temporalizes Space, the existence of Work in the World is the existence in this World of Time. Now, if Man is the Concept, and if the Concept is Work, Man and the Concept are also *Time*.

If all this holds true, it must *first* be said that there is conceptual understanding only where there is an essentially temporal, that is, historical, reality; and *secondly*, that only historical or temporal existence can reveal itself by the Concept. Or in other words, conceptual understanding is necessarily *dialectical*.[35]

---

[35] For "dialectical" understanding is nothing other than the historical or temporal understanding of the real. Dialectic reveals the *trinitary* structure of Being. In other words, in and by its dialectic the real reveals itself not *sub specie aeternitatis*—that is, outside of Time or as eternally identical to itself—but as a Present situated between the Past and the Future, that is, as a *Bewegung*, as a

Now, if this holds true and if Nature is only Space and not Time, one would have to conclude that there is no conceptual understanding of Nature. One would understand, in the full sense, only where there is Time—i.e., one would truly understand only History. In any case, it is only History that can and must be understood *dialectically*.

One would have to say so. But Hegel does not. And that, I believe, is his basic error. First of all, there is a vacillation in Hegel. On the one hand, he says that Nature is only Space. On the other, he clearly sees that (biological) life is a temporal phenomenon. Hence the idea that Life (*Leben*) is a manifestation of Spirit (*Geist*). But Hegel also sees, and he is the first to say so in so many words, that truly human existence is possible only by the *negation* of Life (as we know, the Risk of life in the Fight for prestige is *constituent* of Man). Hence an *opposition* of *Leben* and *Geist*. But if this opposition exists, Life is not historical; therefore there is no biological *dialectic*; therefore there is no conceptual understanding of Life.

Now, Hegel asserts that there is such an understanding. He imagines (following Schelling) a *dialectical* biology, and he sets ,it forth in the *Phenomenology* (Chapter V, Section A, *a*). To be sure, he denies the conceptual understanding or dialectic of non-vital reality. But this merely leads him to say that the real World is a *living* being. Hence his absurd philosophy of Nature, his insensate critique of Newton, and his own "magical" physics which discredited his System in the nineteenth century.

But there is yet more to say. Dialectical understanding applies only to historical reality—that is, to the reality created by Work according to a Project. To assert, as Hegel does, that *all* understanding is dialectical and that the natural World is understandable is to assert that this World is the work of a Demiurge, of a Creator-God conceived in the image of working Man. And this is what Hegel actually says in the *Logik*, when he says that his "Logic" (that is, his ontology) is "the thought of God before the creation

---

creative movement, or else, again, as a *result* which is a project and as a *project* which is a result—a result which is born of a project and a project engendered by a result; in a word, the real reveals itself in its dialectical truth as a *Synthesis*. (See Chapter 7, "The Dialectic of the Real and the Phenomenological Method in Hegel," in this volume.)

of the World." It would follow that Hegel understands the World because the World is *created* according to the Concept that *Hegel* has. And thus we are in the midst of a paradox. Hegelian anthropo-*theism* ceases to be an image; Hegel is actually God, God the *creator*, and the *eternal* God. Now, (unless he is mad) a man cannot assert that he created the World. If, then, the thought that is revealed in the *Logik* is the thought that *created* the World, it is certainly not Hegel's thought. It is the thought of a Creator *other* than Hegel, *other* than Man in general; it is the thought of *God.* And therefore the *Logik*, in spite of its title, is not simply logic; like Spinoza's *Ethics*, it is *theo*-logy—that is, the logic, thought, or discourse of *God.*[36]

But enough of the natural World. Let us note that Hegel realized an immense philosophical progress by identifying the Concept and Time. For by doing this—that is, by discovering *dialectical* knowledge—he found the means of establishing a phenomenology, a metaphysics, and an ontology of *History*—that is, of Man as we conceive of him today and as he is in reality.

Let us see the decisive consequence for Man following from this discovery.

The Concept is Time. Time in the full sense of the term—that is, a Time in which there is a Future also in the full sense—that is, a Future that will never become either Present or Past. Man is the

---

[36] Personally, I do not believe that this is a necessary consequence. I see no objection to saying that the natural World eludes *conceptual* understanding. Indeed, this would only mean that the existence of Nature is revealed by mathematical algorithm, for example, and not by concepts—that is, by *words* having a meaning. Now, modern physics leads in the end to this result: one cannot *speak* of the physical reality without contradictions; as soon as one passes from algorithm to verbal description, one contradicts himself (particles-waves, for example). Hence there would be no *discourse* revealing the physical or natural reality. This reality (as presented as early as Galileo) would be revealed to Man only by the articulated *silence* of algorithm. Physical matter is understood *conceptually* or dialectically (it can be *spoken* of) only to the extent that it is the "raw material" of a product of human work. Now, the "raw material" itself is neither molecules nor electrons, and so on, but wood, stone, and so on. And these are things which, if not living themselves, at least exist on the scale of Life (and of Man as living being). Now, it does seem that algorithm, being *nontemporal*, does not reveal Life. But neither does dialectic. Therefore, it may be necessary to combine Plato's conception (for the mathematical, or better, geometrical, substructure of the World) with Aristotle's (for its biological structure) and Kant's (for its physical, or better, dynamic, structure), while reserving Hegelian dialectic for Man and History.

empirical existence of the Concept in the World. Therefore, he is the empirical existence in the World of a Future that will never become present. Now, this Future, for Man, is his *death*, that Future of his which will never become his Present; and the only reality or real presence of this Future is the *knowledge* that Man has in the present of his future death. Therefore, if Man *is* Concept and if the Concept *is* Time (that is, if Man is an *essentially temporal* being), Man is *essentially* mortal; and he is Concept, that is, absolute Knowledge or Wisdom incarnate, only if he *knows* this. Logos becomes flesh, becomes Man, only on the condition of being willing and able to *die*.

And this causes us to understand why possibility III, adopted by Hegel, appears so late in the history of philosophy. To deny that the Concept is eternal, to say that it *is* Time, is to deny that Man is immortal or eternal (at least to the extent that he thinks, to the extent that he is truly a human being). Now, Man accepts his death only *in extremis*; and it was also *in extremis* that philosophy accepted possibility III.[37]

"*Alles* endliche *ist dies, sich selbst aufzuheben,*" Hegel says in the *Encyclopaedia*. It is only *finite* Being that dialectically overcomes itself. If, then, the Concept is Time, that is, if conceptual understanding is *dialectical*, the existence of the Concept—and consequently of Being revealed by the Concept—is essentially *finite*. Therefore History itself must be essentially finite; collective Man (humanity) must die just as the human individual dies; universal History must have a definitive *end*.

We know that for Hegel this end of history is marked by the coming of Science in the form of a Book—that is, by the appearance of the Wise Man or of *absolute* Knowledge in the World. This absolute Knowledge, being the *last* moment of Time—that is, a moment without a *Future*—is no longer a temporal moment. If absolute Knowledge *comes into being* in Time or, better yet, as Time or History, Knowledge that *has come into being* is no longer temporal or historical: it is *eternal*, or, if you will, it is *Eternity*

---

[37] Thus we see that the expression "anthropo-theism" is but a metaphor: circular—that is, dialectical—absolute Knowledge reveals *finite* or mortal being; this being, therefore, is not the *divine* being; it is indeed, the *human* being; but Man can know that this is *his* being only provided that he knows that he is *mortal*.

revealed to itself; it is the Substance of Parmenides-Spinoza which reveals itself by a *Discourse* (and not by Silence), precisely because it is the *result* of a historical *becoming*; it is Eternity *engendered* by Time.

And this is what Hegel is going to explain in the text of the Second Stage of the Second Section of the Second Part of Chapter VIII.

6

INTERPRETATION OF THE THIRD PART OF CHAPTER VIII OF THE *PHENOMENOLOGY OF SPIRIT* (CONCLUSION)

Complete Text of the Twelfth Lecture of the Academic Year 1938–1939

In the passage where Hegel spoke of the circularity of the "System," it was said that in coming to the end of the *Logik*, one is brought around to its beginning, and that having effected this circular movement, one sees the necessity of going beyond it— that is, of going to the *Phenomenology*.

To proceed from the *Logik* to the *Phenomenology* is to proceed from the identity or perfect coincidence of the Subject and the Object, of the Concept and Reality, of *Bewusstsein* and *Selbstbewusstsein*, to their opposition or "difference" (*Unterschied*), as Hegel says.

Now, the distinction between external-Consciousness and Self-Consciousness which characterizes the *Phenomenology* presupposes a real difference between Consciousness in general and the non-conscious Reality or, if you please, a real distinction between Man and the World.

Consequently, a System that necessarily breaks up into two Parts, namely a *Logik* and a *Phenomenology*, must necessarily be "realist," as we say. This fact is decisive for understanding Hegel. For, deceived by the Hegelian expression "absolute Idealism" (*absoluter Idealismus*), people have often asserted that Hegel's System is "idealist." Now in fact, Hegelian absolute Idealism has nothing to do with what is ordinarily called "Idealism." And if terms are used in their usual senses, it must be said that Hegel's System is "realist."

To convince oneself of this, one need only cite several texts found in the essay of his youth entitled "Difference between Fichte's and Schelling's Systems" (1801).

In it, for example, Hegel says the following (Volume 1, pages 47, 48, 77):

> Neither the Subjective by itself, nor the Objective [by itself], fills up Consciousness. The pure Subjective is [just] as much [an] abstraction as the pure Objective . . . It is in view of the identity of the Subject and the Object that I posit things outside of me with as much [subjective] certainty as I posit myself: things exist just as [subjectively] certainly as I myself exist (*So gewiss Ich bin, sind die Dinge*). [Hence Hegel is even more "realist" than Descartes.] . . . One finds in both [namely, in the Subject and the Object] not only the same right [to existence], but also the same necessity. For if only the one had been related to the Absolute, and the other not, their essential-reality would then be supposed unequally (*ungleich*); and the union of the two [would therefore be] impossible; [also impossible,] consequently, the task of philosophy, [the aim of which is, precisely,] to overcome-dialectically the division-or-opposition (*Entzweiung*) [of the Subject and the Object].

This is clear. But the "demonstration" of "Realism" in Chapter VIII of the *Phenomenology* reveals aspects of the problem that are little known, although very important.

Hegel posits the principle of metaphysical "realism" in the passage immediately following the one in which he demonstrated the necessity of proceeding from the *Logik* to the *Phenomenology*. Having demonstrated this necessity, Hegel continues as follows (page 563, lines 11–14):

> However, this alienation-or-externalization (*Entäusserung*) is as yet imperfect. It expresses the *relation* (*Beziehung*) of the [subjective] Certainty of self to the Object; which Object, precisely because it is found in the relation [to the Subject], has not yet attained its full freedom-or-autonomy (*Freiheit*).

It is not sufficient to proceed from the *Logik* to the *Phenomenology*. The *Phenomenology* deals with the *relation* between *Bewusstsein* and *Selbstbewusstsein*, between Thought and Reality. The Object appears in it only to the extent that it is related to the Subject. Now, for a Reinhold, for a Fichte, this relation of the Subject and the Object is effected within the Subject, the Object being but one of the aspects of subjective activity. For Hegel, on the other hand, the dialectic of the Subject and Object, which is effected inside of the Subject and is described in the *Phenomenology*, is meaningful only if one supposes the existence of an Object properly so-called—that is, an Object external to and independent of the Subject. Or, as Hegel says, one must give the Object "its full freedom (*seine völlige Freiheit*)."

In short, relying on Schelling here, Hegel has just posited (against Fichte) the absolute necessity of a "realist" metaphysics.

In the text that follows (page 563, lines 14–21), Hegel briefly indicates the nature of this "realist" metaphysics, the necessity of which he has just proclaimed.

> Knowledge knows (*kennt*) not only itself, but also its Negative, [i.e., it knows] its limit (*Grenze*). To know-or-understand (*wissen*) its limit means: to know (*wissen*) how to sacrifice itself. This sacrifice (*Aufopferung*) is the alienation-or-externalization in which Spirit represents (*darstellt*) its becoming Spirit in the form of a *free contingent process* (*Geschehens*), by intuitively-contemplating (*anschauend*) its pure *Self* (*Selbst*) as *Time* outside of itself, and likewise its *Given-Being* (*Sein*) as Space.

The passage contains, first, a sort of "deduction" of Realism, which can be misunderstood if taken out of context. The passage is directed against Fichte. And in speaking to Fichte, Hegel uses his language here (*Grenze*, and so on). Thus, the text *seems* to speak of an act of the Subject, which posits the Object by positing its own limit. This seems to be pure Fichte—that is, "Idealism." But a careful reading and a comparison of what Hegel says with what Fichte says elsewhere shows that this is a polemic. First, it is not the *I* or the Subject (*Ich*) that posits the Object or the limit, but *Spirit* (*Geist*). Now, Hegel never tires of repeating (and he will repeat it again a bit further on) that Spirit is not origin or beginning, but end or result. Spirit is revealed Being—that is, a *synthesis* of (objective) Being and its (subjective) Revelation. Not the Subject, but Spirit (and therefore Being) posits itself as Space and Time, or as we shall shortly see, as Nature (= *Sein*) and History (= Man = Subject = *Selbst*). Next, Hegel does not, like Fichte, say that Knowledge "posits" (*setzt*) its "limit" (that is, the Object). He only says that it "knows" (*kennt*) its limit.

Therefore, Hegel means quite simply to say that Knowledge can understand itself—that is, explain or "deduce" itself—only by supposing the existence of a nonknowledge—that is, of a real Object or, better, of an Object external to and independent of the Knowledge that reveals it. And this is exactly the opposite of what Fichte says.

Hence there is no "deduction" of Realism in Fichte's sense of the word. There is only a "deduction" in the Hegelian sense of the word—that is, an *a posteriori* deduction or a conceptual understanding of what *is*. There is no question, as in Fichte, of deducing the Object or the Real from the Subject or the Idea.[1] Therefore, by starting with Spirit—that is, a *synthesis* of the real and the ideal—Hegel foregoes deducing the one from the other (as he says quite plainly in the text that I have cited from the essay of 1801). He posits—that is, he presupposes—both of them. And he "deduces" them only after the fact, from the Spirit which is their common result. In other words, he only tries to *understand* their relation, which is constituted by the becoming of knowledge, by starting with what according to him is the established fact of absolutely true knowledge, in which the real and the ideal coincide. But he says that, in finding oneself in possession of the Truth—that is, of the "Science" or "System"—one must not forget their origin, which is not coincidence, but opposition and interaction of the independent real and ideal. One must not believe that if Science is Knowledge, Being too is Knowledge (or Subject). Being is Spirit, that is, synthesis of Knowledge *and* the Real. And the "System" itself is not a game carried on by the Subject within itself, but the result of an interaction between Subject and Object; and thus it is a revelation of the Object by the Subject and a realization of the Subject in the Object.

Hegel *starts* with Spirit, which he says is a "result." And he wants to understand it as a result—that is, to describe it as resulting from its own becoming (*das Werden des Geistes zum Geiste*). Since Spirit is the coincidence of Subject and Object (or as Hegel says: of the *Selbst* and the *Sein*), its becoming is the road that

---

[1] It is, in fact, absurd to want to "deduce"—that is, to *demonstrate*—Realism. For if one could *deduce* the real from knowledge, Idealism would be right, and there would be no reality *independent* of knowledge.

leads toward this coincidence, along which road, consequently, a *difference* between the two is maintained, an account of which can be given only by a metaphysical *Realism*.

Having said this, Hegel makes two extremely important qualifications. First, Hegel says that "the becoming of Spirit" has the form *"des freien zufälligen Geschehens."* Thus he repeats what we have known for a long while: namely, that the "deduction" is possible only after the fact or *a posteriori*, as we say. To say that the Spirit's becoming is "contingent and free" is to say that, starting with Spirit which is the end or result of becoming, one can reconstruct the path of the becoming, but one can neither foresee its path from its beginning, nor deduce the Spirit from it. Since Spirit is the identity of Being and the Subject, one can deduce from it the earlier opposition of the two and the process that overcomes that opposition. But starting with the initial opposition, one can deduce neither its being finally overcome, nor the process that leads to it. And that is why this process (in particular, History) is a free *(frei)* series of contingent *(zufällig)* events.

Secondly, Hegel says that, in its becoming, Spirit (that is, the revealed Totality of Being) is necessarily double: it is on the one hand Self *(Selbst)* or Time, and on the other, static Being *(Sein)* or Space. And this is very important.

First, it is a new assertion of Realism. For it is quite obvious that Realism is necessarily dualist, and that an ontological dualism is always "realist." [2] The whole question is to know how to define the two terms that are ontologically opposed in Realism. Now, Hegel says that they must be opposed as Time and Space. And, in saying this, he somehow sums up his whole philosophy and indicates what is truly new in it. Now, taken by itself, this assertion seems paradoxical. No one has ever thought of dividing the totality of Being into Space and Time. To the extent that (Western) philosophy has been "realist" or, rather, "dualist," it has divided the totality of Being into Subject and Object, into Thought and Reality, and so on. But we know that for Hegel Time *is* the Concept. With that, instead of being paradoxical, Hegel's division,

[2] The assertion that everything is Object or "matter" is equivalent to the assertion that everything is Subject or "spirit"; the "materialist" and the "idealist" or "spiritualist" assertions coincide, because both are equally empty of meaning.

quite to the contrary, seems commonplace: it is the Cartesian opposition (to mention by name only Descartes) of Extension and Thought. But in fact, Hegel made a great discovery when he replaced the term "Thought" with the term "Time." But I have already tried to show this, and I shall not return to it again.

The text in question is interesting, however, for yet another reason. In it, Hegel identifies Space and *Sein*, static Given Being; this is commonplace and quite Cartesian. On the other hand, the identification of Time and the *Selbst* (the Self)—that is, Man— is new. But this is the Hegelian conception of Man = Action = Negativity, which we know and need not talk about now. What I would like to underline is that Hegel here *opposes* the Self (= Time) to *Sein* (= Space). Man, therefore, is *Nicht-sein*, Nonbeing, Nothingness.[3] To oppose Time to Being is to say that time is nothingness. And there is no doubt that Time must actually be understood as an *annihilation* of Being or Space. But if Man *is* Time, he himself is Nothingness or annihilation of spatial Being. And we know that for Hegel it is precisely in this annihilation of Being that consists the Negativity which *is* Man, that Action of Fighting and Work by which Man preserves himself in spatial Being while *destroying* it—that is, while transforming it by the creation of hitherto unknown new things into a genuine Past—a nonexistent and consequently nonspatial Past. And this Negativity —that is, this Nothingness nihilating as Time in Space—is what forms the very foundation of specifically human existence—that is, truly active or creative, or historical, individual, and free, existence. This Nothingness, too, is what makes Man a *passerby* in the spatial World: he is born and he dies in it as Man. Therefore, there is a Nature without Man—before Man, and after Man—as Hegel will say.

Finally, when this same text is related to Knowledge, it must be said that Man properly so-called—that is, Man *opposed* to single and homogeneous spatial Being, or the historical free Individual whom Hegel calls *Selbst* ("Self")—is necessarily Error and not Truth. For a Thought that does not coincide with Being is

---

[3] Indeed, in the *Logik* the Totality of Being—that is, Spirit—is defined at the outset as Being (*Sein*) and *Nothingness* (*Nichts*)—that is, as their synthesis, which is Becoming.

false. Thus, when specifically human error is finally transformed into the truth of absolute Science, Man ceases to exist as Man and History comes to an end. The overcoming of Man (that is, of Time, that is, of Action) in favor of static Being (that is, Space, that is, Nature), therefore, is the overcoming of Error in favor of Truth. And if History is certainly the history of human errors, Man himself is perhaps only an error of Nature that "by chance" (freedom?) was not immediately eliminated.

In my opinion, the division of the Totality of revealed Being (or as Hegel says, of Spirit) into Space and Time is neither a paradox, nor a commonplace, but a truth discovered by Hegel. And if this truth is accepted, it must be said that "Realism" in philosophy means, finally, nothing but "Historicism." "Realism" means ontological dualism. And calling the two members of the fundamental opposition "Space" and "Time" introduces the notion of History into philosophy, and thus poses not only the problem of an Anthropology or Phenomenology of historical Man, but also the problem of a Metaphysics and an Ontology of History. To say that philosophy must be "realist," therefore, is in the final analysis to say that it must take account and give an account of the fact of *History*.

And I believe that this is quite true: If *per impossible*, what is called ontologically "Negativity," metaphysically "Time" or "History," and anthropologically "Action," did not exist, Idealism (= Monism) would be right: it would be superfluous to *oppose* Being to Thought ontologically, and hence there would be no need to go beyond Parmenides. As a matter of fact, I do not believe that the *Real* properly so-called can be defined otherwise than it has been by Maine de Biran (among others): the Real is what *resists*. Now, it is perfectly wrong to believe that the Real resists Thought. In point of fact, it does not resist it: it does not even resist false thought; and, as for true thought, it is precisely a coincidence with the Real.[4] The Real resists Action, and not Thought. Consequently, there is true philosophical "Realism" only where philosophy takes account and gives an account of Action—

---

[4] Indeed, if I say I can pass through this wall, the wall by no means resists what I say or think: as far as it is concerned, I can say so as long as I please. It begins to resist only if I want to realize my thought by Action—that is, if I actually hurl myself against the wall. And such is always the case.

that is, of History—that is, of Time. And therefore philosophical "Realism," or better, "Dualism," does indeed mean: "Temporalism" or "Historicism." [5]

But let us return to the text.

Having opposed given Being or Space to the Self or Time, Hegel specifies the nature of the two opposed entities, speaking first of Space (page 563, lines 21–25):

> This just-mentioned becoming of Spirit [namely], *Nature*, is its living immediate becoming. Nature, [that is,] the alienated-or-externalized Spirit, is in its empirical-existence nothing [else] but the

[5] It is meaningless to oppose the knowing Subject to the Object which is known, as "Realism" ordinarily does. For, having opposed them, one no longer understands their union or coincidence in true knowledge. If one wants to take account of the "real," one must not oppose the (natural) World to a "Subject," situated who knows where, and whose sole function is to *know* this World—that is, to reveal it by discourse or concept. One must not oppose Being to *Thought* or to the *knowing* Subject. One must oppose *natural* Being to *human* Being. Or, to use Hegel's language: on the phenomenological level, *Sein* is opposed to *Selbst*; on the metaphysical level, Space to Time; on the ontological level, Identity to Negativity. In other words, one must see something else in Man besides a *knowing* Subject; and one must *oppose* Man to the (natural) World precisely to the extent that he is this other thing (*Anderes*).

True knowledge—and that is what we generally talk about—is selfless (*selbstlos*)—that is, inhuman. In it, the Subject (Thought, Concept, and so on) coincides with the *Object*. And we can say that the *Object* is what reveals itself to itself in and by this knowledge. Indeed, let us suppose that a man understood as "knowing subject" is reduced to the (adequate) understanding of a single particular reality: the reality "dog," for example. Then, he would be nothing other than the revelation of this reality "dog." This is to say that we would be faced with the revealed reality "dog." In other words, we would be faced with the *dog* that is conscious *of itself*, and not a *man* who is acquiring knowledge *of* the dog. And in this case we would be faced with a true dog (a *natural* being) and not a *man* in canine form. Putting it otherwise, to use Hegel's language, there would only be (dumb) *Sentiment* of self (*Selbst-gefühl*) and not (speaking) *Consciousness* of self (*Selbst-bewusstsein*). Or, to put it otherwise again, the concept would be embodied in the thing that it reveals and would not exist outside of it as word. Hence "Realism" would not be meaningful, since there would be no separation between the Subject and the Object.

For there to be "Realism," the concept (knowledge) must be opposed to the thing (the object). Now, it is only *human* or "subjective" knowledge that opposes itself to the object to which it is related, by being materialized outside of the object in discourse. But this "subjective" knowledge is by definition a knowledge that does not coincide with the object. Therefore, it is a *false* knowledge. The problem which calls for a "realist" solution, therefore, is the problem of error and not of truth. Now, citing the fact of error makes it necessary to pose the problem of its origin. And, clearly, passive cognitive contemplation, which opens eternal alienation-or-externalization of its *stable-continuity* (*Bestehens*) and the [dialectical] movement which produces the *Subject*.

Sein or Space is Nature, the nonconscious natural World. And this World is *eternal* in the sense that it is outside of Time. Nature is the *ewige Entäusserung* of the Spirit. Here too there is becoming (*Werden*) or movement: but as in Descartes, the movement in question is nontemporal or geometrical; and the natural changes (biological coming into being) do not transform the *essence* of Nature, which therefore remains eternally identical to itself. This natural "movement" ("evolution") produces, to be sure, the "*Subjekt*"—that is, Man, or more exactly, the animal that will become Man. But Man, once constituted in his human specificity, *opposes* himself to Nature and thus engenders a *new* becoming which essentially transforms natural given Being and is the Time that annihilates it—i.e., he engenders the history of negating Action.

Hegelian "Realism," therefore, is not only ontological, but also metaphysical. Nature is *independent* of Man. Being eternal, it subsists before him and after him. It is in it that he is *born*, as we have just seen. And as we shall soon see, Man who *is* Time also *disappears* in spatial Nature. For this Nature *survives* Time.[6]

---

itself to the object and makes it accessible, cannot explain the origin of error that eludes and conceals the object. If, then, the seat of error or false knowledge, or rather, knowledge opposed to the object, is man or the "subject," he must have something else for support in addition to passive contemplation of the given. And this other thing, in Hegel, is called Negativity, Time, and Action (*Tat, Tun, Handeln*). (Hence it is not by chance that man makes errors when he loses his *sang-froid*, hurries, or hasn't enough time, or when he obstinately persists in saying no).

Therefore, "Realism" is meaningful only to the extent that one opposes the natural World or given Being (*Sein*) revealed by the Concept—that is, Being with the Knowledge of Being—to Man understood as Action that negates given Being. To put it otherwise, it can also be said that Knowledge (Revelation) is indifferently related both to natural Being and to human Being, both to Space and to Time, both to Identity and to Negativity; hence there is no opposition between Being and Knowledge; an opposition exists only between (known) *natural* Being or *Sein*, and (known) *human* Being or *Tun*; as for error and "subjective" knowledge in general—they *presuppose* this *ontological* opposition.

[6] The disappearance of Man at the end of History, therefore, is not a cosmic catastrophe: the natural World remains what it has been from all eternity. And therefore, it is not a biological catastrophe either: Man remains alive as animal in *harmony* with Nature or given Being. What disappears is Man properly so-called—that is, Action negating the given, and Error, or in general, the Subject

Sein or *Raum* is eternal, or rather nontemporal, Nature. The opposite entity, which is *Selbst* (that is, Man) or *Zeit*, is nothing other than History.

This is what Hegel now says (page 563, lines 26–30):

> As for the other aspect of the Spirit's becoming, [which is] *History*, [it] is the becoming which *knows-or-understands* [and which] *mediates* itself;—[it is] Spirit alienated-or-externalized in (*an*) Time. But this alienation-or-externalization is just as much the alienation-or-externalization of itself;—the negative-or-negating-entity (*Negative*) is the negative-or-negating-entity of itself.

The *Selbst*—that is, Man properly so-called or the free Individual, *is* Time; and Time is History, and *only* History. (Which,

---

opposed to the Object. In point of fact, the end of human Time or History— that is, the definitive annihilation of Man properly so-called or of the free and historical Individual—means quite simply the cessation of Action in the full sense of the term. Practically, this means: the disappearance of wars and bloody revolutions. And also the disappearance of *Philosophy*; for since Man himself no longer changes essentially, there is no longer any reason to change the (true) principles which are at the basis of his understanding of the World and of himself. But all the rest can be preserved indefinitely; art, love, play, etc., etc.; in short, everything that makes Man *happy*. Let us recall that this Hegelian theme, among many others, was taken up by Marx. History properly so-called, in which men ("classes") fight among themselves for recognition and fight against Nature by work, is called in Marx "Realm of necessity" (*Reich der Notwendigkeit*); *beyond* (*jenseits*) is situated the "Realm of freedom" (*Reich der Freiheit*), in which men (mutually recognizing one another without reservation) no longer fight, and work as little as possible (Nature having been definitively mastered— that is, harmonized with Man). Cf. *Das Kapital*, Book III, Chapter 48, end of the second paragraph of § III.

Note to the Second Edition

The text of the preceding note is ambiguous, not to say contradictory. If one accepts "the *disappearance* of Man at the end of History," if one asserts that "Man remains alive *as animal*," with the specification that "what *disappears* is Man *properly so-called*," one cannot say that "all the rest can be preserved indefinitely: art, love, play, etc." If Man becomes an animal again, his arts, his loves, and his play must also become purely "natural" again. Hence it would have to be admitted that after the end of History, men would construct their edifices and works of art as birds build their nests and spiders spin their webs, would perform musical concerts after the fashion of frogs and cicadas, would play like young animals, and would indulge in love like adult beasts. But one cannot then say that all this "makes Man *happy*." One would have to say that post-historical animals of the species *Homo sapiens* (which will live amidst abundance and complete security) will be *content* as a result of their artistic, erotic and playful behavior, inasmuch as, by definition, they will be contented with it. But there is furthermore, is *das* wissende *Werden*, "the *knowing* becoming" of the Spirit—that is, in the final analysis, philosophical evolution.) And Man is essentially *Negativity*, for Time is *Becoming*—that is, the *annihilation* of Being or Space. Therefore Man is a Nothingness that nihilates and that preserves itself in (spatial) Being only by *negating* being, this Negation being Action. Now, if Man is Negativity—that is, Time—he is not eternal. He is born and he dies as Man. He is "*das Negative seiner selbst*," Hegel says. And we known what that means: Man overcomes himself as Action (or *Selbst*) by ceasing to *oppose* himself to the World, after creating in it the universal and homogeneous State; or to put it otherwise, on the cognitive level: Man overcomes himself as *Error* (or "Subject" *opposed* to the Object) after creating the Truth of "Science."

In the following texts which end Chapter VIII and thus the *Phenomenology* as a whole, Hegel states his conception of History

---

more. "The *definitive annihilation* of Man *properly so-called*" also means the definitive disappearance of human Discourse (*Logos*) in the strict sense. Animals of the species *Homo sapiens* would react by conditioned reflexes to vocal signals or sign "language," and thus their so-called "discourses" would be like what is supposed to be the "language" of bees. What would disappear, then, is not only Philosophy or the search for discursive Wisdom, but also that Wisdom itself. For in these post-historical animals, there would no longer be any "[discursive] *understanding* of the World and of self."

At the period when I wrote the above note (1946), Man's return to animality did not appear unthinkable to me as a prospect for the future (more or less near). But shortly afterwards (1948) I understood that the Hegelian-Marxist end of History was not yet to come, but was already a present, here and now. Observing what was taking place around me and reflecting on what had taken place in the world since the Battle of Jena, I understood that Hegel was right to see in this battle the end of History properly so-called. In and by this battle the vanguard of humanity virtually attained the limit and the aim, that is, the *end*, of Man's historical evolution. What has happened since then was but an extension in space of the universal revolutionary force actualized in France by Robespierre-Napoleon. From the authentically historical point of view, the two world wars with their retinue of large and small revolutions had only the effect of bringing the backward civilizations of the peripheral provinces into line with the most advanced (real or virtual) European historical positions. If the sovietization of Russia and the communization of China are anything more than or different from the democratization of imperial Germany (by way of Hitlerism) or the accession of Togoland to independence, nay, the self-determination of the Papuans, it is only because the Sino-Soviet actualization of Robespierrian Bonapartism obliges post-Napoleonic Europe to speed up the elimination of the numerous more or less anachronistic sequels to its pre-revolutionary past. Already, moreover, this process of elimination is more advanced in the North American precisely. And this shows that, for Hegel, the introduction of History into philosophy is his principal and decisive discovery. First, Hegel says the following (page 563, lines 30–39):

This becoming [that is, History] represents (*stellt dar*) a [dialecti-cal] sluggish-and-inert (*träge*) movement and succession of Spirits. [It is] a gallery of images, each one of which, [being] endowed with the complete richness of spirit, moves with such sluggishness-and-inertia precisely because the Self must make its way into and digest this total richness of its substance. Given that the completion-or-perfection of Spirit consists in the Knowledge-or-understanding of what *it is*, [that is, of] its substance,—this Knowledge is its *act-of-going-inside-of-itself* in which it leaves its empirical-existence and transmits its concrete-form to internalizing-Memory (*Erinnerung*).

This is plain, and there is little to add: Each stage of Becoming—that is, each historical World—is "*mit dem* vollständigen *Reichtum des Geistes ausgestattet.*" This is to say: never, at any moment of

---

extensions of Europe than in Europe itself. One can even say that, from a certain point of view, the United States has already attained the final stage of Marxist "communism," seeing that, practically, all the members of a "classless society" can from now on appropriate for themselves everything that seems good to them, without thereby working any more than their heart dictates.

Now, several voyages of comparison made (between 1948 and 1958) to the United States and the U.S.S.R. gave me the impression that if the Americans give the appearance of rich Sino-Soviets, it is because the Russians and the Chinese are only Americans who are still poor but are rapidly proceeding to get richer. I was led to conclude from this that the "American way of life" was the type of life specific to the post-historical period, the actual presence of the United States in the World prefiguring the "eternal present" future of all of humanity. Thus, Man's return to animality appeared no longer as a possibility that was yet to come, but as a certainty that was already present.

It was following a recent voyage to Japan (1959) that I had a radical change of opinion on this point. There I was able to observe a Society that is one of a kind, because it alone has for almost three centuries experienced life at the "end of History"—that is, in the absence of all civil or external war (following the liquidation of feudalism by the roturier Hideyoshi and the artificial isolation of the country conceived and realized by his noble successor Yiyeasu). Now, the existence of the Japanese nobles, who ceased to risk their lives (even in duel) and yet did not for that begin to work, was anything but animal.

"Post-historical" Japanese civilization undertook ways diametrically opposed to the "American way." No doubt, there were no longer in Japan any Religion, Morals, or Politics in the "European" or "historical" sense of these words. But *Snobbery* in its pure form created disciplines negating the "natural" or "animal" given which in effectiveness far surpassed those that arose, in Japan or elsewhere, from "historical" Action—that is, from warlike and revolutionary Fights or from forced Work. To be sure, the peaks (equalled nowhere else) of specifically Japa-

Time, is there a Spirit existing outside of the human historical World. Therefore, there is no transcendence; History is the becoming of Spirit, and the Spirit is nothing but this historical becoming of Man.

As for the goal of History—it is *Wissen*, Knowledge of self—that is, Philosophy (which finally becomes Wisdom). Man creates an historical World only in order to *know* what this World is and thus to *understand* himself in it. Now, I have already said that the concept "Dog," for example, can break away from the real *dog* and be materialized in the *word* "Dog," or, in other words, that there can be conceptual or discursive *knowledge* (*Wissen*) of the dog, only because the dog dies or becomes Past. And such is also the case, as Hegel has just said, for Man and his historical World. One can *understand* an historical World only because it is *historical*—that is, temporal and consequently finite or mortal. For one understands it truly—that is, conceptually or philosophically—only in "*Erinnerung*": it is the *memory* (*Erinnerung*) of a past real which is the *internalization* (*Er-innerung*) of this real—i.e., the passing of its "meaning" (or "essence") from the

---

nese snobbery—the Noh Theater, the ceremony of tea, and the art of bouquets of flowers—were and still remain the exclusive prerogative of the nobles and the rich. But in spite of persistent economic and political inequalities, all Japanese without exception are currently in a position to live according to totally *formalized* values—that is, values completely empty of all "human" content in the "historical" sense. Thus, in the extreme, every Japanese is in principle capable of committing, from pure snobbery, a perfectly "gratuitous" *suicide* (the classical épée of the samurai can be replaced by an airplane or a torpedo), which has nothing to do with the *risk* of life in a Fight waged for the sake of "historical" values that have social or political content. This seems to allow one to believe that the recently begun interaction between Japan and the Western World will finally lead not to a rebarbarization of the Japanese but to a "Japanization" of the Westerners (including the Russians).

Now, since no animal can be a snob, every "Japanized" post-historical period would be specifically human. Hence there would be no "definitive annihilation of Man properly so-called," as long as there were animals of the species *Homo sapiens* that could serve as the "natural" support for what is human in men. But, as I said in the above Note, an "animal that is *in harmony* with Nature or given Being" is a *living* being that is in no way human. To remain human, Man must remain a "Subject *opposed* to the Object," even if "Action negating the given and Error" disappears. This means that, while henceforth speaking in an *adequate* fashion of everything that is given to him, post-historical Man must continue to *detach* "form" from "content," doing so no longer in order actively to transform the latter, but so that he may *oppose* himself as a pure "form" to himself and to others taken as "content" of any sort.

external Reality into the Concept which is *in* me, *inside* of the "Subject." And if the totality of History can be thus understood (in and by the *Phenomenology*) only at the end *of* History, a particular historical World can be understood only after its end or death in History.

Hegel himself says so, moreover, in the *Rechtsphilosophie* (Volume VI, page 17):

> As the thought-or-idea (*Gedanke*) of the World, philosophy appears in time only after the objective-reality completes-or-perfects its formative-educational process (*Bildungsprozess*) and has been achieved (*fertig gemacht*) . . . When philosophy paints its grisaille, a concrete-form of life has [already] grown old; and it does not permit itself to be rejuvenated by [a] grisaille, only known-or-understood (*erkennen*):—the owl of Minerva begins its flight only at the coming of dusk.

This celebrated passage, written fifteen years after the *Phenomenology*, is the best commentary on the text which I am interpreting.

In the passage following this text, Hegel develops his idea further (page 563, line 39–page 564, line 13):

> In its act-of-going-inside-of-itself, Spirit is submerged in the night of its Self-Consciousness. But its empirical-existence which has disappeared is preserved in this night. And this dialectically-overcome empirical-existence, [that is, the existence which is already] past, but [which is] engendered-again from the Knowledge, is the new empirical-existence: [it is] a new [historical] World and a new concrete-form of Spirit. In the latter, Spirit must begin again in the immediacy of this form, and it must grow-and-ripen again starting with it; [it must do so, therefore,] in just as naive a manner as if everything that precedes were lost for it and it had learned nothing from the experience of earlier [historical] Spirits. But *internalizing-Memory* (*Er-Innerung*) has preserved this existence, and [this Memory] is the internal-or-private-entity, and in fact a sublimated (*höhere*) form of the substance. Therefore, if this Spirit, while seeming to start only with itself, begins its formative-education (*Bildung*) again from the start, at the same time it begins [it] at a higher (*höhern*) level.

This passage deals with the *phenomenological* aspect of the dialectic of Being, and this aspect is History. As for the rhythm

of History, it is indeed such as I indicated previously: action →
coming to consciousness → action. Historical *progress*, which represents what is truly historical or human in History, is a "mediation"
by Knowledge or by comprehending Memory. In two senses, then,
History is a history of Philosophy: on the one hand, it exists
through Philosophy and *for* Philosophy; on the other, there is
History *because* there is Philosophy and *in order that* there may
be Philosophy, or—finally—Wisdom. For Understanding or
Knowledge of the Past is what, when it is integrated into the
Present, transforms this Present into an *historical* Present, that is,
into a Present that realizes a *progress* in relation to its Past.

This dialectic of Action and Knowledge is essentially temporal.
Or, better still, it *is* Time—that is, a nonidentical Becoming—in
which there is truly and really a *progress* and hence a "before"
and an "after."

This is what Hegel says (page 564, lines 13–16):

> The realm-of-Spirits which is formed-and-educated in this fashion
> in empirical-existence constitutes a succession (*Aufeinanderfolge*)
> in which one [of the historical Spirits] took over from another and
> each received the empire of the World from the one preceding it.

Now, if this dialectical Becoming *is* Time, it is because it has
a beginning and an end. Hence there is a goal (*Ziel*) which can
no longer be surpassed.

Hegel is now going to talk about this goal (page 564, lines
16–23):

> The goal (*Ziel*) of this succession [that is, of universal History] is
> the revelation of depth; and this revelation is the *absolute Concept*.
> This revelation is consequently the dialectical-overcoming of the
> Spirit's depth, that is, its *expansion-or-extension* (*Ausdehnung*); [in
> other words, this revelation is] the negating-Negativity of this ab-
> tract-I (*Ich*) existing-inside-of-itself; [Negativity] which is the aliena-
> tion-or-externalization of this I, that is, its substance. And [this
> revelation is also] the Time of this abstract-I—[Time which con-
> sists in the fact] that this alienation-or-externalization is alienated-or-
> externalized in itself and, [while existing] in its expansion-or-exten-
> tion, thus *likewise* exists as well in its depth, [that is, in] the Self
> (*Selbst*).

The goal of History, its final term, is "the absolute Concept"—
that is, "Science." In this Science, Hegel says, Man dialectically-

overcomes his temporal or "pointlike"—i.e., truly human—exist-ence, *as opposed* to Nature, and he himself becomes Extension (*Ausdehnung*) or Space. For in the *Logik*, Man limits himself to *knowing* the World or *Sein*, and since his knowledge is true, he coincides with the World—that is, with *Sein*—that is, with eternal or nontemporal Space. But, Hegel adds, in and by this Science Man likewise overcomes this extension of his, or his Externalization (*Entäusserung*), and remains "pointlike" or temporal—that is, specifically human: he remains a *Selbst*, a Self. But as Hegel will immediately say, he remains so only in and by *Er-Innerung*, in and by the comprehending Memory of his historical past, the Memory which forms the First Part of the "System"—that is, the *Phe-nomenology*.

Indeed, here is what Hegel says in the final passage (page 564, lines 23–36):

> *The goal*, [which is] absolute Knowledge [or the Wise Man who is the author of *Science*], that is, Spirit which knows-or-understands itself as Spirit, [has as] the path [leading] to it the internalizing-Memory of [historical] Spirits, as they exist in themselves and achieve the organization of their realm. Their preservation in the aspect of their free-or-autonomous empirical-existence, which ap-pears-or-is-revealed in the form of contingency, is History [i.e., the vulgar historical science which merely narrates events]. And their preservation in the aspect of their conceptually-understood organiza-tion, is the *Science* of appearing (*erscheinenden*) *Knowledge* [that is, the *Phenomenology*]. The two [taken] together, [chronicle-his-tory and the *Phenomenology*, that is,] conceptually-understood His-tory, form the internalizing-Memory and the Calvary of the abso-lute Spirit, the objective-Reality, the Truth [or revealed-Reality], and the [subjective] Certainty of its throne, without which it would be lifeless solitary-entity. Only
>> *from the Chalice of this Realm-of-Spirits rises up to it the foam of its infinity.*

"Science" properly so-called—that is, the *Logik* or the Second Part of the "System"—Science that reveals eternal Being or real Eternity, is necessarily preceded by a First Part, which deals with the Becoming of Being in Time or as Time—that is, with History. On the one hand, it is historical Science in the common sense of the word, which is humanity's "naive" Memory; and on the other, it is the conceptual or philosophical *understanding* of the past that is preserved in and by this "naive" Memory, this understanding being the *Phenomenology*. It follows that for Hegel, the *Phenomenology* cannot be understood without a previous knowledge of real history, just as history cannot be truly *understood* without the *Phenomenology*. It was right for me, then, to talk about Athens, Rome, Louis XIV . . . and Napoleon, in my interpretation of the *Phenomenology*. As long as one does not see the historical facts to which this book is related, one understands nothing of what is said in it. But the *Phenomenology* is something other than a "universal history" in the common sense of the word. History *narrates* events. The *Phenomenology explains* them or makes them *understandable*, by revealing their human *meaning* and their *necessity*. This is to say that it *reconstructs* ("deduces") the *real* historical evolution of humanity in its humanly *essential* traits. It reconstructs them *a priori*, by "deducing" them from anthropogenetic Desire (*Begierde*) that is directed toward another Desire (and thus is Desire for Recognition) and that realizes itself through Action (*Tat*) negating given-Being (*Sein*). But, once more, this "*a priori*" construction can be carried out only *after the fact*. It is first necessary that *real* History be completed; next, it must be *narrated* to Man;[7] and only then can the Philosopher, becoming a Wise man, *understand* it by reconstructing it "*a priori*" in the *Phenomenology*. And this same phenomenological *understanding* of History is what transforms the Philosopher into a Wise man; for it is what definitively overcomes Time, and thus makes possible the adequate revelation of *completed* and *perfect*, that is, eternal and immutable, Being—a revelation effected in and by the *Logik*.

One more remark, concerning the quotation from Schiller (taken from his poem "Freundschaft") with which the *Phenomenology* ends. This is not a word-for-word quotation. And the modifications made (consciously or not) by Hegel are revealing.

I shall not dwell on the fact that Hegel says "*Geister*reich" instead of "*Seelen*reich," although this substitution (which is very "modern") is extremely significant. What is especially important

---

[7] Moreover, there is no real history without historical *memory*—that is, without oral or written Memoirs.

is that Hegel says *"dieses* Geisterreich" instead of "das *ganze* Seelenreich." By this change, he means to exclude the "Angels" of which Schiller speaks; he means to underline that eternal or infinite Being—that is, the absolute Spirit (which, in Schiller, is God), arises solely from the totality of human or historical existence. Therefore, the temporal past of eternal Being is *human*, and *only* human. If one wants to talk about "God" in Hegel, therefore, one must not forget that this "God's" past is Man: it is a Man who has become "God," and not a *God* who has become Man (and who, moreover, again becomes God). And the third modification of Schiller's text by Hegel has the same meaning. Schiller says: *"die* Unendlichkeit"; Hegel writes: *"seine* Unendlichkeit." Thus the *Phenomenology* ends with a radical denial of all transcendence. Revealed-infinite-eternal-Being—that is, the absolute Spirit—is the infinite or eternal being of this same Being that existed as universal History. This is to say that the Infinite in question is *Man's* infinite. And hence the "Science" that reveals this infinite-Being is a Science of Man in two ways: on the one hand, it is the result of History— that is, a product of Man; and on the other, it talks about Man: about *his* temporal or historical becoming (in the *Phenomenology*), and about *his* eternal *being* (in the *Logik*). Therefore "Science" is indeed *Selbst-bewusstsein*, and not *Bewusstsein*. And the Wise Man, as he comes to the end of the *Phenomenology*, can say that the "Science" properly so-called that he is now going to develop (in the *Logik*) is truly *his* Science or *his* Knowledge.

But, as I have already said several times, the Wise Man can speak of *Science* as *his* Science only to the extent that he can speak of *death* as *his* death. For, as he proceeds to the *Logik*, the Wise Man *completely* abolishes Time—that is, History—that is, his own truly and specifically human reality, which already in the *Phe-nomenology* is but a *past* reality: he definitively abandons his reality as a free and historical Individual, as Subject opposed to the Object, or as Man who is essentially something other (*Anderes*) than Nature.

Hegel himself knows this full well. And he knew it at least as early as 1802. For in his essay of 1802 entitled *Glauben und Wissen*, there is a passage in which he plainly says so, and which I would like to cite in ending my commentary on the *Phenomenology*.

167

In this passage we read the following (Volume I, pages 303f.):

The whole sphere of finiteness, of one's being something, of the sensual—is swallowed up in true-or-genuine Faith when confronted with the thought and intuition (*Anschauung*) of the Eternal, [thought and intuition] here becoming one and the same thing. All the gnats of Subjectivity are burned in this devouring flame, and *the very consciousness* of this giving-of-oneself (*Hingebens*) and of this annihilation (*Vernichtens*) is annihilated (*vernichtet*).

Hegel knows it and says it. But he also says, in one of his letters, that this knowledge cost him dearly. He speaks of a period of total depression that he lived through between the twenty-fifth and thirtieth years of his life: a "Hypochondria" that went "*bis zur Erlähmung aller Kräfte,*" that was so severe as "to paralyze all his powers," and that came precisely from the fact that he could not accept the necessary abandonment of *Individuality*—that is, actually, of humanity—which the idea of absolute Knowledge demanded. But, finally, he surmounted this "Hypochondria." And becoming a Wise Man by that final acceptance of death, he published a few years later the First Part of the "System of Science," entitled "Science of the Phenomenology of the Spirit," in which he definitively reconciles himself with all that is and has been, by declaring that there will never more be anything new on earth.

7

THE DIALECTIC OF THE REAL AND THE
PHENOMENOLOGICAL METHOD IN HEGEL

*Complete Text of the Sixth through Ninth Lectures
of the Academic Year 1934–1935*

What is Dialectic, according to Hegel?

We can give a first answer to this question by recalling a passage from the *Encyclopaedia*—more exactly, the Introduction to the First Part of the *Encyclopaedia*, entitled "Logik."

In § 79 (third edition) Hegel says this (Volume V, page 104, lines 27–30):

> With regard to its form, *logic* has three aspects (*Seiten*): (a) the *abstract* or *understandable* (*verständige*) aspect; (b) the *dialectical* or *negatively rational* (*vernünftige*) aspect; (c) the *speculative* or *positively rational* aspect.

This well-known text lends itself to two misunderstandings. On the one hand, one might believe that Dialectic reduces to the second aspect of "Logic," isolated from the other two. But in the explanatory Note, Hegel underlines that the three aspects are in reality inseparable. And we know from elsewhere that the simultaneous presence of the three aspects in question is what gives "Logic" its dialectical character in the broad sense. But it must be noted right away that "Logic" is dialectical (in the broad sense) only because it implies a "negative" or negating aspect, which is called "dialectical" in the narrow sense. Nevertheless, dialectical "logic" necessarily implies three complementary and inseparable aspects: the "abstract" aspect (revealed by Understanding, *Verstand*); the "negative," properly "dialectical," aspect; and the "positive" aspect (the last two aspects are revealed by Reason, *Vernunft*).

On the other hand, one might suppose that Dialectic is the

preserve of logical *thought*; or in other words, that this passage is concerned with a philosophical *method*, a way of investigation or exposition. Now, in fact, this is not at all the case. For Hegel's *Logik* is not a logic in the common sense of the word, nor a gnoseology, but an ontology or Science of Being, taken as Being. And "the Logic" (*das Logische*) of the passage we have cited does not mean logical *thought* considered in itself, but *Being* (*Sein*) revealed (correctly) in and by thought or speech (*Logos*). Therefore, the three "aspects" in question are above all aspects of Being itself: they are *ontological*, and not logical or gnoseological, categories; and they are certainly not simple artifices of *method* of investigation or exposition. Hegel takes care, moreover, to underline this in the Note that follows the passage cited.

In this Note, he says the following: (Volume V, page 104, lines 31–33):

> These three aspects do not constitute three *parts* of Logic, but are *constituent-elements* (*Momente*) of *every logical-real-entity* (*Logisch-Reellen*), that is, of every concept or of everything that is true (*jedes Wahren*) in general.

Everything that is true, the true entity, the True, *das Wahre*, is a real entity, or Being itself, as revealed correctly and completely by coherent discourse having a meaning (*Logos*). And this is what Hegel also calls *Begriff*, concept; a term that means for him (except when, as in the writings of his youth and still occasionally in the *Phenomenology*, he says: *nur Begriff*) not an "abstract notion" detached from the real entity to which it is related, but "conceptually understood reality." The True and the Concept are, as Hegel himself says, a *Logisch-Reelles*, something logical and real at the same time, a realized concept or a conceived reality. Now, "logical" thought that is supposed to be true, the concept that is supposed to be adequate, merely reveal or describe Being as it *is* or as it *exists*, without adding anything to it, without taking anything away from it, without modifying it in any way whatsoever. The structure of thought, therefore, is determined by the structure of the Being that it reveals. If, then, "logical" thought has three aspects, if in other words it is dialectical (in the broad sense), this is only because Being itself is dialectical (in the broad sense), because of the fact that it implies a "constituent-element" or an "aspect" that is negative or negating ("dialectical" in the narrow and strong sense of the term). Thought is dialectical only to the extent that it correctly reveals the dialectic of Being that *is* and of the Real that *exists*.

To be sure, pure and simple Being (*Sein*) does not have a three-fold or dialectical structure; but the Logical-real, the Concept or the True—i.e., Being revealed by Speech or Thought—does. Hence one might be inclined to say that Being is dialectical only to the extent that it is revealed by Thought, that Thought is what gives Being its dialectical character. But this formulation would be incorrect, or at least misleading. For in some sense the reverse is true for Hegel: Being can be revealed by Thought; there is a Thought in Being and of Being, only because Being is dialectical; i.e., because Being implies a negative or negating constituent element. The real dialectic of existing Being is, among other things, the revelation of the Real and of Being by Speech or Thought. And Speech and Thought themselves are dialectical only because, and to the extent that, they reveal or describe the dialectic of *Being and of the Real*.

However that may be, philosophic thought or "scientific" thought in the Hegelian sense of the word—i.e., rigorously true thought—has the goal of revealing, through the meaning of a coherent discourse (*Logos*), Being (*Sein*) as it *is* and *exists* in the totality of its objective-Reality (*Wirklichkeit*).[1] The philosophic or "scientific" *Method*, therefore, must assure the adequation of Thought to Being, since Thought must adapt itself to Being and to the Real without modifying them in any way whatsoever. This is to say that the attitude of the philosopher or the "scientist" (= the Wise Man) with respect to Being and to the Real is one of purely passive *contemplation*, and that philosophic or "scientific" activity reduces to a pure and simple *description* of the Real and of Being. The Hegelian *method*, therefore, is not at all "dialectical": it is purely contemplative and descriptive, or better, *phenomenological* in Husserl's sense of the term. In the Preface and the Introduction to the *Phenomenology*, Hegel insists at length

---

[1] The *revealed* real totality of Being is not only Being (*Sein*), but also the *revelation* of being or Thought (*Denken*); and this *revealed* totality is Spirit (*Geist*). What is dialectical or threefold is *Geist* and not *Sein*; Being is but the first constituent-element (*Moment*) of Spirit.

on the passive, contemplative, and descriptive character of the "scientific" method. He underlines that there is a dialectic of "scientific" thought only because there is a dialectic of the Being which that thought reveals. As soon as the revealing description is correct, it can be said that *ordo et connexio idearum idem est ac ordo et connexio rerum*; for the order and the connection of the real are, according to Hegel, dialectical.

Here is what Hegel says, for example, in the Preface to the *Phenomenology* (page 45, lines 7–20):

> But scientific knowledge (*Erkennen*) demands, on the contrary, that one give himself (*übergeben*) to the life of the object (*Gegenstandes*) or, to say the same thing in different words, that one have before oneself and express in speech (*auszusprechen*) the inner necessity of this object. By thus plunging (*sich vertiefend*) into its object, this knowledge forgets that overview (*Übersicht*) [thought to be possible from the outside] which is [in reality] only knowledge's (*Wissens*) own face reflected back into itself from the content. But having plunged into the matter and progressing (*fortgehend*) in the [dialectical] movement of this matter, scientific knowledge comes back into itself; but not before the filling (*Erfüllung*) or the content [of the thought] gathers itself back into itself, simplifies itself to specific determination (*Bestimmtheit*), lowers itself to [being] *an* aspect (*Seite*) [merely] of an empirical-existence (*Daseins*) [the other aspect being thought], and transforms itself (*übergeht*) into its superior (*höhere*) truth [or revealed reality]. By that very process, the simple-or-undivided Whole (*Ganze*) which has an overview of itself (*sich übersehende*) itself emerges from the richness [of the diversity] in which its reflection [into itself] seemed lost.

"Scientific knowledge" gives itself or abandons itself without reserve, without preconceived ideas or afterthoughts, to the "life" and the "dialectical movement" of the Real. Thus, this truly true knowledge has nothing to do with the "Reflection" of pseudo-philosophy (i.e., pre-Hegelian philosophy) and of pseudo-science (Newtonian science), which reflects *on* the Real while placing itself *outside* of the Real, without one's being able to say precisely where; Reflection which pretends to give an "overview" of the Real on the basis of a knowing Subject that calls itself autonomous or independent of the Object of knowledge; a Subject that, according to Hegel, is but an artificially isolated aspect of the known or revealed Real.

To be sure, in the end, "scientific knowledge" comes back toward itself and reveals itself to itself: its final goal is to describe itself in its nature, in its genesis, and in its development. Just like ordinary philosophic knowledge, it is a self-knowledge. But it is a complete and adequate self-knowledge—that is, it is true in the strong sense of the word. And it is true because, even in its return toward itself, it simply follows passively the dialectical movement of its "content" which is the "object"—that is, the Real and Being. The Real itself is what organizes itself and makes itself concrete so as to become a determinate "species," capable of being revealed by a "general notion"; the Real itself reveals itself through articulate knowledge and thereby becomes a known object that has the knowing subject as its necessary complement, so that "empirical existence" is divided into beings that speak and beings that are spoken of. For real Being existing as Nature is what produces Man who reveals that Nature (and himself) by speaking of it. Real Being thus transforms itself into "truth" or into reality *revealed* by speech, and becomes a "higher" and "higher" truth as its discursive revelation becomes ever more adequate and complete.

It is by following this "dialectical movement" of the Real that Knowledge is present at its own birth and contemplates its own evolution. And thus it finally attains its end, which is the adequate and complete understanding of itself—i.e., of the progressive revelation of the Real and of Being by Speech—of the Real and Being which engender, in and by their "dialectical movement," the Speech that reveals them. And it is thus that a *total* revelation of real Being or an entirely revealed Totality (an "undivided Whole") is finally constituted: the coherent whole of Being realized in the real Universe, completely and perfectly described in the "overview" given by the one and unique "Science" or the "System" of the Wise Man, finally emerges from Being which at first was only a natural World formed of separate and disparate entities, an incoherent "richness" in which there was no "reflection," no discursive knowledge, no articulate self-consciousness.

Taken separately, the Subject and the Object are *abstractions* that have neither "objective reality" (*Wirklichkeit*) nor "empirical existence" (*Dasein*). What exists in *reality*, as soon as there is a Reality *of which one speaks*—and since we in fact *speak* of reality, there can be for us only Reality of which one speaks—what exists in reality, I say, is the Subject that knows the Object, or, what is the same thing, the Object known by the Subject. This double Reality which is nonetheless one because it is equally real in each aspect, taken in its whole or as Totality, is called in Hegel "Spirit" (*Geist*) or (in the *Logik*) "absolute Idea." Hegel also says: "*absoluter Begriff*" ("absolute Concept"). But the term *Begriff* can also be applied to a *fragment* of total revealed Being, to a "constituent-element" (*Moment*) of the Spirit or Idea (in which case the Idea can be defined as the integration of all the Concepts—that is, of all the particular "ideas"). Taken in this sense, *Begriff* signifies a particular real entity or a real aspect of being, revealed by the meaning of a word—i.e., by a "general notion"; or else, what is the same thing, *Begriff* is a "meaning" ("idea") that exists empirically not only in the form of an actually thought, spoken, or written word, but also as a "thing." If the (universal or "absolute") "Idea" is the "Truth" or the Reality revealed by speech of the one and unique *totality* of what exists, a (particular) "Concept" is the "Truth" of a particular real entity taken *separately*, but understood as an *integral element* of the Totality. Or else, again, the "Concept" is a "true entity" (*das Wahre*)—that is, a real entity *named* or revealed by the meaning of a *word*, which meaning relates it to all other real entities and thus inserts it in the "System" of the whole Real revealed by the *entirety* of "scientific" Discourse. Or else, finally, the "Concept" is the "essential reality" or the *essence* (*Wesen*) of a concrete entity—that is, precisely the reality which corresponds, in that concrete entity, to the *meaning* of the word that designates or reveals it.

Like the Spirit or the Idea, each Concept is hence double and single at the same time; it is both "subjective" and "objective," both real thought of a real entity and a real entity really thought. The *real* aspect of the Concept is called "object" (*Gegenstand*), "given-Being" (*Sein*), "entity that exists as a given-Being" (*Seiendes*), "In-itself" (*Ansich*), and so on. The aspect *thought* is called "knowledge" (*Wissen*), "act of knowing" (*Erkennen*), "knowledge" (*Erkenntniss*), "act of thinking" (*Denken*), and so on; and occasionally "concept" (*Begriff*) in the common sense (when Hegel says: *nur Begriff*). But these two aspects are inseparable and complementary, and it is of little importance to know which of the two must be called *Wissen* or *Begriff* (in the common sense), and which *Gegenstand*. What is of importance is that— in the Truth—there is perfect *coincidence* of the *Begriff* and the *Gegenstand*, and that—in the Truth—Knowledge is purely *passive* adequation to essential-Reality. And that is why the true Scientist or the Wise Man must reduce his existence to simple *contemplation* (*reines Zusehen*) of the Real and of Being, and of their "dialectical movement." He looks at everything that *is* and verbally describes everything that he sees: therefore, he has nothing to *do*, for he modifies nothing, adds nothing, and takes nothing away.

This, at least, is what Hegel says in the Introduction to the *Phenomenology* (page 71, line 27–page 72, line 11):

> If by *concept* we mean *knowledge* (*Wissen*), and by the essential-reality (*Wesen*) or the *true-entity* (*Wahre*) we mean entity existing as a *given-being* (*Seiende*) or *object* (*Gegenstand*), it follows that verification (*Prüfung*) consists in seeing (*zuzusehen*) if the concept corresponds to the object. But if by *concept* we mean the *essential-reality* of the In-itself (*Ansich*) of the *object*, and by *object*, on the other hand, we understand the object [taken] as *object*, namely, as it is *for another* [i.e., for the knowing Subject], it follows that verification consists in our seeing if the object corresponds to its concept. It is easily seen that both [expressions signify] the same thing. But what is essential is to keep [in mind] for the whole study (*Untersuchung*) that these two constituent-elements (*Momente*), [namely] *concept* and *object, Being for another* and *Being in itself*, are situated within the very knowledge that we are studying, and that consequently we do not need to bring in standards (*Masssäbe*) or to apply *our* [own] intuitions (*Einfälle*) and ideas (*Gedanken*) during the study. By omitting these latter, we attain [the possibility] of viewing the thing as it is *in* and *for itself*.

> Now, any addition (*Zutat*) [coming] from us becomes superfluous not only in the sense (*nach dieser Seite*) that [the] concept and [the] object, the standard and what is to be verified, are present (*vorhanden*) in the Consciousness (*Bewusstsein*) itself [which we, as philosophers, study in the *Phenomenology*]; but we are also spared

the effort of comparing the two and of *verifying* in the strict sense, so that—since [studied] Consciousness verifies itself—in this respect too, only pure contemplation (*Zusehen*) is left for us to do.

When all is said and done, the "method" of the Hegelian Scientist consists in having no method or way of thinking peculiar to his Science. The naive man, the vulgar scientist, even the pre-Hegelian philosopher—each in his way opposes himself to the Real and deforms it by opposing his own means of action and methods of thought to it. The Wise Man, on the contrary, is fully and definitively reconciled with everything that *is*: he entrusts himself without reserve to Being and opens himself entirely to the Real without resisting it. His role is that of a perfectly flat and indefinitely extended mirror: he does not reflect on the Real; it is the Real that reflects itself on him, is reflected in his consciousness, and is revealed in its own dialectical structure by the discourse of the Wise Man who describes it without deforming it.

If you please, the Hegelian "method" is purely "empirical" or "positivist": Hegel looks at the Real and describes what he sees, everything that he sees, and nothing but what he sees. In other words, he has the "experience" (*Erfahrung*) of dialectical Being and the Real, and thus he makes their "movement" pass into his discourse which describes them.

And that is what Hegel says in the Introduction to the *Phenomenology* (page 73, lines 7–11):

> This *dialectical* movement which Consciousness carries out (*ausübt*) in (*an*) itself, both in terms of its knowledge and its object, to the extent that the new [and] true object *arises* (*entspringt*) out of this movement [and appears] before Consciousness, is strictly speaking what is called *experience* (*Erfahrung*).

To be sure, this experience "strictly speaking" is something quite different from the experience of vulgar science. The latter is carried out by a Subject who pretends to be independent of the Object, and it is supposed to reveal the Object which exists independently of the Subject. Now in actual fact the experience is had by a man who lives within Nature and is indissolubly bound to it, but is also opposed to it and wants to transform it: science is born from the desire to transform the World in relation to Man; its final end is technical application. That is why scientific knowledge is never absolutely passive, nor purely contemplative and descriptive. Scientific experience perturbs the Object because of the active intervention of the Subject, who applies to the Object a *method* of investigation that is his own and to which nothing in the Object itself corresponds. What it reveals, therefore, is neither the Object taken independently of the Subject, nor the Subject taken independently of the Object, but only the result of the *interaction* of the two or, if you will, that interaction itself. However, scientific experience and knowledge are concerned with the Object as independent of and isolated from the Subject. Hence they do not find what they are looking for; they do not give what they promise, for they do not correctly reveal or describe what the Real is *for them*. Generally speaking, Truth (= revealed Reality) is the coincidence of thought or descriptive knowledge with the concrete real. Now, for vulgar science, this real is supposed to be independent of the thought which describes it. But in fact this science never attains this autonomous real, this "thing in itself" of Kant-Newton, because it incessantly perturbs it. Hence scientific thought does not attain its truth; there is no scientific *truth* in the strong and proper sense of the term. Scientific experience is thus only a pseudo-experience. And it cannot be otherwise, for vulgar science is in fact concerned not with the concrete real, but with an *abstraction*. To the extent that the scientist thinks or knows his object, what really and concretely exists is the *entirety* of the Object known by the Subject or of the Subject knowing the Object. The isolated Object is but an abstraction, and that is why it has no fixed and stable continuity (*Bestehen*) and is perpetually deformed or perturbed. Therefore it cannot serve as a basis for a Truth, which by definition is universally and eternally valid. And the same goes for the "object" of vulgar psychology, gnoseology, and philosophy, which is the Subject artificially isolated from the Object—i.e., yet another abstraction.[2]

[2] This interpretation of science, on which Hegel insisted very much, is currently admitted by science itself. In quantum physics it is expressed in mathematical form by Heisenberg's relations of uncertainty. These relations show on the one hand that the experience of physics is never perfect, because it cannot achieve a description of the "physical real" that is both complete and adequate (precise). On the other hand, the famous principle of "complementary notions" follows from it, formulated by Bohr: that of the wave and the particle, for example. This means that the (verbal) physical description of the Real necessarily

Hegelian experience is a different story: it reveals *concrete* Reality, and reveals it without modifying or "perturbing" it. That is why, when this experience is described verbally, it represents a Truth in the strong sense of the term. And that is why it has no specific *method* of its own, as experience, thought, or verbal description, that is not at the same time an "objective" structure of the concrete Real itself which it reveals by describing it.

The *concrete* Real (of which we *speak*) is both Real revealed by a discourse, and Discourse revealing a real. And the Hegelian experience is related neither to the Real nor to Discourse taken separately, but to their indissoluble unity. And since it is itself a revealing Discourse, it is itself an aspect of the concrete Real which it describes. It therefore brings in nothing *from outside*, and the thought or the discourse which is born from it is not a reflection *on* the Real: the Real itself is what reflects itself or is reflected in the discourse or as thought. In particular, if the thought and the discourse of the Hegelian Scientist or the Wise Man are dialectical,

---

implies contradictions: the "physical real" is simultaneously a wave filling all of space and a particle localized in one point, and so on. By its own admission, Physics can never attain Truth in the strong sense of the term.—In fact, Physics does not study and describe the concrete Real, but only an artificially isolated aspect of the Real—that is, an abstraction; namely: the aspect of the Real which is given to the "physical Subject," this Subject being Man reduced to his eye (which is, moreover, idealized)—i.e., yet another abstraction. Physics describes the Real to the extent that it is given to this Subject, without describing this Subject itself. Physics, however, is obliged to take account of the act which "gives" the Real to this Subject, and which is the act of seeing (which presupposes the presence of light, in the broad sense). Now this *abstract* description is made not with words having a meaning (Logos), but with the help of algorithms: if concrete Man *speaks* of the Real, the abstract physical Subject uses a mathematical "language." On the level of algorithm, there is neither uncertainty nor contradiction. But neither is there any *Truth* in the proper sense, since there is no genuine *Discourse* (Logos) that reveals the Real. And as soon as one wants to move from algorithm to *physical* Discourse, one introduces contradictions and an element of uncertainty. Hence there is no Truth in the domain of Physics (and of science in general). Only philosophic Discourse can achieve Truth, for it alone is related to the *concrete* Real—that is, to the *totality* of the reality of Being. The various sciences are always concerned with abstractions: on the one hand, because they relate the Real not to living man, but to a more or less simplified, or better, abstract, "knowing Subject"; on the other hand, because they neglect in their descriptions either the (abstract) Subject which corresponds to the (abstract) Object which they describe, or the (abstract) Object which is given to the (abstract) Subject which they study. And that is why they have their own peculiar *methods* of thought and of action.

it is only because they faithfully reflect the "dialectical movement" of the Real of which they are a part and which they *experience* adequately by giving themselves to it without any preconceived *method*.

Hegel's *method*, then, is not at all dialectical, and Dialectic for him is quite different from a method of thought or exposition. And we can even say that, in a certain way, Hegel was the first to abandon Dialectic as a philosophic *method*. He was, at least, the first to do so voluntarily and with full knowledge of what he was doing.

The dialectical method was consciously and systematically used for the first time by Socrates-Plato. But in fact it is as old as philosophy itself. For the dialectical method is nothing but the method of dialogue—that is, of discussion.

Everything seems to indicate that Science was born in the form of Myth. A Myth is a theory—that is, a discursive revelation of the real. Of course, it is supposed to be in agreement with the given real. But in fact, it always goes beyond its givens, and once beyond them, it only has to be coherent—i.e., free of internal contradictions—in order to make a show of truth. The period of Myth is a period of monologue, and in this period one *demonstrates* nothing because one "discusses" nothing, since one is not yet faced with a contrary or simply different opinion. And that is precisely why there is true or false "myth" or "opinion" (*doxa*), but no "science" or "truth" properly so-called.

Then, by chance, the man who has an opinion, or who has created or adopted a myth, comes up against a different myth or a contrary opinion. This man will first try to get rid of it: either by plugging up his ears in some way, by an internal or external "censoring"; or by overcoming (in the *non*dialectical sense of the term) the adverse myth or opinion, by putting to death or banishing its propagators, for example, or by acts of violence that will force the others to *say* the same thing as he (even if they do not *think* the same thing).

But it can happen (and we know that this actually did happen one day, somewhere) that the man begins to *discuss* with his adversary. By an act of freedom he can decide to want to "convince" him, by "refuting" him and by "demonstrating" his own point of view. To this end he *speaks* with his adversary, he engages in a *dialogue* with him: he uses a *dialectical method*. And it is by becoming a dialectician that the man of myth or opinion becomes a scientist or a philosopher.

In Plato (and probably already in Socrates) all this became conscious. If Plato has Socrates say that not the trees, but only the men in the city can teach him something, it is because he understood that, starting from (false or true) myth and opinion, one can attain science and truth only by way of discussion—that is, by way of dialogue or dialectic. In fine, according to Socrates-Plato, it is from the collision of diverse and adverse opinions that the spark of the one and the only truth is finally struck. A "thesis" is opposed to an "anti-thesis," which, by the way, the thesis generally provokes. They confront each other, correct one another mutually—that is, destroy each other—but also combine and finally engender a "synthetic" truth. But this latter is still just one opinion among many others. It is a new thesis that will find or arouse a new anti-thesis, in order to associate itself with it by negating it— i.e., by modifying it—in a new synthesis, in which it will be different from what it was at the start. And so on, until one achieves a "synthesis" that will no longer be the thesis of a discussion or a "thesis" that can be discussed; an indisputable "truth" that will no longer be a simple "opinion" or *one* of the possible opinions; or, speaking objectively, the single One which is not in opposition to an Other because it is the Whole—the Idea of the ideas, or the Good.

In philosophy or science born from discussion—that is, in dialectical (or synthetic) truth which realizes the Good in man by verbally revealing the One-Whole—the intermediate theses, anti-theses, and syntheses are *aufgehoben*, as Hegel will later say. They are "overcome," in the threefold sense of the German word *Aufheben*—that is, "overcome dialectically." In the first place, they are *overcome* or annulled with respect to whatever is fragmentary, relative, partial, or one-sided in them—that is, with respect to what makes them false when one of them is taken not for *an* opinion, but as *the* truth. Secondly, they are also *preserved* or safeguarded with respect to whatever is essential or universal in them—that is, with respect to what in each of them reveals one of the manifold aspects of the total and single reality. Finally, they are *sublimated*—that is, raised to a superior level of knowledge and of reality, and therefore of truth; for by completing one another, the thesis and the antithesis get rid of their one-sided and limited or, better, "subjective" character, and as synthesis they reveal a more comprehensive and hence a more comprehensible aspect of the "objective" real.

But if dialectic finally attains the adequation of discursive thought to Reality and Being, nothing in Reality and Being corresponds to dialectic. The dialectical movement is a movement of human thought and discourse; but the reality itself which one thinks and of which one talks is in no way dialectical. Dialectic is but a *method* of philosophic research and exposition. And we see, by the way, that the method is *dialectical* only because it implies a negative or negating element: namely, the antithesis which *opposes* the thesis in a verbal *fight* and calls for an *effort* of demonstration, an effort, moreover, indistinguishable from a *refutation*. There is truth properly so-called—that is, scientific or philosophic truth, or better, dialectical or synthetical truth—only where there has been discussion or dialogue—that is, antithesis *negating* a thesis.

In Plato, the dialectical method is still quite close to its historical origins (the sophistic discussions). In his writings we are dealing with genuine dialogues, in which the thesis and the antithesis are presented by different persons (Socrates generally incarnates the antithesis of all theses asserted by his interlocutors or expressed successively by one of them). And as for the synthesis, it is generally the auditor who must make it—the auditor who is the philosopher properly so-called: Plato himself or that disciple who is capable of understanding him. This auditor finally attains the absolute truth which results from the entirety of the dialectic or from the coordinated movement of all the dialogues, a truth that reveals the "total" or "synthetical" Good which is capable of fully and definitively "satisfying" the one who knows it and who is consequently *beyond* discussion or dialectic.[3]

---

[3] For Plato, it must be added, there is a gap, a break in continuity. Dialectic only prepares the vision of the Good, but does not necessarily lead to it: this vision is a sort of mystic illumination or ecstasy. (Cf. the Seventh Letter). Perhaps the vision is silent, and the Good ineffable (in which case Plato would be a Mystic). In any case, it is more than, and different from, the integration of the dialectical movement of thought: it is an intuition *sui generis*. Objectively speaking, God or the One is something other than the Totality of the Real: it is *beyond* Being; it is a *transcendent* God. Plato is certainly a Theologian. (Cf. above, the Course of the year 1938–39, Note on Eternity, Time, and the Concept.)

In Aristotle the dialectical method is less apparent than in Plato. But it continues to be applied. It becomes the aporetic method: the solution of the problem results from a discussion (and sometimes from a simple juxtaposition) of all possible opinions—that is, of all opinions that are coherent and do not contradict themselves. And the dialectical method was preserved in this "scholastic" form until our time in both the sciences and philosophy.

But along a parallel line there was something else.

Like all opinion, the Myth arises spontaneously and is accepted (or rejected) in the same way. Man creates it in and by his ("poetical") imagination, content if he avoids contradictions when he develops his initial idea or "intuition." But when the confrontation with a different opinion or myth engenders the desire for a *proof*, which cannot as yet be satisfied by a *demonstration* through *discussion*, one feels the need to found one's opinion or the myth that one is proposing (both being supposed to be unverifiable empirically—i.e., by an appeal to common sense experience) on something more than simple personal *conviction* or "subjective certainty" (*Gewissheit*)—which is visibly of the same type and weight as the adversary's. A foundation of superior or "divine" value is sought and found: the myth is presented as having been "revealed" by a god, who is supposed to be the guarantee for its truth—that is, for its universal and eternal validity.

Just like dialectical truth, this "revealed" mythical truth could not have been found by an isolated man confronted with Nature. Here too "trees teach man nothing." But "the men in the city" do not teach him anything either. It is a God who reveals the truth to him in a "myth." But in contrast to dialectical truth, this mythical truth is not the result of a *discussion* or a dialogue: God alone spoke, while man was content to listen, to understand, and to transcribe (and to do this far from the city, on the top of a mountain, and so on).

Even after having been a Platonic philosopher, man can still sometimes return to the "mythological" period. Such was the case of Saint Augustine. But this "return" is in reality a "synthesis": the myth-revealing God becomes a quasi-Socratic interlocutor; man engages in *dialogue* with his God, even if he does not go so far as to have a discussion with him (Abraham, however, *discusses* with Jehovah!). But this divine-human "dialogue" is but a hybrid and transitory form of the dialectical method. Accordingly, it assumed an infinite variety of forms among the diverse "Mystics," ranging from true dialogue in which "God" is but a title for the human interlocutor with whom one *discusses*, to diverse "revelations" on the tops of mountains in which the human partner is only a mute auditor, "convinced" beforehand.

In any case, the divine interlocutor is, in fact, fictitious. It all happens in the soul itself of the "scientist." And that is why Saint Augustine had "dialogues" with his "soul." And a distant disciple of that Platonic (or Plotinian) Christian, Descartes, deliberately dropped God and was content to have dialogue and discussion with himself. Thus Dialectic became "Meditation." It was in the form of Cartesian meditation that the dialectical method was used by the authors of the great philosophical "systems" of the seventeenth and eighteenth centuries: from Descartes to Kant-Fichte-Schelling. At first sight, this is a step backwards in relation to Socrates-Plato-Aristotle. The great modern "Systems" are like so many "Myths" which are juxtaposed without being discussed, which are created out of nothing by their authors without coming from an earlier dialogue. But in fact, this is not at all the case. On the one hand the author himself *discusses* his "theses" and *demonstrates* their veracity by *refuting* possible objections or "antitheses": thus he applies a dialectical method. On the other hand, in fact, the Platonic Dialogues preceded these Systems, which come from them "dialectically" through the intermediary of the aporetic discussions of Aristotle and the scholastic Aristotelians. And just as in a Platonic Dialogue, the auditor (who in this case is a historian-philosopher of philosophy) discovers the absolute truth as the result of the implicit or tacit "discussion" between the great Systems of history, hence, as the result of their "dialectic."

Hegel was the first of these auditor-historian-philosophers. In any case, he was the first to be so consciously. And that is why he was the first who could knowingly abandon Dialectic conceived as a philosophical *method*. He is content to observe and describe the dialectic which was effected throughout history, and he no longer needs to *make* a dialectic himself. This dialectic, or the "dialogue" of the Philosophies, took place before him. He only has to have the "experience" of it and to describe its synthetical final result in a coherent discourse: the expression of the absolute truth is

INTRODUCTION TO THE READING OF HEGEL

nothing but the adequate verbal description of the dialectic which engendered it. Thus, Hegel's Science is "dialectical" only to the extent that the Philosophy which prepared it throughout History *has been* (implicitly or explicitly) dialectical.

At first sight, this attitude of Hegel is a simple return to Plato. If Plato lets Parmenides, Protagoras, Socrates, and still others have dialogues, while being content to record the result of their discussions, Hegel records the result of the discussion which he organizes between Plato and Descartes, Spinoza and Kant, Fichte and Schelling, and so on. Hence, here again we would seem to be dealing with a dialectical *method* in the search for truth or in its exposition, which in no way affects the Real which that truth reveals. And Hegel does actually say somewhere that he is only rediscovering the ancient or, rather, Platonic, dialectic. But a closer examination shows that this is not at all the case, and that when Hegel speaks of Dialectic, he is talking about something quite different from what is found in his predecessors.[4]

One can say, if one pleases, that the eternal light of absolute Hegelian truth, too, comes from the collision of all the philosophic opinions which preceded it. However, this *ideal* dialectic, the dialogue of the Philosophies, took place, according to Hegel, only because it is a reflection of the *real* dialectic of Being. And only because it reflects this real dialectic does it finally achieve, in the person of Hegel, the truth or the complete and adequate revelation of the Real. Each philosophy correctly reveals or describes a turning point or a stopping place—thetical, antithetical, or synthetical— of the real dialectic, of the *Bewegung* of existing Being. And that is why each philosophy is "true" in a certain sense. But it is true only relatively or temporarily: it remains "true" as long as a new philosophy, also "true," does not come along to demonstrate its "error." However, a philosophy does not by itself transform itself into another philosophy or engender that other philosophy in and by an autonomous dialectical movement. The Real corresponding to a given philosophy itself becomes really other (thetical, antithetical, or synthetical), and this other Real is what engenders

---

[4] Hegel is nonetheless right in saying that he rediscovers Plato; for Platonic dialectic, the dialectical *method*, actually is an aspect of the dialectic of the *real* which Hegel discovered.

another adequate philosophy, which, as "true," replaces the first philosophy which has become "false." Thus, the dialectical movement of the history of philosophy, which ends in the absolute or definitive truth, is but a reflection, a "superstructure," of the dialectical movement of the *real* history of the Real. And that is why all philosophy that is "true" is also essentially "false": it is false in so far as it presents itself not as the reflection or description of a constituent element or a dialectical "moment" of the real, but as the revelation of the Real in its totality. Nonetheless, even while being or becoming "false," all philosophy (worthy of the name) remains "true," for the total Real implies and will always imply the aspect (or the "moment") which that philosophy revealed. The absolute truth or the Science of the Wise Man, of Hegel—that is, the adequate and complete revelation of the Real in its Totality—is indeed, therefore, an integral synthesis of all the philosophies presented throughout history. However, neither these philosophies through their discussions, nor the historian-philosopher who observes them, effects the synthesis in question: *real* History is what does it, at the end of its own dialectical movement; and Hegel is content to record it without having to *do* anything whatsoever, and consequently, without resorting to a specific mode of operation or a *method* of his own.

"*Weltgeschichte ist Weltgericht*" ("World History is a tribunal that judges the World"). History is what judges men, their actions and their opinions, and lastly their philosophical opinions as well. To be sure, History is, if you please, a long "discussion" between men. But this *real* historical "discussion" is something quite different from a philosophic dialogue or discussion. The "discussion" is carried out not with verbal arguments, but with clubs and swords or cannon on the one hand, and with sickles and hammers or machines on the other. If one wants to speak of a "dialectical method" used by History, one must make clear that one is talking about methods of war and of work. This real, or better, active, historical dialectic is what is reflected in the history of philosophy. And if Hegelian Science is dialectical or synthetical, it is only because it describes that *real* dialectic in its totality, as well as the series of consecutive philosophies which corresponds to that dialectical *reality*. Now, by the way, reality is dialectical only because it implies a negative or negating element: namely, the active negation of the given, the negation which is at the foundation of every bloody fight and of all so-called "physical" work.

Hegel does not need a God who would reveal the truth to him. And to find the truth, he does not need to hold dialogues with "the men in the city," or even to have a "discussion" with himself or to "meditate" *à la Descartes*. (Besides, no purely verbal discussion, no solitary meditation, can lead to the truth, of which Fighting and Work are the only "criteria.") He can find it all alone, while sitting tranquilly in the shade of those "trees" which taught Socrates nothing, but which teach Hegel many things about themselves and about men. But all this is possible only because there *have been* cities in which men had discussions against a background of fighting and work, while they worked and fought for and because of their opinions (cities, moreover, which were surrounded by these same trees whose wood was used in their construction). Hegel no longer discusses because he benefits from the discussion of those who preceded him. And if, having nothing more *to do*, he has no *method* of his own, it is because he profits from all the actions effected throughout history. His thought simply reflects the Real. But he can do so only because the Real is dialectical— that is, imbued with the negating action of fighting and work, which engenders thought and discourse, causes them to move, and finally realizes their perfect coincidence with the Real which they are supposed to reveal or to describe. In short, Hegel does not need a dialectical *method* because the truth which he incarnates is the final result of the real or active dialectic of universal History, which his thought is content to reproduce through his discourse.

From Socrates-Plato until Hegel, Dialectic was only a philosophical method without a counterpart in the real. In Hegel there is a real Dialectic, but the philosophical method is that of a pure and simple description, which is dialectical only in the sense that it describes a dialectic of reality.

In order better to understand the meaning of and the reason for this truly revolutionary transposition, one must be willing to make the philosophical experiment which Hegel proposes to the reader of the *Phenomenology* in its first Chapter. Look at your watch, he says, and note that it is, let us say, noon. Say it, and you will have enunciated a truth. Now write this truth on a piece of paper: "It is now noon." At this point Hegel remarks that a truth cannot cease to be true because of being formulated in writing. And now look at your watch again and reread the sentence you have written. You will see that the truth has been transformed into error, for it is *now* five minutes past noon.

What can be said, except that real being can transform a human truth into an error—at least in so far as the real is temporal, and Time has a reality.

This observation was made a long time ago: since Plato or, rather, since Parmenides, and perhaps even earlier. But one aspect of the question was neglected until Hegel; namely, the fact that, through his discourse, through his written discourse in particular, man succeeds in *preserving* error in the very heart of reality. If Nature happens to commit an error (the malformation of an animal, for example), it eliminates it *immediately* (the animal dies, or at least does not propagate). Only the errors committed by man *endure* indefinitely and are propagated at a distance, thanks to language. And man could be defined as an error that is preserved in existence, that *endures* within reality. Now, since *error* means *disagreement* with the real; since what is *other* than what is, is *false*, one can also say that the man who errs is a Nothingness that nihilates in Being, or an "ideal" that is present in the real.[5]

Only man can err without thereby having to become extinct: he can continue to exist, making mistakes all the while about what exists; he can *live* his error or in error; and the error or the false which is nothing in itself becomes *real* in him. And the experiment mentioned above shows us how, thanks to man, the nothingness of the noon which is past can be really present, in the form of an erroneous sentence, in the real present of five minutes past twelve.

But this preservation of error in the real is possible only because its transformation into a truth is possible. It is because error can be corrected that it is not pure nothingness. And experience shows that human errors are actually corrected in the course of time and become truths. One can even say that every *truth* in the proper sense of the term is an *error* that has been *corrected*. For the truth

---

[5] Parmenides' assertion: "Being and Thought are the same thing," can at best be applied only to *true* thought, but certainly not to *false* thought. The false is certainly *something other* than Being. And yet, one cannot say that the false "is nothing," that "there is no" error. Error "exists" in its way: *ideally*, so to speak.

is more than a reality: it is a *revealed* reality; it is the reality *plus* the revelation of the reality through discourse. Therefore, in the heart of the truth, there is a *difference* between the real and the discourse which reveals it. But a difference is *actualized* in the form of an *opposition*, and a discourse *opposed* to the real is, precisely, an error. Now a difference that was never actualized would not really be a difference. Therefore, there is really a *truth* only where there *has been* an error. But error exists really only in the form of human discourse. If man, then, is the only one who can err really and live in error, he is also the only one who can incarnate truth. If Being in its totality is not only pure and simple Being (*Sein*), but Truth, Concept, Idea, or Spirit—this is only because it implies in its real existence a human or articulate reality, which is capable of erring and of correcting its errors. Without Man, Being would be mute: it would be *there* (*Dasein*), but it would not be *true* (*das Wahre*).

The example given by Hegel shows how man manages to create and to preserve an error in Nature. Another example, which is not found in Hegel but which illustrates his thought well, permits us to see how man succeeds in transforming into truth the error which he was able to preserve as error in the real.

Let us suppose that, in the Middle Ages, a poet wrote in a poem: "*at this moment* a man is flying over the ocean." This was without a doubt an error, and it remained such for many centuries. But if we now reread that sentence, we are most likely reading a truth, for it is almost certain that *at this moment* some aviator is over the Atlantic, for example.

We previously saw that Nature (or given Being) can make a human truth false (which man nonetheless succeeds in preserving indefinitely as error). And now we see that man can transform his own error into truth.[6] He began with an error (whether voluntary or not is unimportant) by speaking of the terrestrial animal of the species *homo sapiens* as a flying animal; but he finished with the statement of a truth by speaking of the flight of an animal of that species. And it was not the (erroneous) discourse that changed

[6] One could say that, by inventing the airplane, man corrects the "error" of Nature, which created him without wings. But that would only be a metaphor: to say that is to anthropomorphize Nature. Error, and hence truth, exists only where there is language (*Logos*).

in order to conform to given Being (*Sein*); it was that Being that was transformed in order to conform to the discourse.

The action which transforms the given real so as to make true a human error—that is, a discourse that was in disagreement with this given—is called *Work*: it was by working that man constructed the airplane which transformed the poet's (voluntary) error into truth. Now, work is a real *negation* of the given. Hence Being which exists as a World in which men work implies a negative or negating element. This is to say that it has a dialectical structure. And because it has this structure, it contains in it a discourse that reveals it; it is not only given Being, but revealed Being or Truth, Idea, Spirit. The truth is an error that has become true (or has been "dialectically overcome" as error); now, the real negation of the given by Work is what transforms the error into truth; the truth, therefore, is necessarily dialectical in the sense that it results from the *real* dialectic of work. Accordingly, the truly adequate verbal expression of the truth must take account and give an account of its dialectical origin, of its birth from the *work* which man carries out within Nature.

This applies to truth that is related to the natural World—that is, to discourse that reveals the reality and being of Nature. But truth related to man—that is, discourse that reveals the human reality—is equally dialectical, in the sense that it results from a real negation of the human (or social, historical) given and must give an account of that fact.

To become aware of this, one must imagine a case in which a "moral error" (= a crime) is transformed into "truth" or virtue. For every morality is an implicit anthropology, and man is speaking of his very being when he judges his actions morally.[7]

Let us suppose, then, that a man assassinates his king for political reasons. He believes he is acting well. But the others treat him as a criminal, arrest him, and put him to death. In these conditions he actually is a criminal. Thus the given social World, just like the natural World, can transform a human truth (a "subjective" truth—i.e., a "certainty") into error.

But let us suppose that the assassin in question starts a victorious

---

[7] Inversely, every anthropology is an implicit morality. For the "normal" man of which anthropology speaks is always a "norm" for the behavior or the appreciation of empirical man.

revolution. At once society treats the assassin as a hero. And in these conditions he actually is a hero, a model of virtue and good citizenship, a human ideal. Man can therefore transform a crime into virtue, a moral or anthropological error into a truth.

As in the example of the airplane, here too there is a real transformation of the existing World—that is, an active negation of the given. But the former concerned the natural World, whereas here it is a question of the human or social, historical World. And if in the former case the negating action was Work, here it is Fighting (Fighting to the death for recognition, *Anerkennen*). But in both cases there is effective active negation of the given, or as Hegel says: "dialectical movement" of the real.

This active or *real* negation of the given, effected in Fighting and by Work, is what constitutes the negative or negating element determining the dialectical structure of the Real and of Being. Hence we are indeed dealing with a dialectical *Real* and a *real* Dialectic. But this Dialectic has an ideal "superstructure," a kind of reflection in thought and in discourse. In particular, throughout history, there was always a philosophy (in the broad sense) ready to give an account of the state of things realized at every decisive turning point in the dialectical evolution of the World. Thus, the history of philosophy and of "culture" in general is itself a "dialectical movement," but it is a secondary and derivative movement. Finally, insofar as Hegel's thought and discourse reveal and describe the totality of the real in its becoming, they too are a "dialectical movement"; but this movement is in some sense tertiary. Hegelian discourse is dialectical to the extent that it describes the real Dialectic of Fighting and of Work, as well as the "ideal" reflection of this Dialectic in thought in general and in philosophical thought in particular. But in itself Hegelian discourse is not at all dialectical: it is neither a dialogue nor a discussion; it is a pure and simple "phenomenological" description of the real dialectic of the Real and of the verbal discussion which reflected this dialectic in the course of time. Accordingly, Hegel does not need to "demonstrate" what he says, nor to "refute" what others have said. The "demonstration" and the "refutation" were effected *before* him, in the course of the History which preceded him, and they were effected not by verbal arguments, but in the final analysis by the proof (*Bewährung*) of Fighting and Work. Hegel only has to record the final result of that "dialectical" proof and to describe it correctly. And since, by definition, the content of this description will never be modified, completed, or refuted, one can say that Hegel's description is the statement of the absolute, or universally and eternally (i.e., "necessarily") valid, truth.

All this presupposes, of course, the *completion* of the real Dialectic of Fighting and of Work, that is, the definitive stopping of History. It is only "at the end of time" that a Wise Man (who happened to be named Hegel) can give up all dialectical *method*—that is, all real or ideal negation, transformation, or "critique" of the given—and limit himself to describing the given—that is, to revealing through discourse the given precisely as it is given. Or more exactly, it is at the moment when Man, having become Wise, is fully satisfied by such a pure and simple description, that the active or real negation of the given no longer takes place, with the result that the description remains valid or true indefinitely and consequently is no longer open to discussion, and never again engenders polemical dialogues.

As a philosophical *method*, therefore, Dialectic is abandoned only at the moment when the *real* Dialectic of the active transformation of the given definitively stops. As long as this transformation endures, a description of the given real can only be partial or provisional: to the extent that the real itself changes, its philosophical description must also change in order to continue to be adequate or true. In other words, as long as the real or active dialectic of History endures, errors and truths are dialectical in the sense that they are all sooner or later "dialectically overcome" (*aufgehoben*), the "truth" becoming partially, or in a certain sense, false, and the "error" true; and they are changed thus in and by discussion, dialogue, or dialectical *method*.

In order to give up the dialectical method and to lay claim to absolute truth by limiting oneself to pure description without any "discussion" or "demonstration," one must therefore be sure that the real dialectic of History is truly completed. But how is this to be known?

At first sight, the answer is easy. History stops when Man no longer acts in the full sense of the term—that is, when he no longer negates, no longer transforms the natural and social given through bloody Fighting and creative Work. And Man no longer does this when the given Real gives him full satisfaction (*Befriedigung*), by fully realizing his Desire (*Begierde*, which in Man is a Desire for universal recognition of his unique personality—*Anerkennen* or *Anerkennung*). If Man is truly and fully satisfied by what *is*, he no longer desires anything real and therefore no longer changes reality, and thus he himself ceases really to change. The only "desire" which he can still have—if he is a *philosopher*—is the "desire" to *understand* what is and what he is, and to reveal it through discourse. Therefore Man, even as philosopher, is definitively satisfied by the adequate description of the real in its totality which is given by the Science of the Wise Man: hence he will never again oppose what has been said by the Wise Man, just as the Wise Man no longer opposed the real which he was describing. Thus the Wise Man's nondialectical (i.e., nonnegating) description will be the absolute truth, which will engender no philosophical "dialectic" and will never be a "thesis" against which an antithesis will come in opposition.

But how can it be known whether Man is truly and fully *satisfied* by what is? According to Hegel, Man is nothing but Desire for recognition ("*der Mensch* ist *Anerkennen*," Volume XX, page 206, line 26), and History is but the process of the progressive satisfaction of this Desire, which is fully satisfied in and by the universal and homogeneous State (which, for Hegel, was the Empire of Napoleon). But first Hegel had to anticipate the historical *future* (which, by definition, is unforeseeable because it is free—that is, it arises from a *negation* of the present given), for the State that he had in mind was only in the process of formation; and we know that today it is still far from having an "empirical existence" (*Dasein*) or from being an "objective reality" (*Wirklichkeit*) or a "present real" (*Gegenwart*). Furthermore, and this is much more important, how can one know that the satisfaction given in and by this State is truly a definitive satisfaction for Man as such, and not merely for one of his possible Desires? How can one know that the stabilization of the historical "movement" in the Empire is not simply a pause, the result of a momentary lassitude? By what right can one assert that this State will not engender in Man a new Desire, other than the Desire for Recognition, and that this State will not consequently be negated some day by a negating or creative Action (*Tat*) other than the Action of Fighting and Work?

One can make this assertion only by supposing that the Desire for recognition exhausts *all* the human *possibilities*. But one has the right to make that supposition only if one has a complete and perfect knowledge of Man—that is, a universally and definitively ("necessarily") valid—i.e., *absolutely true*—knowledge. Now, by definition, the absolute truth can be attained only at the end of History. But the problem is precisely to determine this end of History.

One is caught, then, in a *vicious circle*. And Hegel was perfectly aware of this. But he believed he had found a criterion both for the absolute truth of his description of the real—that is, for its correct and complete character—and for the end of the "movement" of this real—that is, for the definitive stopping of History. And, curiously enough, this criterion is precisely the *circularity* of his description—that is, of the "System of science."

Hegel starts with a more or less ordinary description of the real (represented by a philosophy set forth in the course of history); he chooses, however, the one which seems the simplest, the most elementary, and which reduces, for example, to a single word (in fact it is a very ancient philosophy; that of Parmenides, for example, which reduces to saying: Being *is*). The correct presentation of that description shows that it is incomplete, that it reveals only one of the aspects of Being and the Real, that it is only a "thesis" that necessarily engenders an "antithesis," with which it is necessarily going to combine in order to give a "synthesis," which will be only a new "thesis," and so on.[8] Proceeding

---

[8] The philosopher who set forth the "thesis" did not know that it was only a thesis that had to engender an antithesis, and so on. In other words, even the *aspect* of the real which he in fact described was not described correctly. Now, he thought he was describing the *totality* of the real. Hegel, on the other hand, knows that it is only an *aspect* of the real, and that is why he describes it correctly—that is, in such a way as to show the necessity of the antithesis which describes the complementary aspect, and so on. (He knows this, because he no longer *opposes* the given real which he is describing, since he is *satisfied* by it and desires only its correct description, and not its transformation; the inoperative desire to transform the real is what engenders error in the philosopher). Hegel sees all this because he already knows the *final* synthesis of *all* the intermediate theses, antitheses, and syntheses, since he has described the *completed*,

in this fashion step by step, by simple adequate descriptions, or by a correct descriptive repetition of the (derivative) dialectic of the history of philosophy, in which each step is just as *necessary* or inevitable as are the various elements in the description of a complex real (the description of the trunk, the branches, the leaves, and so on, in the description of a tree, for example)— proceeding in this fashion, Hegel finally comes to a point that is none other than his point of departure: the *final* synthesis is also the *initial* thesis. Thus he establishes that he has gone around or described a *circle*, and that if he wants to continue, he can only *go around again*: it is impossible to *extend* his description; one can only *make it again* as it has already been made once.

This means that Hegel's discourse exhausts *all* the *possibilities* of thought. One cannot bring up any discourse in opposition to him which would not already be a part of his own discourse, which would not be reproduced in a paragraph of the System as a constituent element (*Moment*) of the whole. Thus we see that Hegel's discourse sets forth an *absolute* truth, which cannot be negated by anyone. And therefore we see that this discourse is not dialectical, in the sense that it is not a "thesis" that can be "dialectically overcome." But if Hegel's thought cannot be surpassed by thought, and if it itself does not surpass the given real but is content to describe it (for it knows and says that it is *satisfied* by what is), no ideal or real negation of the given is any longer possible. The real, then, will remain eternally identical to itself, and its entire History will forever belong to the past. A complete and correct description of this real will therefore be universally and eternally valid—that is, absolutely true. Now, the circularity of the Hegelian description proves that it is complete and hence correct: for an erroneous or incomplete description, which stopped at a lacuna or ended in an impasse, would never come back upon itself.

Thus, by demonstrating the absolute truth of the System without "discussion"—that is, without "refutation" or "demonstration"

---

truly *total* real created by the *whole* of the real dialectic which the history of philosophy reflects. But the presentation of that history (and of History in general) as a series of theses, antitheses, and syntheses is what will show him that he has actually described (in a correct and complete way) the *totality* of the real— i.e., that his description is a *final* or *total* synthesis.

—the circularity which was simply observed by the Wise Man justifies his purely descriptive or non*dialectical method.*

There is no reason to insist upon the character of Hegel's non-dialectical method. There is not much to be said about it. And what can be said has already been said by Edmond Husserl about his own "phenomenological" method, which he quite wrongly opposed to the Hegelian method with which he was not familiar. For in fact Hegel's method is nothing but the method that we nowadays call "phenomenological."

On the other hand, there is good reason to speak at greater length about the DIALECTIC which Hegel has in mind—that is, the dialectical structure of the Real and of Being, as he conceives of it and describes it in the *Phenomenology* and the *Encyclopaedia*.

First let us see what the threefold structure of Being itself is, as it is described in Hegel's Ontology—that is, in the "Logik" which forms the first part of the *Encyclopaedia*. Next, we shall have to consider the significance of the dialectical triplicity of Being in the "appearance" (*Erscheinung*) of its "empirical existence" (*Dasein*), as it is described in the *Phenomenology*.

Let us take up again the general definition of Dialectic given in § 79 of the third edition of the *Encyclopaedia* (Volume V, page 104, lines 27–30):

With regard to its form, *logic* has three aspects: (a) the *abstract* or *understandable* aspect; (b) the *dialectical* [in the narrow sense] or *negatively rational* aspect; (c) the *speculative* or *positively rational* aspect.

"Logic" or "the logical Real" (*das Logisch-Reelle*)—that is, Being and the Real correctly described by a coherent Discourse (*Logos*), necessarily has three "aspects" (*Seiten*) or "constituent-elements" (*Momente*). These three elements are constituent of revealed Being, and are also found in the Discourse which correctly reveals this threefold or dialectical Being.

Let us now see what these three constituent elements or aspects of real Being and of the Discourse that reveals Being are.

The first aspect is defined in § 80 of the *Encyclopaedia* (Volume V, page 105, lines 2–5):

Thought (*Denken*) [taken] as *Understanding* (*Verstand*) stops at fixed (*festen*) specific-determination (*Bestimmtheit*) and at the distinction-or-differentiation (*Unterschiedenheit*) of this determination in relation to the others [the other fixed determinations]; such a limited (*beschranktes*) abstract-entity (*Abstraktes*) is valid for the Understanding as something enduring (*bestehend*) and existing for itself [that is, independently of the existence of the other determinations and of the thought which thinks or reveals them].

Thought, in the mode of Understanding, is the common thought of man: of the "naive" man, of the vulgar scientist, of the pre-Hegelian philosopher. This thought does not reveal Being in its totality; it does not reflect the three constituent-elements of Being and of every being, but stops at the first; it describes (correctly, in principle) only the "abstract" aspect of Being, which is precisely the "understandable" (*verständig*) constituent-element.

The thought of the Understanding is exclusively dominated by the primordial ontological (and hence "logical") category of *Identity*. Its logical ideal is the perfect agreement of thought with itself or the absence of all internal contradiction—that is, the homogeneity, or better, the identity, of its content. Every identity is true by definition, and every truth has a content that is identical to itself and in itself. And as truth is an adequate revelation of Being or the Real, Being and the Real are, for the Understanding, always and everywhere *identical* to themselves and in themselves. Now what is true of Being and the Real taken in their totality must also be true for everything that *is* or exists, for every particular entity that exists really. For the Understanding, every real entity always remains *identical* to itself; it is *determined* once for all in its specificity (*feste Bestimmtheit*), and it distinguishes *itself* in a precise, fixed, and stable manner from all other real entities, which are just as fixedly determined as it is (*Unterschiedenheit gegen andere*). In short, it is a *given* entity, which can be neither engendered nor destroyed, nor modified in any way whatsoever. That is why one can say that it exists *for itself* (*für sich*)—that is, independently of the rest of existing Being, and in particular independently of the Understanding which thinks it.

Now, according to Hegel, real Being actually is such as it is revealed by the Understanding. *Identity* is indeed a fundamental ontological category, which applies both to Being itself and to everything that *is*. For everything is actually *identical* to itself and *different* from all others, and precisely this allows (scientific or "naive") thought to "define" it or to reveal its "specificity"—that is, to recognize it as remaining "the same thing" and as being "something other" than what it is not. The thought of the Understanding, therefore, is *true* in principle. If there were no Identity in Being and of Being, no *science* of the Real would be possible (as the Greeks saw very clearly), and there would have been no *Truth* or Reality that is revealed by a coherent Discourse. But this "coherent" or identical thought is also false, if it claims to reveal the *totality* of Being and not only one of its (three) aspects. For in fact, Being and the Real are something else in addition to Identity with self.

Furthermore, the thought of the Understanding itself manifests its own insufficiency. For in pursuing its ideal of Identity, it finally leads to a universal tautology which is empty of meaning or of content, and its "discourse" in the end reduces to the single *word*: "Being," or "One," and so on. As soon as it wants to develop this word into genuine *discourse*, as soon as it wants to *say something*, it introduces diversity, which contradicts Identity and makes it decrepit or false from its own point of view.

This insufficiency of the thought of the Understanding was already pointed out by Plato (notably in the *Parmenides*). Hegel spoke of it in the *Phenomenology* (notably in Chapter III) and elsewhere. And in our time Meyerson insisted upon it at great length. Hence there is no reason to go over it again. What must be underlined is that for Hegel this thought is insufficient because Being itself is more, and something other, than Identity; and because Being is something more than Identity, thought can get beyond the stage of the Understanding or of tautological "discourse." [9] This thought does not attain the Truth because it cannot develop into *discourse* that reveals real Being; and it is not circular, it does not *come back* to its point of departure, because it does not

---

[9] Tautology reduces to a single word; therefore it is not a genuine Discourse (*Logos*). But it allows for an indefinite algorithmic development, and in this form it can be considered as a "revelation" of the Real or a "truth." But tautology (mathematical or otherwise) can reveal only the *identical* aspect of Being and of the Real. One could say that it correctly and completely reveals given-Being (*Sein*) or the natural Reality—that is, the natural World excluding Man and his social or historical World. But Hegel himself does not say this.

succeed in going beyond this point. But if this thought is not a Truth, then real Being is something else in addition to what this thought reveals of it. Hence one must go beyond the Understanding in order to reveal real Being in its totality. Or more exactly, the thought of the Understanding is surpassed because the discursive auto-revelation of real Being reveals not only its Identity with itself, but also its other fundamental ontological aspects.

To attain the truth—that is, to reveal the totality of real Being—thought must therefore go beyond the stage of Understanding (*Verstand*) and become Reason (*Vernunft*) or "rational-or-reasonable" (*vernünftig*) thought. This thought reveals the other fundamental aspects of Being as such and of everything that is real. And first of all, as "negative" Reason, it reveals by its discourse the "negatively rational" aspect of what *is*—i.e., the constituent-element of (revealed) Being and the (revealed) Real which Hegel calls "dialectical" in the narrow or proper sense of the term, precisely because it involves a negative or negating element.

Here is how this second constituent-element of Being (actually, of revealed Being) is defined in § 81 of the *Encyclopaedia* (Volume V, page 105, lines 7–9):

> The [properly] *dialectical* constituent-element is the act-of-dialectical-self-overcoming (*eigene Sichaufheben*) of these finite specific-determinations (*Bestimmungen*) and their transformation (*Übergehen*) into their opposites (*entgegengesetzte*).

It is important at the outset to state that negatively rational thought (or Reason) is not what introduces the negative element into Being, thus making it dialectical: the determined and fixed *real* entities (revealed by Understanding) themselves negate themselves "dialectically" (i.e., while preserving themselves) and thus become *actually* other than they are or were. "Negatively rational" or "dialectical" thought merely describes this *real* negation of the "understandable" given and of its fixed "specific-determinations."

Hegel himself insists on this, moreover, in the second explanatory Note which he adds to the cited paragraph.

Among other things, he says the following (Volume V, page 105, lines 13–37):

> Dialectic is generally considered as an external art [that is, as a "method"]. . . . Often Dialectic is actually nothing more than a

subjective see-saw of a reasoning that goes back and forth (*hin-und-herübergehendem Räsonnement*). . . . [But] in its authentic (*eigentümlichen*) specific-determination Dialectic is, all to the contrary, the proper (*eigene*), true (*wahrhafte*) nature of the specific-determinations of the Understanding, of things (*Dinge*), and of the finite-entity as such (*Endlichen Überhaupt*). . . . Dialectic . . . is this *immanent* going beyond (*Hinausgehen*), in which the one-sidedness and the limitation (*Beschränktheit*) of the specific-determinations of the Understanding are represented (*darstellt*) as what they are, namely, as their [own] negation. Everything that is finite (*alles Endliche*) is an act of dialectical self-overcoming. Consequently, the Dialectical (*das Dialektische*) constitutes the moving soul of scientific progress (*Fortgehens*), and it is the only principle thanks to which an *immanent connection* (*Zusammenhang*) *and a necessity* penetrate (*kommt*) into the content of Science. . . .

Therefore, it is the Real itself that is dialectical, and it is dialectical because it implies in addition to Identity a second fundamental constituent-element, which Hegel calls *Negativity*.

Identity and Negativity are two primordial and universal ontological categories.[10] Thanks to Identity every being remains *the*

---

[10] In the *Encyclopaedia* Hegel says that *every* entity can "overcome" itself and consequently is dialectical. But in the *Phenomenology* he asserts that only the *human* reality is dialectical, while Nature is determined by Identity alone (Cf. for example page 145, lines 22–26 and page 563, lines 21–27). Personally I share the point of view of the *Phenomenology* and do not accept the dialectic of natural Being, of *Sein*. I cannot discuss that question here. I would, however, say this: the implication of Negativity in identical Being (*Sein*) is equivalent to the presence of Man in Reality; Man, and he alone, reveals Being and Reality through Discourse; therefore *revealed* Being in its *totality* necessarily implies Negativity; hence it is indeed a *universal* onto-logical category; but within the total Reality one must distinguish, on the one hand, the purely identical *natural* reality, which therefore is not dialectical in itself, which does not overcome itself dialectically, and, on the other hand, the *human*, essentially negating reality, which dialectically overcomes both itself and the natural identical reality which is "given" to it; now, the dialectical overcoming of the given (by Fighting and Work) necessarily leads to its revelation through Discourse; therefore Reality *revealed* by discourse—i.e., Reality taken in its *totality* or *concrete* Reality—is indeed dialectical. Example: the acorn, the oak, and the transformation of the acorn into the oak (as well as the evolution of the species "oak") are not dialectical; on the other hand, the transformation of the oak into an oak table is a *dialectical* negation of the natural given, that is, the creation of something *essentially* new: it is because Man "works" with the oak that he has a "science" of the oak, of the acorn, and so on; this science is dialectical, but not insofar as it reveals the acorn, its transformation into the oak, and so on; it is dialectical insofar as it evolves as a science (of

same being, eternally *identical* to *itself* and *different* from the *others*; or, as the Greeks said, every being represents, in its temporal existence, an immutable eternal "idea," it has a "nature" or "essence" given once and for all, it occupies a fixed and stable "place" (*topos*) in the heart of a World ordered from all eternity (*cosmos*). But thanks to Negativity, an identical being can negate or overcome its identity with itself and become other than it is, even its own opposite. In other words, the negating being, far from necessarily "representing" or "showing" (as a "phenomenon") its given identical "idea" or "nature," can *negate* them itself and become opposite to them (that is, "perverted"). Or again, the negating being can break the rigid ties of the fixed "differences" that distinguish it from the other identical beings (by "freeing" itself from these ties); it can leave the place that was assigned to it in the Cosmos. In short (as Hegel puts it in the first edition of the *Logik*), the being of negative or negating Being, dominated by the category of Negativity, consists in "not being what it is and being what it is not" (*das nicht zu sein, was es ist, und das zu sein, was es nicht ist*).

Concrete (revealed) real Being is both Identity and Negativity. Therefore it is not only static given-Being (*Sein*), Space, and Nature, but also Becoming (*Werden*), Time, and History. It is not only Identity or equality to itself (*Sichselbstgleichheit*), but also Other-Being (*Anderssein*) or negation of itself as given and creation of itself as other than this given. In other words, it is not only empirical-Existence (*Dasein*) and Necessity (*Notwendigkeit*), but also Action (*Tat, Tun, Handeln*) and Freedom (*Freiheit*).

Now, to be other than one is (Negativity) while at the same time continuing to be oneself (Identity), or to identify oneself with something other while at the same time distinguishing oneself from it, is at the same time to *be* (and to *reveal* through Discourse) both what one is oneself and what one is not.[11] To become other

---

Nature) in the course of History; but it evolves thus dialectically only because Man engages in real dialectical negations of the given through Work and Fighting.

[11] The Being which "overcomes" itself as Being while continuing to be itself— i.e., Being—is the *concept* "Being." To identify oneself with the tree without *becoming* a tree is to form and to have the (adequate) *concept* of the tree. To become other while continuing to be oneself is to have and to preserve the *concept* of one's I (in and by "memory").

than one is is to adopt a posture with respect to oneself, to exist (as one has been) *for oneself* (as one is now). The being which negates the given real dialectically also preserves it as negated— that is, as unreal or "ideal": it preserves what is negated as the "meaning" of the discourse by which it reveals it. Hence it is "conscious" of what it negates. And if it negates itself, it is self-conscious. The simply identical being, on the other hand, exists only *in itself* and *for the others*—that is, in its identity with itself and through the relations of difference which tie it to the rest of the identical beings within the cosmos: it does not exist *for itself*, and the others do not exist *for it*.

Thus, Being which is both *Identity* and *Negativity* is not only homogeneous and immutable *Being in itself* (*Ansichsein*), and fixed and stable *Being for another entity* (*Sein für Anderes*); but also *Being for itself* (*Fürsichsein*) split into real being and revealing Discourse, and *Other-Being* (*Anderssein*) in perpetual transformation which frees it from itself as *given* to itself and to others.

The identical and negating being, therefore, is "free" in the sense that it is more than its given being, since it is also the revelation of this being by Discourse. But if this Discourse reveals Being in its totality, if it is truly true, it reveals not only the Identity but also the Negativity of Being. That is why Discourse is not only the Discourse of the Understanding (dominated by the single onto-logical category of Identity), but also a Discourse of negative or properly "dialectical" Reason (dominated by the onto-logical category of Negativity). But we shall see at once that this is not yet sufficient: Discourse is truly true, or reveals the concrete totality of (revealed) Being, only provided that it is also a Discourse of positive or "speculative" Reason.

Indeed, negating Being *itself* negates itself. Therefore, it is as *same* that it negates itself or becomes and is *other*: it is negating as identical and identical as negating. Hence one cannot say that Being is Identity *and* Negativity: being both at the same time, it is neither the one nor the other taken separately. Concrete (revealed) real Being is neither (pure) *Identity* (which is Being, *Sein*) nor (pure) *Negativity* (which is Nothingness, *Nichts*), but *Totality* (which is Becoming, *Werden*). Totality is, therefore, the third fundamental and universal onto-logical category: Being is real or concrete only in its *totality*, and every concrete real entity is the *totality* of its constituent elements (identical or negating). And it is in the aspect of Totality that Being and the Real are revealed by the "positively rational" thought which Hegel terms "speculative." But this thought is possible only because there is, in Being and the Real themselves, a "speculative" or "positively rational" real constituent element, which "speculative" thought limits itself to revealing.

Here is how Hegel defines this real "speculative" constituent-element in § 83 of the *Encyclopaedia* (Volume V, page 105, line 41–page 106, line 2):

> The *speculative* or *positively rational* comprehends (*fasst auf*) the unifying-unity (*Einheit*) of the specific-determinations in their opposition (*Entgegensetzung*), [that is,] the *affirmative* which is contained in their dissolution (*Auflösung*) and transformation (*Übergehen*).

The negating being negates its identity to itself and becomes its own opposite, but it continues to be the same being. And *this*, *its* unity within opposition to itself, is its *affirmation* in spite of its negation or "dissolution," or, better, "transformation." It is as this negating affirmation of itself, as reaffirmation of its original identity to itself, that the being is a "speculative" or "positively rational" entity. Thus, Being which reaffirms itself as Being identical to itself, after having negated itself as such, is neither Identity nor Negativity, but Totality. And it is as Totality that Being is truly and fully dialectical. But Being is dialectical Totality and not tautological Identity because it is also Negativity. Totality is the unifying-unity of Identity and Negativity: it is affirmation by negation.

In other words, taken as Totality, Being is neither simply *Being in itself*, nor simply *Being for itself*, but the integration of the two or *Being in and for itself* (*An-und-Fürsichsein*). This is to say that Totality is revealed Being or self-conscious Being (which Hegel calls "absolute Concept," "Idea," or "Spirit"): it is split by Negativity into given static Being (*Sein*) and its discursive "ideal" opposite; but it is, or again becomes, one and homogeneous in and by this doubling (*Entzweiung*) when the Totality of Being is correctly revealed by the "total" or circular Discourse of the Wise Man. Thus, in spite of the *Negativity* which it encloses and presupposes, the final *Totality* is just as much one and unique, homo-geneous and autonomous, as the first and primordial *Identity*. As the *Result* of Negation, Totality is as much an Affirmation as is the Identity which was negated in order to *become* Totality.

In the first explanatory Note added to § 82, Hegel explains why Negativity is not Nothingness, why it does not lead to the pure and simple destruction of the auto-negating being, but ends in a new *positive* determination of this being, which *in its totality* once more becomes absolutely identical to itself. (The Synthesis is a new Thesis).

This is what he says (Volume V, page 106, lines 3-8):

> Dialectic has a *positive* result because it has a *specifically-determined* (*bestimmten*) *content*; that is, because its result is not truly (*wahr-haft*) empty [and] *abstract Nothingness* (*Nichts*), but the Negation of *certain specific-determinations* (*gewissen Bestimmungen*), which are contained in the result precisely because this latter is not an *immediate* (*unmittelbares*) *Nothingness*, but a result.

(Dialectical) Negation is the negation of an Identity—that is, of something *determined*, *specific*, which corresponds to an eternal "idea" or a fixed and stable "nature." Now, the specific-determina-tion (*Bestimmtheit*) of what is negated (and identical) determines and specifies both the negation itself and its (total) result. The negation of A has a *positive* or specifically determined content because it is a negation of A, and not of M or N, for example, or of some undetermined X. Thus, the "A" is *preserved* in the "non-A"; or, if you please, the "A" is "*dialectically* overcome" (*aufge-hoben*) in the "non-A." And that is why the non-A is not pure Nothingness, but an entity that is just as "positive"—i.e., deter-mined or specific, or better, identical to itself—as the A which is negated in it: the non-A is all this because it *results* from the nega-tion of a determined or specific A; or, again, the non-A is not nowhere because the A has a fixed and stable place in the heart of a well-ordered Cosmos.

If Identity is incarnated in the "A" which is identical to itself (A = A), Negativity is made concrete in and by (or as) the *non* of the "non-A." Taken in itself, this *non* is pure and simple Nothingness: it is something only because of the A which it negates. The isolated *non* is absolutely *undetermined*: it represents, in absolute *freedom*, independence with regard to *every* given determination, to *every* "nature" fixed once for all, to *every* localization in an ordered Cosmos. The presence of the *non* in the "non-A" is what permits that which was "A" to go anywhere starting from the place which "A" occupied in the Cosmos, to create for itself any "nature" other than the innate "nature" of "A," to determine itself otherwise than "A" was determined by its fixed difference from what it was not. But the presence of "A" in the "non-A" limits the absolute liberty of the "non" and makes it concrete—that is, determines or specifies it. One can, to be sure, go anywhere: but only starting from the place *which "A" occupied*; one can, to be sure, create any "nature" for oneself: but only on the condition that it be other than *that of "A."* In short, if the point at which (dialectical) negation will end is indifferent, its point of departure is fixed and stable, or determined and specific—that is, *given.* Thus, the negation is not just any negation, but the negation *of "A."* And this "A" in the "non-A" is what *makes concrete* or determines the *absolute* freedom of the "non," which, as *absolute*, is only pure Nothingness, or death.

Moreover, as soon as "non-A" exists, the purely negating "non" is just as much an *abstraction* as the purely identical A. What really exists is the unity of the two—that is, the "non-A" as *totality* or entity that is as much one and unique, determined and specific, as the "A" itself—the "non-A" which is a "B."

A is preserved in B (= non-A). But the *non* which negates A is equally maintained in it. Therefore A is preserved only in its negation (just as the *non* is maintained only as the non of A). Or more exactly, B *is* the negation of A: a negation that preserves itself in positive existence (*Bestehen*). Or still more exactly, B is the (positive) result of the *negation* of A. Thus, B is an A that has not only been *overcome* and at the same *preserved*, but also *sublimated* (*aufgehoben*) by this preserving negation. For if A is *immediate* (*unmittelbar*), B is *mediated* (*vermittelt*) by negation; if A is pure *Identity*, B is *Totality* implying *Negativity*; if A is purely and simply *given*, B is the result of a negating action—that is, *created*; if A exists only *in itself* (*an sich*) or for others (*für Anderes*), B exists also *for itself* (*für sich*), for in it A takes a position with respect to itself, by negating itself as given and by affirming itself as created by this auto-negation.

But B does not exist only *for itself*; it exists *in and for itself* (*an und für sich*). For in it A affirms itself as totality, by maintaining its identity with itself taken as negated, negating, and resulting from negation: it is A itself that negates itself by the *non*, and it itself becomes the "non-A" which is B. That is why B is not only Totality that results from negation and thus implies Negativity, but also Identity. And as such, B too is *given* and *in itself*: it too has a specific determined "nature" and a fixed place in the Cosmos.

This is to say that B can stir up a new "non," that Negativity can be made concrete in and by a "non-B." This "non-B" will be "C," which will be able to engender a "non-C." And so on, indefinitely. Or more exactly, until the negation of some "N" leads us back to the point of departure: non-N = A. Then all one can do is go indefinitely around the circle which was just closed by that last *creative* negation.

In fact, the *real* (or active) Dialectic *stops* at the "N" of which the "non-N" is "A." This "N" is Totality in the proper and strong sense of the word: it is the integration of *all* that has been affirmed, negated, and reaffirmed, and of all that *can* be affirmed, negated, and reaffirmed: for to negate "N" is to affirm "A," which has already been affirmed, and so on. Now, "N" is Totality—that is, Being in and for itself—that is, real Being perfectly *self-conscious* or completely *revealed* to itself by a coherent Discourse (which is the absolute Science of the Wise Man). In order to negate itself really—that is, actively—total real Being would have to desire to be other than it is. But, being perfectly self-conscious, it knows that by negating itself such as it is, it can only become such as it has been (for non-N = A). But it has negated itself as it has been, and has finally become such as it is now. To want to negate it as it is now, therefore, is in the final analysis to want to make it such as it is now: in other words, it is not to want really to negate it.[12] Therefore "N" does not negate itself *really*, and never becomes "A" again by becoming "non-N."

But the will of total Being to *become again* that which it is is not absurd. And this will too is, if you please, *negating*: it is a

---

[12] We know that the *real* Dialectic (History) progresses by the negation which is implied by Man's Fighting and Work. Now, the *total* Reality (our "N") implies *satisfied* Man—that is, Man who no longer acts by *negation* of the given. Hence the definitive stopping of the *real* Dialectic.

will to *become again* what one is, in a different way from that way in which one *became* it. Now, every negation transforms the In-itself into For-itself, the unconscious into the conscious. The will in question, therefore, is simply the desire of the totality of the Real to understand itself in and by a coherent Discourse, and to understand itself in its real *becoming* by *reproducing* this becoming through Discourse or thought. From the *real* "N" one goes through negation (or the renunciation of *life* in favor of *knowledge*) to the *ideal* "non-N = A," and one reconstructs in thought the route which ended at "N," this final term too being here *ideal* (the "Idea" of the "Logik"). And this last negating action of real Being is incarnated in the will of the Wise Man to produce his Science.

However, the Wise Man's negation is ideal and not real. Therefore it creates no new *reality* and is content to reveal the Real in the totality of its becoming. The movement of Science, therefore, is dialectical only to the extent that it reproduces or describes the Dialectic of reality. And that is why this movement is not only circular, but also cyclical: coming to the ideal "N," one negates it ideally (this negation being the desire to rethink the Science or to reread the book which contains it) and thus one comes again to the initial "A," which forces one to go ahead until one comes again to "N." In other words, the Discourse of the Science which describes the whole of the real Dialectic can be repeated indefinitely, but it cannot be modified in any way whatsoever. And this is to say that this "dialectical" Discourse is the absolute Truth.

Concrete real Being is Totality. Hence it implies Identity and Negativity, but as "dialectically overcome" in and by Totality. Identity and Negativity do not exist really in an isolated state; just like Totality itself, they are only complementary *aspects* of one and the same real being. But in the discursive *description* of this concrete real being, its three aspects must be described *separately* and *one after another*. Thus, the correct description of the *three fold* dialectical Real is a "dialectical" discourse accomplished in *three phases*: the *Thesis* precedes the *Antithesis*, which is followed by the *Synthesis*; this latter is then presented as a new Thesis; and so on.

The Thesis describes the Real in its aspect of Identity. It reveals a being by taking it as *given*—that is, as a static being that remains what it is without ever truly becoming other.[13] The Antithesis, on the other hand, describes the aspect of Negativity in the real being. It reveals a (dialectical) being by taking it as the *act* of negating itself as it is given and of becoming *other*. If the Thesis describes the *being* (*Sein*) of the Real, the Antithesis describes its *action* (*Tun*); and also the *consciousness* which it has of itself and which is nothing but the doubling of the Real into a real that is *negated* in its given being (thus this being becomes "abstract notion" or "meaning") and a real that *negates* this given being by a spontaneous action. Finally, the Synthesis describes the being as Totality. It reveals a (dialectical) being by considering it as *resulting* from its action, by which it overcame itself as the *given* being, of which given being it became aware in and by that very overcoming. If in the Thesis the being *is* simply, in itself and for others, in the Antithesis it exists for itself as well, as a *given* which it is in the process of really or actively overcoming; and in the Synthesis it is in itself and for others as existing for itself (i.e., as self-conscious) and as resulting from its own negating action. If you please, the Thesis describes the *given* material to which the action is going to be applied, the Antithesis reveals this *action* itself as well as the thought which animates it (the "project"), while the Synthesis shows the result of that action—that is, the completed and objectively real *product* (*Werk*). This product *is*, just as the initial given is; however, it exists not as *given*, but as *created* by action that negates the given.

But the transformation of the *given* being into a product *created* by negating action is not accomplished all at once. Certain elements or aspects of the given material are preserved as they are in the product—that is, without active transformation that negates or creates. In certain of its aspects, in certain of its elements, the product too is a pure and simple *given*, liable to be actively negated and to serve as material for a new product. And that is why the Synthesis must describe the being not only as a *product* or a result

---

[13] Identical being can nonetheless *become* what it is. In other words, it can represent its eternal "nature" in the form of a temporal *evolution*: such as the egg which becomes a hen (which lays a new egg). But this evolution is always circular, or rather, cyclical. This is to say that one can always find a segment of the evolution that will remain *identical* to itself indefinitely (the evolution which goes from the egg to the new egg, for example).

of action, but also as a *given* that can provoke other negating actions—that is, as a being to be revealed in a (new) Thesis. That is, unless the being described in the Synthesis (which then would be the final Synthesis) is such that it no longer implies *givens* that can be transformed into *products* by negating *action.*

Hegel expresses the difference between "thetical" Being and the Real (Identity) and "synthetical" Being and the Real (Totality) by saying that the former are *immediate* (*unmittelbar*), whereas the latter are *mediated* (*vermittelt*) by "antithetical" action (Negativity) which negates them as "immediate." And one can say that the fundamental categories of *Immediacy* (*Unmittelbarkeit*) and *Mediation* (*Vermittlung*) sum up the whole real Dialectic which Hegel has in mind. The *immediate entity* (*das Unmittelbare*) is given static being (*Sein*), necessity (*Notwendigkeit*), fixed and stable continuity (*Bestehen*) which is deprived of all true action and of self-consciousness. The *mediated entity* (*das Vermittelte*), on the other hand, is action realized in a product, freedom, dialectical movement, and discursive understanding of itself and of its world. However, there are degrees of Immediacy and Mediation. Each progress in the real Dialectic represents a (partial) mediation of a (relative) immediacy, and this Dialectic stops when *everything* that is immediate (and can be mediated) actually is mediated by (conscious) negating action. And as for the "ideal" Dialectic of Science, it only describes this "movement" or this process of progressive mediation, starting from its beginning which is the absolute Immediate, and continuing until its end, which is the same Immediate completely mediated.

But one can say that the Hegelian Dialectic is entirely summed up by a single fundamental category, which is that of *dialectical Overcoming* (*Aufheben*). For what is to be "overcome" is precisely the Immediate, and the "overcoming" itself is Mediation through negating action which creates the Mediated, this latter being nothing but the Immediate taken, or posited, as dialectically "overcome." And of course, it is real Being itself that finally is entirely "overcome": the verbal "overcomings" of Science serve only to describe the real process of the active "overcoming" or Mediation of given Being or the Immediate by Action.[14]

[14] Hegel often speaks of "Negativity," but he rarely uses the terms "Identity" and "Totality." The expressions "Thesis," "Antithesis," "Synthesis" almost never

One can say that in the final analysis Hegel's philosophy has a dialectical character because it tries to give an account of the phenomenon of Freedom, or, what is the same thing, of Action in the proper sense of the term—that is, conscious and voluntary human action; or, and this is again the same thing, because it wants to give an account of History. In short, this philosophy is "dialectical" because it wants to give an account of the fact of *Man's* existence in the World, by revealing or describing Man as he is really—that is, in his irreducible specificity or as *essentially* different from all that is only Nature.

If freedom is something other than a dream or a subjective illusion, it must make its mark in objective reality (*Wirklichkeit*), and it can do this only by realizing itself as *action* that operates in and on the real. But if action is *free*, it must not be an automatic result, so to speak, of whatever the real given is; therefore it must be *independent* of this given, even while acting on the given and amalgamating with it to the extent that it realizes itself and thus itself becomes a given. Now, it is Hegel's merit to have understood that this union in independence and this independence in union occur only where there is *negation* of the given: Freedom = Action = Negativity. But if action is independent of the given real because it *negates* it, it creates, in realizing itself, something essentially *new* in relation to this given. Freedom *preserves* itself in the real, it *endures* really, only by perpetually creating new things from the given. Now, truly creative evolution, that is, the materialization of a future that is not a simple prolongation of the past through the present, is called History: Freedom = Negativity = Action = History. But what truly characterizes Man, what distinguishes him essentially from the animal, is precisely his *historicity*. To give an account of History, therefore, is to give an account of Man understood as a free and historical being. And one can give an account of Man thus understood only by taking

---

appear in his writings. The "dialectical" expressions he commonly uses are: "Immediacy," "Mediation," "Overcoming" (and their derivatives). Sometimes, Hegel expresses the dialectical structure of Being and the Real by saying that they are a "Syllogism" (*Schluss*, or *dialektischer Schluss*), in which the "middle term" (*Mitte*) mediates the two "extremes" (*Extreme*) of the Immediate and the Mediated. When Hegel wants to speak of the real dialectical process, he says simply: "movement" (*Bewegung*; very rarely: *dialektische Bewegung*).

account of the Negativity which he implies or realizes—that is, by describing the "dialectical movement" of his real existence, which is the movement of a being that continues to be itself and yet does not remain the same. And that is why the descriptions in Hegelian Science have a dialectical character.

To be sure, it is not only Hegel's Anthropology (set forth in the *Phenomenology*) which is dialectical (with regard to its content); his Ontology and his Metaphysics (set forth in the *Encyclopaedia*) are equally dialectical. But in order to discover the dialectical character of Being as such and of the Real in general, it was sufficient for Hegel to take the notion of the *concrete* seriously and to remember that philosophy must describe the *concrete* real instead of forming more or less arbitrary *abstractions*. For if Man and his historical World exist really and concretely, on an equal level with the natural World, the *concrete* Real and Being itself which actually *is* imply a human reality and hence Negativity in addition to the natural reality. And this is to say, as we know, that Being and the Real are dialectical.

On many occasions Hegel insisted on the fact that philosophy must be concerned with *concrete* reality; notably in the second explanatory Note of § 82 of the *Encyclopaedia* (Volume V, page 106, lines 9–15):

> This [positive or speculative] rational [i.e., Being as Totality], although it is a [rational which is] thought and abstract, is at the same time a *concrete-entity* (*ein Konkretes*). . . . Consequently, in general, philosophy has absolutely nothing to do with pure (*blossen*) abstractions or formal ideas (*Gedanken*); on the contrary, [it is concerned] only with concrete ideas [that is, with notions that correspond to the concrete reality].

Now Hegel does not merely say that his philosophy refers to the *concrete reality*. He also asserts that the philosophy which preceded him, and the vulgar sciences and "naive" man as well, are all concerned with *abstractions*. Now, the concrete real is dialectical. Abstractions are not. And that is why only Hegelian Science reveals or describes the real Dialectic.

To understand this assertion, which is at first glance paradoxical, let us take a simple example:

Let us consider a *real* table. This is not *Table* "in general," nor just *any* table, but always *this concrete* table right here. Now, when "naive" man or a representative of some science or other speaks of *this* table, he isolates it from the rest of the universe: he speaks of *this* table without speaking of what is not this table. Now, *this* table does not float in empty space. It is on *this* floor, in *this* room, in *this* house, in *this* place on Earth, which Earth is at a determined distance from the Sun, which has a determined place within the galaxy, etc., etc. To speak of this table without speaking of the rest, then, is *to abstract* from this rest, which in fact is just as real and concrete as this table itself. To speak of *this* table without speaking of the whole of the Universe which implies it, or likewise to speak of this Universe without speaking of *this* table which is implied in it, is therefore to speak of an *abstraction* and not of a *concrete reality*. And what is true in relation to space is also true in relation to time. *This* table has a determined "history" and not some other "history," nor a past "in general." It was made at a given moment with *this* wood, taken at a given moment from *this* tree, which grew at a given moment from *this* seed, etc., etc. In short, what exists as a *concrete reality* is the spatial-temporal *totality* of the natural world: everything that is *isolated* from it is by that very fact an *abstraction*, which exists as isolated only in and by the *thought* of the man who thinks about it.

All this is not new, for Parmenides was already aware of it. But there is another aspect of the question that Parmenides and all the pre-Hegelian philosophers forgot: *this* table (and even every *table*) implies and presupposes something real and concrete that is called a completed work. As soon as *this* table exists, then, to speak of the *concrete* Real is also to speak of Work. The *concrete*—that is, *total*—Real implies human work just as well as it implies this table, the wood from which it is made, and the natural world in general. Now the concrete Real which implies Work has precisely that threefold dialectical structure which is described by Hegelian Science. For the real Work implied in the Real really *transforms* this Real by actively negating it as given and preserving it as negated in the finished product, in which the given appears in a "sublimated" or "mediated" form. And this is to say that this concrete Real is precisely the real Dialectic or the "dialectical movement" which Hegel has in mind. And if the naive man, the vulgar scientist, or the pre-Hegelian philosopher can ignore this Dialectic, it is precisely because they are concerned not with the *concrete* Real, but with *abstractions*.

Now, to introduce Work into the Real is to introduce Negativity and hence Consciousness and Discourse that reveals the Real. In fact, *this* table is the table of which I am speaking at this moment, and my words are as much a part of this table as are its four legs or the room which surrounds it. One can, to be sure, *abstract* from these words and from many other things besides, as, for example, from so-called "secondary" qualities. But in doing this one must not forget that then one is no longer concerned with the concrete reality, but with an *abstraction*. The concrete Real implies *this* table, all the sensations which it has provoked, all the words which have been said about it, and so on. And *the* abstract Table is truly *this* table—i.e., a concrete reality—only in and by its inseparable union with these sensations, words, and so on, and in general with all that exists and has existed really. Once more, the *concrete* Real is nothing other than the spatial-temporal *Totality* of the real, this totality implying, in addition to Nature, the entirety of real actions and discourses—that is, History.

In the course of History, Man speaks of the Real and reveals it by the meaning of his discourses. Therefore the *concrete* Real is a Real revealed by Discourse. And that is what Hegel calls "Spirit" (*Geist*). Consequently, when he says (for example in the *Phenomenology*, page 24, line 11) that Nature is only an *abstraction* and that only Spirit is *real* or *concrete*, he is stating nothing paradoxical. He is simply saying that the concrete Real is the *totality* of the real from which nothing has been taken away by abstraction, and that this totality, as it exists really, implies that something which is call History. To describe the concrete Real, therefore, is to describe its *historical* becoming too. Now this becoming is precisely what Hegel calls "Dialectic" or "Movement." To say that the concrete Real is Spirit, then, is to assert that it has a dialectical character, and to say that it is a Real *revealed* by discourse, or Spirit.[15]

---

[15] Hegel's reasoning is certainly correct: if the real Totality implies Man, and if Man is dialectical, the Totality itself is dialectical. But as he goes on from there, Hegel commits, in my opinion, a grave error. From the fact that the real Totality is dialectical he concludes that its two fundamental constituent-elements, which

Like all genuine philosophy, Hegel's Science is developed on three superposed levels. First it describes the totality of real Being as it "appears" (*erscheint*) or shows itself to real Man who is a part of the Real, who lives, acts, thinks, and speaks in it. This description is made on the so-called "phenomenological" level: the *Phänomenologie* is the "Science of the appearances of Spirit"— that is, of the totality of real Being which is revealed to itself through the Discourse of Man, whom this Being implies (*Wissenschaft der Erscheinungen des Geistes* is the subtitle of the *Phenomenology*). But the philosopher is not content with this *phenomenological* description (which is *philosophical* because it refers to the *Concrete*—i.e., to the *totality* of the Real, in contradistinc-

---

are Nature and Man (= History), are dialectical. In doing this, he just follows the tradition of ontological monism which goes back to the Greeks: everything that *is*, is in one and the same manner. The Greeks, who philosophically discovered Nature, extended their "naturalistic" ontology, dominated by the single category of Identity, to Man. Hegel, who (in continuing the efforts of Descartes, Kant, and Fichte) discovered the "dialectical" ontological categories of Negativity and Totality by analyzing the human being (Man being understood in conformity with the Judaeo-Christian pre-philosophic tradition), extended his "anthropological" dialectical ontology to Nature. Now, this extension is in no wise justified (and it is not even discussed in Hegel). For if the final foundation of Nature is identical given static Being (*Sein*), one finds in it nothing comparable to the negating Action (*Tun*) which is the basis of specifically human or historical existence. The classic argument: everything that *is*, is in one and the same manner, should not have obliged Hegel to apply one and the same ontology (which, for him, is a dialectical ontology) to Man and Nature, for he himself says (in the *Phenomenology*) that "the true being of Man is his *action*." Now, Action (= Negativity) *acts* otherwise than Being (= Identity) *is*. And in any case there is an essential difference between Nature on the one hand, which is revealed only by Man's Discourse—i.e., by *another* reality than that which it is itself—and Man on the other hand, who *himself* reveals the reality which he is, as well as the (natural) reality which he is not. Therefore it seems necessary to distinguish, within the dialectical ontology of revealed Being or Spirit (dominated by Totality), a nondialectical ontology (of Greek and traditional inspiration) of Nature (dominated by Identity), and a dialectical ontology (of Hegelian inspiration, but modified accordingly) of Man or of History (dominated by Negativity). Hegel's monistic error has two serious consequences. On the one hand, using his single dialectical ontology as a basis, he tries to elaborate a dialectical metaphysic and a dialectical phenomenology of Nature, both clearly unacceptable, which should, according to him, replace "vulgar" science (ancient, Newtonian, and hence our own science too). On the other hand, by accepting the *dialecticity* of *everything* that exists, Hegel had to consider the *circularity* of knowledge as the only criterion for truth. Now we have seen that the circularity of knowledge relative to Man is possible only at the end of History; for as long as Man *changes* radically—that is, *creates* himself as *other* than he is—even his correct description

213

tion to "vulgar" descriptions that relate to *abstractions*). The philosopher also asks himself what the objective Reality (*Wirklichkeit*)—that is, the real (natural and human) World—must be in order that it "appear" in the way in which it actually does "appear" as "phenomenon." The answer to this question is given by the *Metaphysics*, which Hegel calls *Philosophie der Natur* and *Philosophie des Geistes* (*Geist* here being taken as meaning Man). Finally, going beyond this level of *metaphysical* description, the philosopher rises to the *ontological* level, in order to answer the question of knowing what Being itself, taken as *being*, must be, in order that it *realize* itself or *exist* as this natural and human World described in the Metaphysics, which *appears* as described in the

---

is but a partial or entirely provisional "truth." If, then, Nature, as well as Man, is creative or historical, truth and science properly so-called are possible only "at the end of time." Until then there is no genuine *knowledge* (*Wissen*), and one can only choose between *skepticism* (relativism, historicism, nihilism, and so on) and *faith* (*Glauben*).

But if one accepts that the traditional "identical" ontology actually does apply to Nature, a truth relative to Nature, and hence a science of nature, are in principle possible at any moment of time. And since Man is nothing but an active negation *of Nature*, a science of Man is also possible, to the extent that he belongs to the past and the present. Only Man's *future* would then be given over to skepticism or faith (that is, to the certainty of hope, in Saint Paul's expression): since it is a "dialectical"—i.e., creative or free—process, History is essentially unforeseeable, in contrast to "identical" Nature.

Moreover, it seems that an ontological dualism is indispensable to the explanation of the very phenomenon of History. As a matter of fact, History implies and presupposes an *understanding* of past generations by the generations of the present and future. Now if Nature, as well as Man, changed, Discourse could not be communicated throughout time. If stones and trees, and also the bodies and the animal "psychism" of the men of the time of Pericles, were as different from ours as the citizens of the ancient city are from us, we would be able to understand neither a Greek treatise on agriculture and architecture nor Thucydides' history, nor Plato's philosophy. Generally speaking, if we can understand any language which is not our own, it is only because it contains words that are related to realities that are everywhere and always *identical* to themselves: if we can know that "*Hund*" and "*canis*" mean "dog," it is because the real dog exists, which is the same in Germany and in France, in Rome in the time of Caesar and in contemporary Paris. Now these *identical* realities are precisely *natural* realities. An image can show that an attempt at a dualistic ontology is not absurd. Let us consider a gold ring. There is a hole, and this hole is just as essential to the ring as the gold is: without the gold, the "hole" (which, moreover, would not exist) would not be a ring; but without the hole the gold (which would nonetheless exist) would not be a ring either. But if one has found atoms in the gold, it is

Phenomenology. And this description of the structure of Being as such is made in the *Ontology*, which Hegel calls *Logik* (and which he presents before the Metaphysics, but after the Phenomenology).[16]

Now, (in the *Phenomenology*) Hegel described the *dialectical* character of "phenomenal" empirical-Existence (*Dasein*). And he can explain it only by supposing a dialectical structure of objective-Reality and of Being as such. Consequently, if the method of Hegelian philosophy is one of simple description, the content of this philosophy is dialectical not only in the "Phenomenology," but also in the "Metaphysics" and the "Ontology."

Up to now I have talked mostly about the Dialectic of Being and of the Real (which Hegel describes in the *Logik* and the *Encyclopaedia*). But I must also talk about the real Dialectic of empirical Existence, that is, of the "Phenomena" or the "appearances" (*Erscheinungen*) of dialectical Being in its reality. For if, objectively speaking, this "phenomenal" Dialectic is only the "appearance" of the "metaphysical" and "ontological" Dialectics of the Real and of Being, subjectively speaking, it is the only dialec-

---

not at all necessary to look for them in the hole. And nothing indicates that the gold and the hole *are* in one and the same manner (of course, what is involved is the hole as "hole," and not the air which is "in the hole"). The hole is a nothingness that subsists (as the presence of an absence) thanks to the gold which surrounds it. Likewise, Man who *is* Action could be a nothingness that "nihilates" in being, thanks to the being which it "negates." And there is no reason why the final principles of the description of the nihilation of Nothingness (or the annihilation of Being) have to be the same as the principles of the description of the being of Being.

The first attempt (a very insufficient one, by the way) at a *dualistic* ("identical" and "dialectical") ontology (or more exactly, metaphysic) was made by Kant, and it is in this that his unequaled greatness resides, a greatness comparable to that of Plato, who established the principles of "identical" (monistic) ontology. Since Kant, Heidegger seems to be the first to have posed the problem of a dual ontology. One does not get the impression that he has gone beyond the dualistic *phenomenology* which is found in the first volume of *Sein und Zeit* (which is only an introduction to the ontology that is to be set forth in Volume II, which has not yet appeared). But this is sufficient to make him recognized as a great philosopher. As for the dualistic ontology itself, it seems to be the principal philosophic task of the future. Almost nothing has yet been done.

[16] In the *dualistic* hypothesis, Ontology would describe *Being* that realizes itself as Nature separately from *Action* that negates Being and realizes itself (in Nature) as History.

tical given which can be described directly, and it is from it or from its description that one can describe or reconstruct the other two "basic" Dialectics.

But before indicating what the "phenomenological" Dialectic (described by the whole of the *Phenomenology*) is in Hegel, I must make a general remark.

What is dialectical, according to Hegel, is the concrete Real—that is, Totality or the total Synthesis, or, better, Spirit. In other words, it is not *given* Being (*Sein*) itself that has a dialectical structure, but *revealed* Being (*Begriff*). Now, revealed Being implies, on the ontological level, two constituent elements: Being as *revealed* (Identity, Thesis) and Being as *revealing* (Negativity, Antithesis). Consequently, on the metaphysical level, two Worlds must be distinguished, which are inseparable but essentially different: the natural World and the historical or human World. Finally, the phenomenological level is constituted by the reflection of *natural* empirical existence in *human* empirical existence (external Consciousness, *Bewusstsein*), which is in turn reflected in itself (Self-Consciousness, *Selbstbewusstsein*).

Now Hegel expressly says that Negativity is the specifically dialectical constituent element. Identity is not at all dialectical, and if Totality is dialectical, it is only because it implies Negativity. Moving from this ontological level to the metaphysical level, one would then have to say that the Real is dialectical only because the natural World implies a human World, Nature being not at all dialectical in itself. And concerning the "Phenomena," one would have to say that there is a phenomenal Dialectic because the Real "appears" *to Man*: only Man's "phenomenal" existence is dialectical in itself, and the natural "phenomena" are dialectical only to the extent that they are implied in the human "phenomenology" (as natural sciences, for example).

In the *Phenomenology* Hegel seems to accept this view. On several occasions he underlines the *essential* difference between Man and Animal, between History and Nature. And by so doing, he always calls attention to the dialectical character of the human and the nondialectical character of the natural. Thus, when (in Chapter VIII) he identifies Nature with Space and History (that is, Man) with Time, this means for him that Nature is dominated by Identity alone, whereas History implies Negativity and is consequently dialectical (Cf. for example the first paragraph of page 145; likewise page 563, lines 21–27).

But even in the *Phenomenology* Hegel's position lacks clarity. On the one hand, he opposes specifically human existence (*Bewusstsein* or *Geist* in the sense of "Man"), which is dialectical, to animal life (*Leben*), which is not. But on the other hand, he gives (in Chapter V, A, *a*) a vitalistic "phenomenological" description of Nature, which presents Nature as a dialectical "phenomenon." To be sure, there what is involved is a description of Nature by a certain type of "bourgeois" Intellectual, represented by Schelling. And Hegel does not completely identify himself with Schelling, in the sense that he considers Schelling's *Naturphilosophie* only a *phenomenological* description, whereas Schelling himself believed he had given a *metaphysics* of Nature. But Hegel believes that, as "phenomenon," Nature actually is as it "appeared" to Schelling, and he would like to replace the vulgar natural sciences with Schellingian vitalism. Now, from Hegel's pen, this vitalism takes on a clearly dialectical character.

In the *Encyclopaedia* this view is asserted without ambiguity. On the one hand, Hegel sets forth in it a metaphysics of Nature, in which Nature is described as a frankly dialectical reality having the same threefold structure as the human reality, which is described in the metaphysics of Man or of "Spirit." On the other hand, in the Ontology itself, that is, in the *Logik*, Hegel does not, so to speak, take account of the fact that the total Being or the "Idea" (= *Geist*) which he is describing presents on the one hand a dialectical aspect, which transmits its dialectical character to the totality of *Being*, but which is itself *Action* (*Tun*) and not Being (*Sein*), and on the other a fundamentally nondialectical aspect, which is static *given*-Being or *natural* Being.

All this, in my opinion, is an error on Hegel's part. Of course, I cannot make any sort of convincing critique of Hegelian philosophy here. But I should like to indicate that in my opinion the real (metaphysical) and "phenomenal" Dialectic *of Nature* exists only in Hegel's ("Schellingian") imagination.

In these conditions it would be difficult for me to sum up the Dialectic of *natural* "phenomena" which is found in the *Phenomenology* (Chapter V, A, *a*) and which, I confess, I understand very poorly. And I am not anxious, moreover, to propagate this error of Hegel's, which can only harm his philosophical authority and which could cast doubt on the value of Dialectic in general and particularly on the value of the Hegelian description of the "phenomenal" Dialectic of *human* existence. Now in my opinion, this description (contained in the *Phenomenology*) is Hegel's principal title to glory. Hence it is only of this description that I now wish to speak, by setting forth the phenomenological transposition of the metaphysical and ontological Dialectic which I have talked about up to now. To be sure, in order to know what the phenomenological Dialectic of *human* empirical existence is according to Hegel, one must read the whole *Phenomenology*, which is *entirely* devoted to its description.[17] But there are several very short passages in the *Phenomenology* which reveal the true significance of the Dialectic in question very well, and which show how the three fundamental dialectical categories of Ontology and Metaphysics "appear" to man on the phenomenological level as fundamental categories of the "Anthropology" in which human empirical existence is described.

I would now like to cite and interpret these passages.

Hegel sets forth the fundamental principles of his phenomenological anthropology by criticizing Gall's *Phrenology*—that is, in fact, all naturalistic anthropology which assimilates Man to animal because it sees no *essential* difference between them (Chapter V, A, *c*). It is against this static and monistic conception of Man that he opposes his dialectical and "threefold" conception.

He says the following (page 227, lines 28–30 and page 227, line 36–page 228, line 5):

> The [human] individual is in and for himself: he is *for himself*, that is, he is a free action (*Tun*); but he is also *in himself*, that is, he himself has a specifically determined *innate given-being* (*ursprüngliches bestimmtes Sein*) . . . This *given-being* [that is,] the *body* (*Leib*) of the specifically-determined individuality, is its *innateness* (*Ursprünglichkeit*), that which it itself has not done (*Nichtgetan-*

---

17 The (dialectical) phenomenology of Nature set forth in Chapter V, A, *a* can be considered as an element of the phenomenology of Man: it is the description of Man who (in certain social and historical conditions) devotes himself entirely to the observation (*Beobachtung*) of Nature and interprets it as vitalistic, in Schelling's way. Thus understood, the description of Chapter V, A, *a* remains valid.

haben). But given that at the same time the individual is only what he has done (*getan*), his body is also the expression (*Ausdruck*) of himself *produced* (*hervorgebrachte*) by himself; [his body] is at the same time a *sign* (*Zeichen*), which has not remained an immediate thing (*unmittelbare Sache*), but [which is something] by which the individual only makes known (*erkennen*) what he *is* in the sense that he puts his innate nature to work (*ins Werk richtet*).

To say that Man is, exists, and "appears" (*erscheint*) as being and existing "in and for himself" is to say that he is Being in and for itself—i.e., Totality or Synthesis; therefore, it is to say that he is a dialectical (or "spiritual") entity, that his real and "phenomenal" existence is a "movement." [18] Now every dialectical Totality is also, and above all, Identity—that is, Being in itself or Thesis. Ontologically speaking this Identity is *Sein*, given-Being; and metaphysically speaking, it is Nature. In Man who is in the process of "appearing," the aspect (*Seite*) or constituent-element (*Moment*) of Identity, *Sein*, or Nature, is his "body" (*Leib*) or his "innate nature" (*ursprüngliche Natur*) in general.

By the aspect of his *body*, Man is a natural being with fixed characteristics, a "specifically determined" animal which lives in the bosom of Nature, having its "natural place" (*topos*) in it. And it is immediately clear that dialectical anthropology leaves no place for an "afterlife" for Man outside of the natural World. Man is truly dialectical—that is, human—only to the extent that he is also Nature, "identical" spatial or material entity: he can become and be truly human only by being and remaining at the same time an animal, which like every animal is *annihilated* in death.

But in Man the Identity or the In-itself is not only his body in the strict sense: it is his "innateness" in general—that is, "That which he has not himself *done*." First of all, it is Man's "innate nature"—that is, everything that exists in him through biological heredity alone: his "character," his "talents," his "tastes," and so on. And it is also the simple fact of *being born* "slave" or "free" (*als Freier geboren*). For Hegel, this purely *innate* would-be "freedom" (as well as hereditary nobility and belonging to a "class" in gen-

---

[18] By accepting that only the human being is *dialectical* in the Hegelian sense of the term, one can say that Hegel's Dialectic is an *existential* dialectic in the modern sense of the word. In any case, this is what the Dialectic described in the *Phenomenology* is.

eral) is only a natural or animal characteristic, which has nothing to do with true human freedom, *actively acquired* by Fighting or Work: a man is free only when he himself has *made (getan)* himself free. But in Man this "identical" and "natural" That-which-he-has-not-himself-*made* is also everything that penetrates into him in a purely passive way, everything that he is and does "by habit" or "automatically," by tradition, by imitation, and so on—that is, by simple "inertia." If *per impossibile* Man stopped negating the given and negating himself as given or innate—that is, stopped creating new things and creating himself as "new man"—and were content to maintain himself in identity to himself and to preserve the place he already occupied in the Cosmos (or in other words, if he stopped living in relation to the future or to the "project" and allowed himself to be dominated exclusively by the past or by "memory"), he would cease to be truly human; he would be an animal, perhaps a "knowing" and surely a very "complicated" animal, very different from all other natural beings, but not essentially "something other" than they. And, consequently, he would not be "dialectical." [19]

Man is "total" or "synthetical," or, better, "dialectical"; he exists "for himself" or consciously and articulately, hence he is "spiritual" or truly human, only to the extent that he implies the constituent-element of Negativity in his being, in his existence, and

[19] I said: *"per impossibile,"* because according to Hegel Man always negates the given sooner or later, as long as he has not realized the total Synthesis which "appears" as his definitive "satisfaction" *(Befriedigung)*. Personally, I accept the possibility of a stopping along the way. But I think that in this case Man would actually cease to be human. Hegel accepts the final stopping of the historical "movement": after the end of History Man no longer negates, properly speaking (that is, *actively*). However Man does not become an animal, since he continues to speak (negation passes into the "dialectical" *thought* of the Wise Man). But post-historical Man, omniscient, all-powerful, and satisfied Man (the Wise Man) is not a Man in the strict sense of the word either: he is a "god" (a mortal god, admittedly). All education implies a long series of *auto-negations* effected by the child: the parents only encourage him to negate certain aspects of his innate animal nature, but he is the one who must actually do so. (The puppy need only refrain from doing certain things; the child must in addition *be ashamed* to do them; and so on.) And it is only because of these *auto*-negations ("repressions") that every "educated" child is not only a trained animal (which is "identical" to itself and in itself), but a truly human (or "complex") being: although, in most cases, he is human only to a very small extent, since "education" (that is, auto-negations) generally stops too soon.

in his "appearances." Taken in itself, Negativity is pure nothingness: it *is* not, it does not exist, it does not appear. It *is* only as *negation of Identity*—that is, as Difference.[20] Therefore it can *exist* only as a real negation *of Nature*. Now this existence of Negativity is, precisely, specifically human existence, and we see why Man is reduced to nothingness when he dies as animal—that is, when he puts himself so to speak outside of Nature and hence can no longer negate it *really*. But as long as Negativity *exists* in the form of a real negation of the identical natural given, it also *appears*, and its "appearance" is nothing other than the "free action" (*freies Tun*) of Man, as Hegel says in the passage cited above. On the "phenomenal" (human) level, therefore, Negativity is real *freedom* which realizes itself and manifests or reveals itself as *action*.

In the passage cited above Hegel also says that "the [human] individual *is* only what he has *done* (*getan hat*)."

And further on he says (page 236, lines 25–26 and 28–31):

> The *true being* (*Sein*) of Man is in fact (*vielmehr*) *his action or act* (*Tat*); it is in it that Individuality is *objectively real* (*wirklich*) . . . Individuality presents itself [or manifests itself, or appears] (*stellt sich dar*) in effective-action (*Handlung*) as the *negative-or-negating* essential-reality (*Wesen*), which *is* only to the extent that it dialectically-overcomes (*aufhebt*) given-Being (*Sein*).

If *given-Being* (*Sein*) corresponds on the ontological level to Nature, *Act* (*Tat*) is what represents Man as Man on this level. Man as Man is not given Being, but creative Action. If the "objective reality" of Nature is its real *existence*, that of Man properly so-called is his effective *action*. The animal only *lives*; but living Man *acts*, and it is through his effective activity (*Handeln*) that he "manifests" his humanity and "appears" as truly human being. To be sure, Man is also given-Being and Nature: he also exists "in himself," as animals and things exist. But it is only in and by Action that he *is* specifically human, and that he *exists* and *appears* as such—that is, as Being-for-itself or as a self-conscious being that

[20] Parmenides was right in saying that Being *is* and that Nothingness *is not*; but he forgot to add that *there is* a "difference" between Nothingness and Being, a difference which to a certain extent *is* as much as Being itself *is*, since without it, if there were no *difference* between Being and Nothingness, Being itself would not be.

speaks of itself and of what it is not: "he is *for himself*, that is, he is a free action." And by acting, he realizes and manifests Negativity or his Difference from natural given Being.

On the "phenomenological" level, then, Negativity is nothing other than human *Freedom*—that is, that by which Man differs from animal.[21] But if Freedom is ontologically Negativity, it is because Freedom can *be* and *exist* only as *negation*. Now in order to negate, there must be something to negate: an existing *given* and hence an identical given-Being. And that is why man can exist freely—that is, humanly—only while living as an animal in a given natural World. But he lives *humanly* in it only to the extent that he *negates* this natural or animal given. Now negation is *realized* as accomplished *action*, and not as thought or simple desire. Hence it is neither in his more or less "elevated" "ideas" (or his imagination), nor by his more or less "sublime" or "sublimated" "aspirations" that Man is truly free or really human, but only in and by effective—i.e., active—negation of the given real. Freedom does not consist in a *choice* between two *givens*: it is the *negation* of the given, both of the given which one is oneself (as animal or as "incarnated tradition") and of the given which one is not (the natural and social *World*). Moreover, these two negations are in reality only one. To negate the natural or social World dialectically—that is, to negate it while preserving it—is to transform it; and then one must either change oneself to adapt to it, or perish. Inversely, to negate oneself while maintaining oneself in existence is to change the aspect of the World, since this World then implies a modified constituent-element. Thus, Man exists humanly only to the extent that he really transforms the natural and social World by his negating action and he himself changes because of this transformation; or, what is the same thing, to the extent that he transforms the World as a result of an active auto-negation of his animal or social "innate nature."

The freedom which is realized and manifested as dialectical or *negating* Action is thereby essentially a *creation*. For to negate the given without ending in nothingness is to produce something that did not yet exist; now, this is precisely what is called "creating."

[21] Cf. Rousseau: "Therefore it is not so much understanding which constitutes the distinction of man among the animals as it is his being a free agent." (*Discourse on the Origin of Inequality*, translation by R. Masters; New York, 1964, page 114.)

Inversely, one can truly create only by *negating* the given real. For this real is somehow omnipresent and dense, since there is nothing (nothing but Nothingness) outside of it or other than it; hence there is, so to speak, no place for newness in the World; rising up from Nothingness, newness can penetrate into Being and exist only by taking the place of given-Being—that is, by negating it.

In the dialectical interpretation of Man—i.e., of Freedom or Action—the terms "negation" and "creation" must, moreover, be taken in the full sense. What is involved is not replacing one given by another *given*, but overcoming the given in favor of what does not (yet) *exist*, thus realizing what was never *given*. This is to say that Man does not change himself and transform the World for himself in order to realize a conformity to an "ideal" *given* to him (imposed by God, or simply "innate"). He creates and creates himself because he negates and negates himself "without a preconceived idea": he becomes other solely because he no longer wants to be the same. And it is only because he no longer wants to be *what he is* that what he will be or will be able to be is an "ideal" for him, "justifying" his negating or creative action—i.e., his change—by giving it a "meaning." Generally speaking, Negation, Freedom, and Action do not arise from thought, nor from consciousness of self or of external things; on the contrary, thought and consciousness arise from Negativity which realizes itself and "reveals" itself (through thought in Consciousness) as effective free action.

In fine, Negativity (or Freedom) which realizes and manifests itself as creative Action is Man who, while living in the natural World, continues to be himself and yet is not always (or "necessarily") the same. Hence we can say that dialectical Anthropology is the philosophic science of Man as he appears in the (pre-philosophic) Judaeo-Christian conception—that is, of Man who is supposed to be able to *convert himself*, in the full sense of the word, or to become essentially and radically *other*. According to this conception, Man who was created perfect can nevertheless radically pervert this innate or given nature; but essentially perverted Man can repudiate the "old Adam" and thus become the "new Adam," different from the first but still more perfect than he; Man can "overcome" the hereditary sin which nonetheless determines his nature and thus become a saint, who is nonetheless something other than Man before the fall; a pagan whose "natural place" is Hell can "convert himself" to Christianity and thus win his way to Heaven; etc., etc. Now in the Hegelian or dialectical conception of Man, things work out in exactly the same way: the steps of the Dialectic described in the *Phenomenology* are nothing but a series of successive "conversions" that Man carries out in the course of history and that are described by the Wise Man who lives at the end of history and who is himself "converted" to the absolute truth (incarnated in the Napoleonic Empire).

In agreement with Aristotle, Hegel accepts a radical difference between Master and Slave. According to Hegel, Man can appear in Nature or create himself as Man from the animal that he was, only if a Fight to the death for the sake of Recognition (*Anerkennen*) leads to a relation between a free man and a man who is enslaved to him. Hence, from the beginning, Man is necessarily either Master or Slave. And this is what Aristotle said. But according to Aristotle (who did not see the dialecticity of human existence), this will always be the case: Man is *born* with a slavish or free "nature," and he will *never* be able to overcome or modify it; Masters and Slaves form something like two distinct animal "species," irreducible or "eternal," neither of which can leave its "natural place" in the immutable Cosmos. According to Hegel, on the other hand, the radical difference between Master and Slave exists only *at the beginning*, and it can be overcome in the course of time; because for him, Mastery and Slavery are not *given* or *innate* characteristics. In the beginning at least, Man is not *born* slave or free, but *creates* himself as one or the other through free or voluntary Action. The Master is the one who went all the way in the Fight, being ready to die if he was not recognized; whereas the Slave was afraid of death and voluntarily submitted, by recognizing the Master without being recognized by him. But it was one and the same innate animal nature that was transformed by the free Action of the Fight into slavish or free human "nature": the Master could have created himself as Slave, and the Slave as Master. There was no "reason" for one of the two animals (of the species *Homo sapiens*) to become Master rather than Slave. Mastery and Slavery have no "cause"; they are not "determined" by any *given*; they cannot be "deduced" or foreseen from the past which pre-

The Dialectic of the Real and the Phenomenological Method in Hegel

ceded them: they result from a *free* Act (*Tat*). That is why Man can "overcome" his slavish "nature" and *become* free, or better, (freely) *create himself* as free; even if he is born in Slavery, he can negate his innate slavish "nature." And all of History—that is, the whole "movement" of human existence in the natural World— is nothing but the progressive negation of Slavery by the Slave, the series of his successive "conversions" to Freedom (which, how- ever, will not be the "identical" or "thetical" freedom of the Mas- ter, who is free only *in himself*, but the "total" or "synthetical" freedom, which also exists *for itself*, of the Citizen of the universal and homogeneous State).[22]

If Negativity is Freedom which realizes itself as Action negating the given, and if it is the very humanity of Man, Negativity and Man can "appear" for the first time in Nature only as a being that negates or "overcomes" its innate animal nature: Man creates his humanity only by negating himself as animal. And that is why the first "appearance" of Negativity is described in the *Phenome- nology* (Chapter IV) as a Fight to the death for Recognition, or more exactly, as the Risk of life (*Wagen des Lebens*) which this Fight implies. The Desire for Recognition which provokes the Fight is the desire for a desire—that is, for something that does not *exist* really (since Desire is the "manifest" presence of the *absence* of a reality): to want to be "recognized" is to want to be accepted as a positive "value"—that is, precisely speaking, to cause oneself to be "desired." To want to risk one's *life*, which is the *whole* reality of a living being, in favor of something that does not *exist* and cannot exist as inert or merely living real *things* exist—this, then, is indeed to *negate* the given which one is oneself, this is to be *free* or *independent* of it. Now, to negate oneself, in this full sense, and nevertheless to preserve oneself in existence, is indeed

[22] In truth, only the Slave "overcomes" his "nature" and finally becomes Citizen. The Master does not change: he dies rather than cease to be Master. The final fight, which transforms the Slave into Citizen, overcomes Mastery in a *nondialectical* fashion: the Master is simply killed, and he dies as Master. Hence it is only in its slavish aspect that human existence is dialectical or "total": the Master represents, fundamentally, only Identity (human Identity, admittedly). Therefore one can say that Aristotle correctly described the Master. He erred only in believing that the Master is Man in general—that is, in denying the humanity of the Slave. He was right in saying that the Slave as Slave *is* not truly human; but he was wrong in believing that the Slave could not *become* human.

225

to *create* oneself as new and therefore to exist as created by oneself —that is, as free or autonomous.

It is this risk of life, incurred in a fight for pure prestige—i.e., in a fight absolutely without any *raison d'etre*, any "vital interest"— it is this risk of the life in which the living being integrates the totality of the given (and which is also the supreme natural or biological "value"), I say, which is creative or free negating Action, which realizes and "manifests" Negativity or Freedom, and hence Man. Man realizes (= creates) and "manifests" his humanity (= freedom) by risking his life, or at least by being able and willing to risk it, solely "for glory" or for the sake of his "vanity" alone (which by this risk, ceases to be "vain" or "nonexistent" and becomes the specifically human value of *honor*, fully as real as animal "values" but essentially different from them); or, what is the same thing, by risking his life for the sake of "duty" alone (which is *Ought-to-be* precisely because it is not given-*Being*, and which consequently *exists* only as *recognized*, this recognition presupposing and implying, or requiring, the risk of life).[23] No animal commits suicide out of simple shame or pure vanity (as Kirilov would have it in Dostoievsky's *The Possessed*); no animal risks its life to capture or recapture a flag, to win officer's stripes, or to be decorated; animals never have bloody fights for pure prestige, for

---

[23] One acts only according to the duty which one *recognizes*. But it is always supposed that the duty which one recognizes oneself ought to be recognized by the others, who by definition ought also to recognize the value of him who acts in conformity to this duty. To want to act according to duty is in fact, therefore, to want to be "recognized." But it is possible not to be aware of this; one can *think* of duty without *thinking* of "recognition." Often the being which is supposed to "recognize" the man who acts "through duty" is God. Thus, while acting, one can *believe* that one wants to be "recognized" by God alone. But in fact "God" is only the "social milieu" substantialized and projected into the beyond. It sometimes *seems* that one does one's duty only in order not to fall in one's own esteem. But this too is only an illusion. In this case there is a division of individuality into its two components: the one which acts represents the Particularity of the agent; the one which judges him "morally" represents his Universality—that is, the *social* aspect of his existence; the man judges his own "particular" actions in terms of the "universal" values accepted by the society of which he is a part. To be sure, it is possible not to recognize the "accepted" values. But if one takes one's "nonconformity" seriously—that is, if one *realizes* it through action—one transforms or wants to transform the given society in precisely such a way as to make it accept the values in the name of which one is acting. Here again, therefore, one acts, in fact, because of the desire for "recognition"; but one is not always aware of it.

which the only reward is the resulting glory and which can be explained neither by the instinct of preservation (defense of life or search for food) nor by that of reproduction; no animal has ever fought a duel to pay back an insult that harmed none of its vital interests, just as no female has died "defending her honor" against a male. Therefore it is by negating acts of this kind that Man realizes and manifests his freedom—that is, the humanity which distinguishes him from the animals.

But Fighting and Risk are not the only "appearance" of Negativity or of Freedom—that is, of Humanity—in the natural World: Work is another. No animal works, strictly speaking, for it never transforms the world in which it lives according to projects that cannot be explained by the given conditions of its real existence in this world. A land animal never constructs machines to allow it to live in an element other than its natural one: under water, for example, or in the air. Now, Man by his work has constructed the submarine and the airplane. Actually, Work essentially transforms the given natural World and removes the worker from his "natural place" in this World, and thus essentially changes him too, only to the extent that the action in question is truly negating—that is, to the extent that it does not come from some "instinct" or from a given or innate tendency, but negates a hereditary instinct and overcomes innate "nature," which then "manifests" itself as "laziness" that opposes the action. An animal at liberty is never lazy, for if it were, it would die of hunger or not propagate. Man can be lazy only *at work*, precisely because work, properly so-called, corresponds to no *vital* necessity.

Since it is a realization and a "manifestation" of Negativity, Work is always a "forced" work. Man must force himself to work, he must do violence to his "nature." And, at least at the beginning, it is *another* who forces him to it and thus does him violence. In the Bible it was God who imposed Work on fallen man (but that was just a "necessary" consequence of the fall, which was "free"; here too, then, work is the consequence of a free act, the manifestation of the negating action by which Man negated his innate "perfect" nature). In Hegel, Work "appears" for the first time in Nature in the form of slavish work imposed by the first Master on his first Slave (who submitted to him, moreover, voluntarily, since he could have escaped from slavery and work by accepting death in combat or by killing himself after his defeat). The Master makes the Slave work in order, by the Slave's work, to satisfy his own desires, which as such are "natural" or animal desires (in satisfying them the Master differs from an animal only in that he satisfies them without effort, the necessary effort being supplied by the Slave; thus, unlike an animal, the Master can live a life of "enjoyment"). But, to satisfy those desires of the Master, the Slave had to repress his own instincts (to prepare food that he will not eat, even though he desires to eat it, and so on), he had to do violence to his "nature," hence to negate or "overcome" himself as *given*—that is, as animal. Consequently, as an auto-negating Act, Work is an auto-creative act: it realizes and manifests Freedom— that is, autonomy toward the given in general and the given which one is oneself; it creates and manifests the humanity of the worker. In and by Work, Man negates himself as animal, just as he does in and by Fighting. That is why the working Slave can essentially transform the natural World in which he lives, by creating in it a specifically human technical World. He works according to a "project" which does not necessarily result from his own innate "nature"; he realizes through work something that does not (yet) *exist* in him, and that is why he can create things that exist nowhere else but in the World produced by his work: artifacts or works of art—that is, things that Nature never produces.

The "manufactured objects" created by the active auto-negations of the working Slave enter into the natural World and hence transform it *really*. In order to preserve himself in the reality of this transformed (= humanized) World, the Slave himself must change. But since *he* is the one who transformed the given World by working in it, the change which he seems to *undergo* in consequence is in fact an *auto-creation*: it is he who changes himself, who *creates* himself as other than he was *given* to himself. And that is why Work can raise him up from Slavery to Freedom (which will, however, be different from the freedom of the idle Master).

Thus, in spite of appearances, the Slave works *for himself* (also). To be sure, the Master profits from his work. Having negated his animal nature by the Risk accepted in the Fight for Recognition, the Master realized his humanity. He can therefore, like a Man— as opposed to an animal—assimilate the specifically human products of the Slave's work, although he did not "order" them: he is capable of using the artifacts and enjoying the works of art, although at the start he did not "desire" them. And that is why he too changes with the modifications which the Slave's Work brings to the given World. But since he himself does not work, he is not the one who produces these changes outside of himself and hence in himself. The Master evolves because he consumes the products of the Slave's work. But the Slave supplies him with something more than and different from what he desired and ordered, and hence he consumes this surplus (a truly human, "nonnatural" surplus) involuntarily, as if forced: he undergoes a sort of training (or education) by the Slave, if he must do violence to his nature in order to consume what the Slave offers him. Hence he undergoes History, but does not create it: if he "evolves," he evolves only passively, as Nature or an animal species does. The Slave, on the other hand, evolves humanly—that is, voluntarily and consciously, or, better, actively or freely (by negating himself with knowledge of what he is doing). By negating his own given nature through Work, he raises himself above his given nature and is in a (negating) *relation* to it. This is to say that he becomes self-conscious, and thereby conscious of what is not self. The entities which he *creates* by work and which consequently have no *natural* reality reflect themselves in him as *ideal* entities—that is, as "ideas," which appear to him as "models" or "projects" for the works which he executes.[24] Man who works *thinks* and *talks* about what he is work-

---

[24] An idea (*Gedanke*) is born from Desire—that is, from not yet realized negation of the given. Only the Action of Work realizes this negation. Hence one can say that Work is carried out according to a preconceived Idea or Project: the real is transformed according to the ideal. But the Idea is *a priori* only with respect to actual and accomplished Work, and not with respect to the Man who works: it is not an "innate" or "Platonic" Idea. Man *creates* the Idea by ideally creating the (natural or social) given, and he *realizes* the Idea by actually inserting it into the given through Work which really transforms this given according to the Idea. The evolution of means of transportation, for example, was not carried out according to the "idea" or the "ideal" of the automobile, an "idea" that would be given beforehand and would be more and more closely approximated by succeeding efforts. Man began having himself carried by other men or by animals solely because he no longer wanted to walk "naturally"—that is, on foot. And it was by successively *negating* the various means of transportation which were at first *given* to him that he finally produced the automobile, which is a genuine creation, not only as material object, but also as "idea," which has not "preexisted from all eternity" either in man or anywhere else.

ing on (just as he thinks and talks about Nature as the "raw material" for his works); and it is only by thinking and speaking that Man can truly *work*. Thus, the working Slave is conscious of what he is doing and of what he has done: he *understands* the World which he has transformed, and he *becomes aware* of the necessity of changing himself in order to adapt to it; hence he *wants* to "keep up with progress," the progress which he himself realizes and which he reveals through his discourse.[25]

Work, therefore, is the authentic "appearance" of Negativity or Freedom, for Work is what makes Man a dialectical being, which does not eternally remain the same, but unceasingly becomes other than it is really in the given and as given. The Fight, and the Master who incarnates it, are only the catalysts, so to speak, of History or of the dialectical "movement" of human existence: they engender this movement, but are not affected by it themselves. All (true) Masters are of equal worth as Masters, and none of them has by himself (to the extent that he is a Master) overcome his

[25] If he is truly self-conscious, Man who has created a technical World *knows* that he can live in it only by living in it (also) as a worker. That is why Man can *want* to continue working even after ceasing to be a Slave: he can become a free Worker. Actually, Work is born from the Desire for Recognition (by the intermediary of the Fight), and it preserves itself and evolves in relation to this same Desire. To realize a technical progress, humanity must work more or better—that is, it must supply an increase of effort "against nature." To be sure, there have always been men who knew that they worked "for glory." (By itself, the desire to know the given leads to scientific "observation" of it, but not to its transformation by Work; not even to "experimental" intervention, as the example of the Greeks shows.) But most people think that they work more in order to gain more money or to augment their "well-being." However, it is easy to see that the surplus gained is absorbed by expenses of pure prestige and that the supposed "well-being" consists mostly in living better than one's neighbor or no worse than the others. Thus, the surplus of work and hence technical progress are in reality a function of the desire for "recognition." To be sure, the "poor" profit from technical progress. But they are not the ones who create it, nor do their needs or desires. Progress is realized, started, and stimulated by the "rich" or the "powerful" (even in the socialist State). And these men are "materially" satisfied. Therefore, they act only according to the desire to increase their "prestige" or their power, or, if you please, from duty. (Duty is something quite different from the love of one's neighbor or "charity," which has never engendered a technical progress nor, consequently, really overcome misery. This is precisely because "charity" is not a negating action, but the instinctive outpouring of an innate "charitable nature," a nature in fact perfectly compatible with the "imperfections" of the given World which nonetheless cause it to "suffer." Kant refused to see a "virtue"—i.e., a specifically human manifestation—in an action that results from an "instinctive inclination," a *Neigung*.)

Master's nature so as to become something other than he is (since he could only have become a Slave); if the Masters have evolved, their evolution has only been purely external or "material," and not truly human—that is, willed; and the human content of the Fight—that is, the Risk of Life—has not changed through the ages, in spite of the fact that more or less slavish workers have supplied the combatants with ever new types of weapons of war. Only the Slave can *want* to cease to be what he is (i.e., Slave), and if he "overcomes" himself through Work, which can vary indefinitely, he always becomes other, until he becomes truly free—that is, fully satisfied by what he is. Therefore it can be said that Negativity "manifests" itself as Fighting only so that it can "appear" as Work (which otherwise could not have been engendered). At the end, to be sure, in order definitively to free himself or to become truly *other*, the working Slave or ex-Slave must again take up the Fight for prestige against the Master or ex-Master: for there will always be a remnant of Slavery in the Worker as long as there is a remnant of idle Mastery on earth. But this last transformation or "conversion" of Man takes the form of a Fight to the death only because the idle Master is uneducable, since the peaceful educative-transformation (*Bildung*) of Man is accomplished only by Work. The Slave is obliged to overcome Mastery by a nondialectical overcoming of the Master who obstinately persists in his (human) identity to himself—that is, by annulling him or putting him to death. And this annulling is what is manifested in and by the final Fight for Recognition, which necessarily implies the Risk of life on the part of the freed Slave. This Risk, moreover, is what completes the liberation which was begun by his Work, by introducing in him the constituent-element (*Moment*) of Mastery which he lacked. It is in and by the final Fight, in which the working ex-Slave acts as combatant for the sake of glory alone, that the free Citizen of the universal and homogeneous State is created; being both Master and Slave, he is no longer either the one or the other, but is the unique "synthetical" or "total" Man, in whom the thesis of Mastery and the antithesis of Slavery are dialectically "overcome"—that is, *annulled* in their one-sided or imperfect aspect, but *preserved* in their essential or truly human aspect, and therefore *sublimated* in their essence and in their being.

Therefore, to say that Man is dialectical and "appears" as such is to say that he is a being that continues to be itself without remaining the same, because, through Fighting and Work, he *negates* himself as *given*—that is, either as animal or as man born in a certain social or historical milieu and *determined* by it—but also preserves himself in existence or, if you please, in human identity to himself, in spite of these auto-negations. This, then, is to say that Man is neither Identity nor Negativity alone, but Totality or Synthesis; that he "overcomes" himself while preserving and sublimating himself; or that he "mediates" himself in and by his very existence. Now, to say this is to say that he is an essentially *historical* being.

If Identity or Being-in-itself is "manifested" in Man as his *Animality* in the broad sense—that is, as everything in him that is given or innate, or better, inherited; if Negativity or Being-for-itself "appears" in the World as human *Freedom*, which realizes itself as the negating Action of Fighting and Work; Totality or Being-in-and-for-itself "reveals" itself on the human "phenomenal" level as *Historicity*. Indeed, Man who fights and works, thus negating himself as animal, is an essentially historical being, and only he is such a one: Nature and the animal have no history properly so-called.[26]

For History to exist, there must be not only a given reality, but also a negation of that reality and at the same time a ("sublimated") preservation of what has been negated. For only then is evolution *creative*; only then do a true *continuity* and a real *progress* exist in it. And this is precisely what distinguishes human History from a simple biological or "natural" evolution. Now, to preserve oneself as negated is to *remember* what one has been even while one is becoming radically other. It is by historical memory that Man's *identity* preserves itself throughout History, in spite of the *auto-negations* which are accomplished in it, so that he can realize himself by means of History as the integration of his contradictory past or as *totality*, or, better, as dialectical entity. Hence history is always a conscious and willed *tradition*, and all real history also manifests itself as a historiography: there is no History without conscious, lived historical memory.

It is by memory (*Er-innerung*) that Man "internalizes" his past

[26] In the *Phenomenology*, Hegel *opposes* History to Nature (Cf. page 563, lines 21–27).

by making it truly his own, by preserving it in himself, and by really inserting it into his present existence, which at the same time is an active and actual radical negation of this preserved past. Thanks to memory, the man who "converts himself" can remain "the same" man, whereas an animal species that is converted by "mutation" into another has nothing more to do with that species from which it emerged. And memory is what makes Man's auto-negation *concrete*, by making a new *reality* from that negation. For by remembering the given which he was and which he negated, Man remains "specifically determined" (*bestimmt*) by the concrete characteristics of this given, while nonetheless being free with respect to it because he has *negated* it. It is only thus that Man becomes *specifically* other through his auto-negation and preserves himself as real and, consequently, *concrete*: an *other* man in a *new* World, but always a *man* with specific and specifically human characteristics, living in a *human* World which is always a specifically organized historical *World*. Therefore it is by History which is created, lived, and really remembered as "tradition" that Man *realizes* himself or "appears" as dialectical totality, instead of *annihilating himself* and "disappearing" by a "pure" or "abstract" negation of every given whatsoever, real or thought.[27]

Total or dialectical Man—that is, real or concrete Man—is not only *negating* Action: he is a *creative* Action that has been accomplished—that is, a *product* (*Werk*)—in which the negated given is preserved, as the raw material is preserved in the finished product. And that is why Hegel said, at the end of the passage of the *Phenomenology* that I have cited, that Man exists humanly only to the extent that he "puts his innate nature to work" (*ins Werk*

[27] It is in the lack of historical memory (or understanding) that the mortal danger of Nihilism or Skepticism resides, which would negate everything without preserving anything, even in the form of memory. A society that spends its time listening to the radically "nonconformist" Intellectual, who amuses himself by (verbally!) negating any given at all (even the "sublimated" given preserved in historical remembrance) solely because it is a given, ends up sinking into inactive anarchy and disappearing. Likewise, the Revolutionary who dreams of a "permanent revolution" that negates every type of tradition and takes no account of the concrete past, except to overcome it, necessarily ends up either in the nothingness of social anarchy or in annulling himself physically or politically. Only the Revolutionary who manages to maintain or reestablish the historical tradition, by preserving in a positive memory the given present which he himself has relegated to the past by his negation, succeeds in creating a new historical *World* capable of *existing*.

richet). Man "did not remain an immediate thing" (*unmittelbare Sache*), Hegel says in that passage, because "he *is* only what he has *done*" (*getan*)—that is, because he *acted* by *negating* himself as given. But he is a concrete *reality*, which "appears" or "makes itself known" (*erkennen lässt*) through a "sign" (*Zeichen*), because he is a product (*Werk*) produced with the given, in which what is negated, consequently, was *preserved*. Now, this preservation of what is negated in Man is accomplished in and by the remembrance of the very one who negated it. And that is why Man is a dialectical human *reality* only to the extent that he is *historical*, and he is historical only by *remembering* his past which he has surpassed.

In short, to describe Man as a *dialectical* entity is to describe him as a negating *Action* that negates the given within which it is born, and as a *Product* created by that very negation, on the basis of the given which was negated. And on the "phenomenological" level this means that human existence "appears" in the World as a continuous series of *fights* and *works* integrated by *memory*—that is, as *History* in the course of which Man *freely* creates himself.

Thus Hegelian Dialectic gives a philosophic account of the two fundamental categories implied in pre-philosophic Judaeo-Christian anthropology, which, when secularized, became modern anthropology: namely, the categories of Freedom and Historicity. This Dialectic also permits us to understand why these two categories are in fact inseparable. It is obvious, indeed, that there is History—i.e., creative or unforeseeable evolution—only where there are free agents; and that Freedom is *realized* only by the creation of a specifically human, i.e. historical, World. Now, Dialectic shows us that Negativity (= Freedom) differs from Nothingness only to the extent that it is inserted into Totality (= historical synthesis, in which the future is incorporated in the present through the intermediary of the past), and that the real is Totality, instead of pure Identity, only to the extent that it implies its own negation (which, precisely, frees it from itself taken as given). History is what it is—that is, Totality or Synthesis, or, better, creative evolution or progress, and not a pure and simple tautology or an "eternal return"—because it is the unity of *essentially* different constituent elements—i.e., elements created *by negation* of the elements which preceded them and hence independent with respect to them, or free.

Now, Judaeo-Christian and modern anthropology (more or less explicitly) implies a third fundamental category, inseparable from the other two, which is the category of *Individuality*: in this anthropology Man is a *historical free Individual*. And Hegel's philosophic anthropology accepts this conception of Man. Thus, in the passages cited, there was always a concern for the Individual, for human Individuality.

In contradistinction to an animal, a plant, or an inanimate thing, a human being is not only a simple "exemplar" or just another representative of a natural "species," interchangeable with the other representatives. (And Hegel often insists on the fact that the French expression *"une espèce de . . . ,"* applied to a man, has a pejorative sense.) A man is supposed to be "the only one of his kind," by being essentially different from all other men. And at the same time he is supposed to have, in his irreplaceable uniqueness, a positive value even more absolute or universal than that which belongs to a "species" as such.[28] Now, this universal value attributed to something absolutely unique is precisely the value which characterizes Individuality, since such a value is attributed only to it.

In Hegel's terminology, the *Individuality* which characterizes human existence is a synthesis of the *Particular* and the *Universal*. Insofar as this existence "manifests" itself on the "phenomenal" level, Individuality "appears" as active realization of the specifically human desire for *Recognition* (*Anerkennen*). According to Hegel, Man is truly human (that is, free and historical) only to the extent that he is *recognized* as such by others (at the limit, by *all* others) and that he himself recognizes them in turn (for one can be truly "recognized" only by a man whom one recognizes oneself). And we can say that social Recognition is what distinguishes Man, as spiritual entity, from animals and everything that is merely Nature. Now, it is in and by the *universal* recognition of human *particularity* that Individuality realizes and manifests itself.

[28] Thus, for example, it does not seem evil at all to kill or destroy some representative or other of an animal or vegetable species. But the extermination of an entire species is considered almost a crime.

Hegel said this very clearly at Jena, in 1805–1806 (Volume XX, page 206, lines 16–19 and 22–27):

> In the act-of-recognizing (*Anerkennen*) the Self ceases to be this isolated-particular (*Einzelne*) here; it exists (*ist*) juridically [that is, *universally* or as *absolute* value] in the act-of-recognizing, that is, it is no longer in its immediate [or natural] empirical-existence (*Dasein*). . . . Man is necessarily recognized, and he is necessarily recognizing. This necessity is his own, not that of our thought in opposition to the content. As act-of-recognizing, Man himself is the [dialectical] movement, and it is precisely this movement that dialectically-overcomes (*hebt auf*) his state of nature: he is [the] act-of-recognizing; the natural-entity (*Natürliche*) only *exists* (*ist*); it is not [a] *spiritual-entity* (*Geistiges*).

Every man, to the extent that he is human (or "spiritual"), would like, on the one hand, to be different from all others and "the only one of his kind in the world." [29] But on the other hand he would like to be recognized, in his unique particularity itself, as a positive value, and he would like this to be done by the greatest number, if possible by all. And this is to say, in Hegel's terminology, that the truly human Man, radically different from an animal, always searches for Recognition and realizes himself only as actually recognized. Which means that he (actively) desires Individuality and can be real only by (actively) realizing himself through Recognition as Individual.

Hence Man can be truly human only by living in society. Now, Society (and membership in a Society) is real only in and by the actual interaction of its members, which interaction "manifests" itself as, among other things, political existence or State. Hence Man is truly human—that is, "individual"—only to the extent that he lives and acts as "recognized" citizen of a State. (Cf. Volume VII, page 475, lines 23–25.) But at the moment of its appearance, and during its whole historical evolution as well, the State does not fully satisfy the human desire for Recognition and hence does

---

[29] Napoleon was profoundly annoyed and saddened when his Malayan gardener took him for a legendary conqueror of the Far East. A woman of fashion is annoyed and saddened when she sees a friend wearing the dress that was sold to her as "the only one of its kind." Generally speaking, no one wants to be that "average man" whom one often talks about, but always as someone other than oneself.

not perfectly realize Man as Individual. Such is the case because, in the real historical conditions of his existence, a man is never only "this particular man here," recognized by the State as citizen in his unique and irreplaceable particularity. He is always also an interchangeable "representative" of a sort of human "species": of a family, a social class, a nation, or a race, and so on. And only as such a "representative" or as "*specific*-particularity" (*Besonderheit*) is he *universally* recognized: recognized by the State as a Citizen enjoying all political rights and as a "juridical person" of the civil law. Therefore Man is not truly *individual*, and that is why he is not fully *satisfied* (*befriedigt*) by his social and political existence. That is also why he actively and freely (i.e., by negation) transforms the given social and political reality, in order to make it such that he can realize his true Individuality in it. And this progressive realization of *Individuality*, by the active and *free* progressive satisfaction of the desire for Recognition, is the "dialectical movement" of *History* which Man himself is.

In fact, Individuality can be fully realized, the desire for Recognition can be completely satisfied, only in and by the universal and homogeneous State. For, in the *homogeneous* State, the "*specific*-differences" (*Besonderheiten*) of class, race, and so on are "overcome," and therefore this State is directly related to the particular man as such, who is recognized as citizen in his very particularity. And this recognition is truly universal, for, by definition, the State embraces the whole of the human race (even in its past, through the total historical tradition which this State perpetuates in the present; and in its future, since henceforth the future no longer differs from the present in which Man is already fully satisfied).

By fully realizing Individuality, the universal and homogeneous State completes History, since Man, satisfied in and by this State, will not be tempted to negate it and thus to create something new in its place. But this State also presupposes that the totality of the historical process has gone by, and cannot be realized by Man from the outset (for the State, and Man himself, are born from the Fight, which presupposes a *difference* and cannot take place in universal *homogeneity*). In other words, a being can be truly *individual* (and not merely particular) only provided that it is also *historical*. And we have seen that it can be historical only if it is really *free*. Inversely, a really *free* being is necessarily *histori-cal*, and a historical being is always more or less *individual*, finally becoming completely individual.[30]

Already, then, the "phenomenological" description of human empirical existence reveals the three fundamental categories (implicitly discovered by the Judaeo-Christians) which dominate this existence, by distinguishing it from purely natural existence: the categories of Individuality, Freedom, and History. And this same description brings to light their indissoluble union, by showing that Man cannot "appear" as an individual without "manifesting" himself as the free agent of History, that he can "reveal" himself as free only by "appearing" as a historical individual, and that he can "manifest" himself historically only provided that he "appears" in his individual freedom or his free individuality. Now, by revealing this union of the three fundamental categories, the "phenomenological" description presents Man as a being that is dialectical in its empirical existence. Or, more exactly, this description must present him as dialectical so that it can give an account both of the union of the three categories in question and of each of them taken separately.

We have already seen that a free or historical being is necessarily dialectical. And it is easy to see that the same holds true for a being that is an Individual in the Hegelian sense of the word.

Indeed, Individuality is a *synthesis* of the Particular and the Universal, the Universal being the *negation* or the *antithesis* of the Particular, which is the *thetical* given, *identical* to itself. In other words, Individuality is a *Totality*, and the being which is individual is, by this very fact, dialectical.

The particularity of an entity, determined by its *hic et nunc* and by its "natural place" (*topos*) in the Cosmos, not only distinguishes it in a rigid manner from everything that is not it, but also fixes it

---

[30] In truth, the Wise Man is no longer "individual" in the sense that he would be essentially different from all others. If Wisdom consists in the possession of the Truth (which is *one*, and which is the *same* for Hegel and for all his readers), a Wise Man is in no respect different from another Wise Man. This is to say that he is not human in the same way as *historical* Man (nor free in the same sense either, since he no longer negates anything through action): rather, he is "divine" (but mortal). The Wise Man is an Individual, however, in the sense that it is in his existential *particularity* that he possesses the *universal* Science. In this sense, he is still *human* (and therefore mortal).

in its Identity with itself. And this Particularity is a *given* or a "thesis," or, better, a given-being (*Sein*). For what exists at the beginning (in spite of the opinion of "creationists" of every sort, beginning with Plato) is not the Universal, but the Particular: not, for example, *table* in general or *any* animal whatsoever, but *this* particular table and *this* particular animal. However (at least in the World *of which one speaks*—that is, in the World in which Man lives), one can *negate* the Particularity of the existing entity by detaching it from its given *hic et nunc* and causing it to move from the natural Cosmos into the Universe of discourse. Thus, for example, *this* table, which is now here, can become the "general" notion of *Table*, which in some way exists always and nowhere (except "in thought"); and *this* animal can become the "abstract" notion of *an* Animal. But what constitutes the concrete reality (of the World inhabited by Man) is neither the particular entities by themselves nor the universal notions which correspond to them, taken separately. The concrete reality is the whole or the Totality of particular entities revealed by discourse having universal (or true) content, and of general (or better, generic) concepts realized in the spatial-temporal World by the *hic et nunc* of particularities. And it is only as particular realization of a universal concept or as "representative" of a species or kind that a given real entity is an "individual." (Likewise, the Concept would be a pure abstraction—that is, pure nothingness—if it did not correspond to given-Being; and the identifying Particularity implied in this Being is what differentiates general concepts by "individualizing" them.)

But when it is a matter of purely natural real particular entities (i.e., animals, plants, or inanimate things), the universalizing negation is accomplished only in and by the thought (or Discourse) of Man—that is, *outside* of the entities themselves. And that is why one can say that the natural entity, in itself, is only particular: it is universal at the same time, and hence "individual," only through and for the Man who thinks or talks about it. Thus Individuality (and hence Dialectic in general) can "appear" only in the human *science* of nature, but not in Nature itself. The purely natural entity *is* not, strictly speaking, an Individual: it is Individual neither in itself, nor through itself, nor for itself. Man, on the contrary, is individual (and hence dialectical) in himself and through himself, as well as for himself. He is individual *for* himself because he knows himself not only as "this particular man here," but also as a "representative" of the human race (and he can *act* as such). He is individual also *through* himself, for it is he himself who negates himself in his given animal particularity so as to conceive and manifest himself (through speech and action) in his human universality. And Man is finally individual *in* himself— that is, *really* or in his very empirical existence—since the universality of his particular being is not only *thought* by him and by others, but *recognized* as a real value, and recognized *really* or actively by a Universal which is real—i.e., embodied in a State (a Universal he himself creates), which universalizes him *really* since it makes him a Citizen acting (and therefore *existing*) in terms of the "*general* interest."

Therefore, to say that Man is an Individual or a (real, or "existential") synthesis of the Particular and the Universal is to say that he himself is the (universalizing) preserving negation of himself taken as (particular) given. And this is to say that an Individual is necessarily a dialectical being. Now, we have seen that dialectical being must be described on the "ontological" level as being simultaneously Identity, Negativity, and Totality. And we have also seen that Negativity "manifests" itself on the "phenomenal" level as human Freedom, while Totality "appears" as Historicity. It is natural, then, to say that Identity "reveals" itself phenomenologically as Individuality, which is the third fundamental anthropological category.

I did say, it is true, that Identity "manifests" itself on the human "phenomenal" level as *Animality*. But this is by no means a contradiction. Indeed, we were dealing not with Animality simply, as it "appears" in Nature, but with Animality *in Man*, that is, his (originally animal) nature given as dialectically overcome or preserved as sublimated in the totality of human existence. Now, a man's (animal and social) given or innate "nature" is precisely what determines his *particularity*, his rigid and irreducible difference from everything that is not he. As dialectically overcome, then, this "nature" appears as a *negated* particularity—that is, as a universality. And to the extent that this "nature" is preserved and sublimated in its negation, Universality in Man implies Particularity and is thus a manifestation of Individuality. Hence it can be said that Individuality actually "reveals" identity in Man, to the extent that his individuality preserves and sublimates the *particularity* of his innate "nature." If Negativity serves as the ontological basis for Freedom, and Totality for Historicity, Identity is the ontological foundation for Individuality. Thanks to Identity implied in Individuality, a man can remain "the same individual" in spite of the fact that he has become "completely other," in spite of the fact that he has *essentially* changed by *negating* the given particularities of his "character" and by thus *freeing* himself from this "character." And it is as such an "individual," who remains the same even while negating himself, that a man has a personal "history."[31]

However, this way of putting it is not absolutely correct. What exists really is neither Identity nor Negativity, but the Totality that implies both of them as constituent-elements. Therefore it is always Totality that "appears" on the human "phenomenal" level as Individuality, Freedom, and Historicity. These three human "phenomena" are only three different but complementary aspects of the "appearance" of one and the same real Totality, which is the existence of Man's very being. Individuality "reveals" Totality to the extent that it implies Identity; Freedom "manifests" this same Totality as implying Negativity; and Historicity is the "appearance" of Totality as such—that is, as synthesis of individual Identity and free, or better yet, liberating, Negativity.

To say that Man is a free and historical Individual is to say that he "appears" (*erscheint*) in his empirical-existence (*Dasein*) as a dialectical entity, and that he is consequently dialectical both in his objective reality (*Wirklichkeit*) and in his very being (*Sein*). This, then, is to say that Man *is* and *exists* only to the extent that he overcomes himself *dialectically*—i.e. while preserving and sublimating himself.

Now in a passage of the *Encyclopaedia* cited above, Hegel said (Volume V, page 105, line 33) that it belongs to every *finite* entity (*alles Endliche*) to overcome itself dialectically.

---

[31] Nowadays we often talk about a man's "personality." Now, "Personality" ("Person" in Hegel) means nothing but "free and historical Individuality": it is not a new anthropological category, but a word that designates the (actually indivisible) whole of the three fundamental categories of Judaeo-Christian anthropology.

Let us abstract from the fact that this passage asserts that *every* finite entity is dialectical and is *necessarily* dialectical. That is an imprecision of language or an extremely serious error, which I would not want to dwell upon. Let us remember only that, taking the context into account, the passage asserts that only a *finite* entity can be dialectical, that every entity that is (or can be) dialectical is necessarily finite in its very being, as well as in its objective reality and in its "phenomenal" empirical existence. To say that Man is dialectical, therefore, is not only to say that he is individual, free, and historical, but also to assert that he is essentially finite. Now, the radical finiteness of being and of reality "appears" on the human "phenomenal" level as that thing which is called *Death*. Consequently to say that Man "reveals" himself as *historical free Individual* (or as "Personality") and that he "appears" as essentially *mortal* in the strict and full sense of the term is to express one and the same thing in different ways: a historical free individual is necessarily mortal, and a truly mortal being is always a historical free individual.

To remove the paradoxical aspect of this assertion, it must immediately be said that for Hegel human death is something essentially other than the finiteness of purely natural beings. Death is a *dialectical* finiteness. The dialectical being—that is, Man—is the only one who is *mortal* in the strict sense of the word. The death of a human being is essentially different from the "end" of an animal or plant, as well as the "disappearance" of a thing by simple "wear and tear."

In a fragment of the young Hegel (1795?), devoted to an analysis of Love (edited by Nohl, *Hegels theologische Jugendschriften*, Tübingen, 1907), we find a passage relating to death, in which the principle themes which he was to develop later already appear (page 379, last paragraph, and page 381):

> Given that Love is a sentiment (*Gefühl*) of the living (*Lebendigen*), Lovers can distinguish themselves [from one another] only in the sense that they are mortal, [that is, in the sense] that they think this possibility of separation, [and] not in the sense that something may really be separated, not in the sense that a possibility joined to an existing being (*Sein*) is a reality (*Wirkliches*). There is no [raw or given] matter in Lovers [as Lovers], they are a living Whole [or a spiritual Whole, for at that time Hegel identified Life and Spirit];

[that] Lovers have an independence-or-autonomy (*Selbständigkeit*), [a] proper-or-autonomous (*eigenes*) vital-principle, means only: they can die. A plant has salts and earthy parts, which bring with them their own or autonomous laws for their action; [a plant] is the reflection of a foreign-entity (*Fremden*), and one can only say: a plant can be corrupted (or rot, *verwesen*). But Love tends to overcome dialectically (*aufzuheben*) even this distinction-or-differentiation (*Unterscheidung*), this possibility [taken] as pure (*blosse*) possibility, and to give unity to mortality (*Sterbliche*) itself, to make it immortal . . . This results in the following stages: a single independent unit (*Einige*), beings that are separated from one another. and those that are again made into a unit (*Wiedervereinigte*). The newly reunited are again separated, but in the child the union (*Vereinigung*) itself remains without separation (*ungetrennt worden*).

To understand the whole bearing of this "romantic" text, one must know that, at the time when it was written, Hegel for a while believed he had found the specifically human content of Man's existence in Love, and that it was by analyzing the relationship of Love that he first described the Dialectic of this existence, which distinguishes it from purely natural existence. To describe Man as Lover was then, for Hegel, to describe Man as specifically human and essentially different from the animal.

In the *Phenomenology*, Love and the desire for love have become Desire for recognition and Fighting to the death for its satisfaction, with all that follows from it—that is, History which ends in the coming of the satisfied Citizen and the Wise Man. Mutual Recognition in Love has become social and political Recognition through Action. And therefore the "phenomenal" Dialectic is described no longer as a dialectic of love, but as a historical dialectic, in which the objective realization (*Verwirklichung*) of Recognition in the sexual act and the child (mentioned in the last sentence of the passage cited) is replaced by its objective realization in Fighting, Work, and historical progress ending in the Wise Man.[32] In the *Phenomenology*, "the single independent unit" of

[32] The "romantic" and "vitalist" origins of the dialectic of Recognition and Fighting appear clearly in the "formal" description of this dialectic found in the Introduction to Chapter IV of the *Phenomenology* (page 135, second line from the bottom—page 138, line 20). The close ties to the passage cited above from his youthful writing are obvious. Love (human Love) too is a desire for Recognition:

the passage just cited is Man (or, more exactly, pre-human man) before the Fight, animated by the Desire for Recognition, which (in the beginning) is the same for all men. "The beings that are separated from one another" are the Master and the Slave who are created in and by the "first" Fight, and who are essentially different from one another. Finally, the "newly reunited" is no longer either the sexual act or the child, but the satisfied Citizen and the Wise Man, who "synthetize" Mastery and Slavery, and who result from the whole of humanity's historical evolution, as integrating totality of the "dialectical movement" of Fighting and Work. Generally speaking, the complete and adequate "revelation" of the dialectical human reality is no longer Love, which is a unified total given "sentiment of the living," but Wisdom or Science—

---

the lover wants to be *loved*, that is, recognized as absolute or *universal* value in his very *particularity*, which distinguishes him from all others. Hence Love realizes (to a certain extent) Individuality, and that is why it can (to a certain extent) procure Satisfaction. In any case it is a specifically human phenomenon, for in Love one desires another *desire* (the *love* of the other) and not an empirical reality (as, for example, when one simply "desires" someone). What Hegel (implicitly) reproaches Love for in the *Phenomenology* is on the one hand its "private" character (one can be *loved* by only a very few persons, whereas one can be universally *recognized*), and on the other hand its "lack of seriousness," since Risk of life is absent (only this Risk is a truly objective realization of the specifically human content which essentially distinguishes Man from the animal). Not presupposing Risk, Love (= amorous Recognition) does not presuppose Action in general. Therefore it is not Action (*Tun*) or Product (*Werk*) that are recognized in Love as absolute values, but given-Being (*Sein*)—i.e., precisely that which is not truly human in Man. (As Goethe said: one loves a man not because of what he *does* but for what he *is*; that is why one can love a dead man, for the man who *does* truly nothing would already be like a dead man; that is also why one can love an animal, without being able to "recognize" the animal: let us remember that there have never been duels between a man and an animal—or a woman; let us also remember that it is "unworthy of a man" to dedicate himself entirely to love: the legends of Hercules, Samson, and so on.) Consequently, even a man "happy in love" is not fully "satisfied" as long as he is not universally "recognized." In accepting the point of view of the *Phenomenology*, one would have to say that Man can truly *love* (which no animal can do) only because he has already created himself *beforehand* as human being through the Risk incurred in a Fight for Recognition. And that is why only Fighting and Work (born from the Desire for Recognition properly so-called) produce a specifically human *objective-reality* (*Wirklichkeit*), a technical and social, or better, historical, World; the *objective-reality* of Love is purely natural (sexual act, birth of the child): its human content always remains purely internal or private (*innerlich*). History, and not Love, is what *creates* Man; Love is only a secondary "manifestation" of Man who already exists as human being.

that is, the discursive or conceptual understanding of the Totality of Being given to Man and created by him.

But in both "phenomenological" descriptions of the human Dialectic, death plays a primordial role. For already, in the writing of his youth, Hegel asserts that Lovers (who "manifest" the human in Man) can distinguish themselves, the one from the other, and from everything that is not they, only to the extent that they are *mortal*: and this is to say that it is only as *mortals* that they possess an *Individuality*, since Individuality necessarily implies and presupposes a Particularity which is "the only one of its kind in the world." Likewise, it is only thanks to *death* that Lovers have an independent or autonomous, or better, *free* existence. Finally, it is again because of the *mortality* of Lovers that Love realizes itself as dialectical "re-union" of the "beings that are separated"— that is, as Synthesis or Totality unfolded and integrated in *Time*, in the form as a series of consecutive generations or a *historical* evolution (the "Synthesis" of Lovers being the Child). Now, we know that, in his mature writings, Hegel maintains this indissoluble bond between Death on the one hand, and Individuality, Freedom, and Historicity on the other.

But what is especially important to underline is that the "romantic" text radically opposes the *death* of Man (= of Lovers) to the simple disappearance or "decomposition" of purely natural entities (everything that Hegel says there about plants applies to animals and inanimate things as well). The finiteness and actual disappearance of natural entities (the "death" of an animal, for example) are determined, in a necessary and unequivocal fashion, by laws that are *alien* (*Fremdes*) to them, or, if you will, by the natural place (*topos*) which they occupy in the given Cosmos. The death of Man (= of Lovers), on the other hand, is an *immanent* law, an *auto-overcoming*: it is truly *his* death—that is, something that is proper to him and belongs to him as his own, and which can consequently be known by him, wanted or negated by him. The "death" of the natural being exists only "in itself or for us"— that is, for Man who is conscious of it: the finite natural being itself knows nothing of its own finiteness. Death, on the other hand, also exists *for* Man, it is "in and for itself": Lovers "*think* of the possibility of separation" in and by their death. And that is why Man (= Lovers) alone is capable of *wanting* the infinity and the immortality of what *is* finite and mortal, just as he alone can kill *himself*: in Nature, death is only a *given*, but in Man and in History it is also (or at least can always be) a product—that is, the result of a conscious and voluntary *action*.

Now, all this means that the "decomposition" or "corruption" of a natural entity which puts an end to its "empirical existence" is a pure and simple (or "identical") annihilation, where as human death is a "dialectical" (or "total") "overcoming," which annuls while preserving and sublimating. This is to oppose to the "identical" natural World of (Aristotelian) "generation and corruption" the "dialectical" human or historical World of (active or negating) *creation* and of *death* (which is always conscious and sometimes willed or voluntary).

We shall see what this *dialectical* character of human death means in Hegel. But we already know that the "preservation and sublimation" which it entails have nothing to do with an *afterlife*, for we know that the *dialectical* being is necessarily *finite* or mortal, in the full sense. If Man, according to Hegel, can be truly human only because he must and can die, he does not die so as to come to life again, nor so as to live in another World than the natural World in which he is born and in which he creates his own historical World through Action.

Generally speaking, the introduction of the notion of Death in no way modifies the Hegelian description of Dialectic with which we are already acquainted. In fine, to say that Man is *mortal* (in the sense that he is conscious of his death, that he can voluntarily kill himself or "negate" his death in a myth of immortality) is to say nothing other or more than what we say in asserting that Man is a Totality or a dialectical entity: Totality always *appears* as a historical free Individual who is necessarily mortal, and the truly mortal being is necessarily a historical free Individual who *is* and *exists* as a Totality or dialectical entity.

But first it is necessary to consider more closely why this is so. First of all, it is obvious that a dialectical or "total" being can only be finite or mortal. Indeed, by definition Dialectic and hence Totality exist only where there is Negativity. Now, Negativity in its isolated state is pure Nothingness. Its "synthesis" with Identity or given-Being (*Sein*), therefore, can only be a penetration of Nothingness into Being—that is, an annihilation of Being or a nihilation of Nothingness in it. But Being is annihilated only in Time, and Nothingness nihilates in Being as Time. Dialectical or total *Being* (that is, *Spirit* in the *Phenomenology*, or *Life* in the young Hegel's terminology) is therefore necessarily *temporal*: it is *realized*, or if you please, *materialized*, Time—i.e., a Time that *lasts* (in Being or Space). Now, to *last* is necessarily to have a beginning and an end (in Time) which "appear" as birth and death. A dialectical or total being, therefore, is always actually mortal, at least in the sense that its empirical-existence is finite or limited in and by Time.

But "dialectical" Death is more than a simple end or limit imposed from the outside. If Death is an "appearance" of Negativity, Freedom is, as we know, another such "appearance." Therefore Death and Freedom are but two ("phenomenological") aspects of one and the same thing, so that to say "mortal" is to say "free," and inversely. And Hegel actually asserts this on several occasions, notably in a passage of his essay on "Natural Right" (1802).

This is what he says there (Volume VII, page 370, lines 10–13):

> This negative-or-negating Absolute, pure freedom, in its appearance (*Erscheinung*) is death; and through the faculty (*Fähigkeit*) of death the Subject [= Man] shows himself (*erweist sich*) as [being] free and absolutely elevated (*erhaben*) above all constraint (*Zwang*).

On the "metaphysical" level, it is easy to see that this is truly the case. If given-Being is determined in its entirety (and otherwise there would be no possibility of either Science or Truth), it determines, by its entirety, everything that is a part of it. A being that could not escape from Being, therefore, could not evade its destiny, and would be fixed once and for all in and by the place which it occupies in the Cosmos. Or in other words, if Man lived eternally and could not die, he could not render himself immune to God's omnipotence either. But if he can kill himself, he can reject any imposed destiny whatsoever, for by ceasing to exist he will not undergo it. And moving to the "phenomenological" level, we see that suicide, or voluntary death without any "vital necessity," is the most obvious "manifestation" of Negativity or Freedom. For to kill oneself in order to escape from a given situation to which one is *biologically* adapted (since one could continue to *live* in it) is to manifest one's independence with respect to it—

that is, one's autonomy or freedom. And once one can commit suicide in order to escape from *any* given situation *whatsoever*, one can say with Hegel that "the faculty of death" is the "appearance" of "pure freedom," or absolute freedom (at least potentially), with respect to every given in general.[33] But if suicide (which obviously distinguishes Man from the animal) "manifests" freedom, it does not *realize* freedom, for it ends in nothingness and not in a free *existence*. What reveals and realizes freedom, according to Hegel, is the Fight for pure prestige, carried on without any biological necessity for the sake of Recognition alone. But this Fight reveals and realizes freedom only to the extent that it implies the Risk of life—that is, the real possibility of dying.[34]

Death, therefore, is only a complementary aspect of Freedom. But to what extent is it also a complement of Individuality?

---

[33] This Hegelian theme was taken up by Dostoievsky in *The Possessed*. Kirilov wants to commit suicide solely in order to demonstrate the possibility of doing it "without any necessity"—that is, *freely*. His suicide is intended to demonstrate the absolute freedom of man—that is, his independence in relation to God. Dostoievsky's theistic objection consists in saying that man cannot do it, that he necessarily shrinks from death: Kirilov commits suicide out of shame for not being able to do it. But this objection is not valid, because a suicide "out of shame" is also a *free* act (no animal does it). And if, by committing suicide, Kirilov annihilates himself, he has, as he wished, overcome the omnipotence of the external (the "transcendent") by dying "prematurely," before it "was written," and has limited infinity or God. I am indebted to Mr. Jacob Klein for this interpretation of the Kirilov episode.

[34] The fight for pure prestige, moreover, is a *suicide* (whose outcome depends on chance), as Hegel says in the *Lectures at Jena* of 1805–1806 (Volume XX, page 211, the last three lines): "it appears [to each adversary, taken] as external-Consciousness, that he is going to the *death* of an other; but he is going to his own [death]; [it is a] suicide, to the extent that he [voluntarily] exposes himself to *danger*." . . . The fact that the adversaries remain alive subjects them to the *necessities* of existence; but this necessity passes into the Slave (who rejected the Risk), whereas the Master (who accepted it) remains free: in his work, the Slave undergoes the laws of the given; but the idle Master who consumes products already "humanized" by work, prepared for Man, no longer undergoes the constraint of Nature (in principle, of course). It could also be said that the Master is actually humanly dead in the Fight: he no longer *acts*, strictly speaking, since he remains idle; therefore he lives as if he were dead; that is why he does not evolve any more in the course of History and is simply annihilated at its end: his existence is a simple "afterlife" (which is limited in time) or a "deferred death." The Slave progressively frees himself through Work which *manifests* his freedom; but he must finally take up the Fight again and accept the Risk in order to *realize* this freedom by creating through victory the universal and homogeneous State of which he will be the "recognized" Citizen.

Individuality is, by definition, a synthesis of the Universal, and of the Particular which is "the only one of its kind in the world." Now, by moving up to the "ontological" level, one can show that *free* Particularity (or particular freedom) is incompatible with infinity.

Aristotle himself saw very clearly that a "possibility" which would *never* (= as long as Time lasts) be actualized or realized, would in fact be an absolute *impossibility*. If, then, some being, and in particular some human being, were infinite in the sense that it lasted *eternally* (= as long as Time lasts), and if it did not realize certain possibilities of Being, these possibilities would be impossibilities for it or in relation to it. In other words, it would be rigorously *determined* by these impossibilities in its being and in its existence, as well as in its "appearance": it would not be truly *free*. While existing *eternally*, a being will necessarily realize *all* its possibilities, and will realize none of its impossibilities. The *given* whole of its possibilities, or, what is the same thing, of its impossibilities, constitutes its immutable "essence," or its eternal "nature," or its innate "character," or its Platonic "idea," and so on, which it can *develop* in Time by realizing and "manifesting" it, but which it can neither modify nor annihilate. In the real and "phenomenal" World, this being would be only the "representative" (possibly the sole representative) of a "species" determined in its "essence" by the given structure of the Being of which it is a part, determined somehow "before" its temporal realization and "manifestation." Or else, to use the language of Calvin, who made this point with implacable logic: the man who existed eternally would be "chosen" or "damned" *before* his "creation," by being absolutely incapable of modifying in any way whatever his "destiny" or "nature" by his "active" existence in the World.

An infinite or eternal being, and in particular a man who is immortal or is the beneficiary of an "afterlife," would be *particularized* by its restricted possibilities or its impossibilities, and it could be distinguished from all other beings, since it has impossibilities that the others do not have. Hence it would be a *particular* being. But this Particular would not be *free*. And therefore it would not be an Individuality in the proper sense of the word. Unable to go beyond its "nature," it could not negate or "overcome," or better, "transcend," its given Particularity and thus rise to the

Universal. And having nothing *universal* in itself, it would be *merely* particular, without being a true *individual*. Accordingly, in this conception of Man, Individuality appears only where human Particularity is projected on *divine* Universality. Calvin's Man is an Individuality distinguished from simple animal and thingish Particularity only by the fact that he is "chosen" or "damned"—that is, "recognized" in his very *particularity* by a *universal* God. But this God *determines* him by "recognizing" him, and "recognizes" him only according to a *pre*-determination, somehow anterior to the very existence and "appearance" of the one destined for "recognition." Taken in himself, the "immortal" Man with *limited* possibilities is hence neither free nor individual in the proper sense of the word. As for the infinite being which realizes *all* the possibilities of Being, one can, if one pleases, say of it that it is "free": at least in the ancient and Spinozan sense, because of the absence in it of all immanent *constraint* or constraint coming from the outside. But if each man realizes and manifests *all* the possibilities of Being (even if only of human Being), there will no longer be any true difference between men, and none of them will represent a Particularity, without which there is no Individuality properly so-called. Aristotle himself understood this, and his discovery was taken up by the Arabs and by Spinoza. The infinite or eternal ("immortal") being, which is "free" in the sense that it is not limited by impossibilities that are realizable elsewhere, is necessarily one and unique: a *universal* divine "substance," which realizes and manifests itself in and by an infinite multitude of *particular* "attributes" and "modes." If you please, Freedom and Individuality do exist, then, in this infinitist conception; but in this case the free Individual is God alone, and there is no longer a purely natural World, and hence no Man in the proper sense of the word; and consequently, there is no longer a "movement" that is called History.[35] Therefore, if Man is immortal, if he "lives after" his biological death, there is no freedom, no individuality, in him. Man's Freedom is the actual *negation* by him of his own given "nature"—that is, of the "possibilities" which he has already realized, which determine his "impossibilities"—i.e., everything incompatible with his "possibilities." And

[35] See the Course of 1938–1939, Note on Eternity, Time, and the Concept (pages 100–148).

his Individuality is a synthesis of his particularity with a universality that is equally his. Therefore Man can be individual and free only to the extent that he implies in his being *all* the possibilities of Being but *does not have the time* to realize and manifest them all. Freedom is the realization of a possibility *incompatible* (as realized) with the entirety of possibilities realized previously (which consequently must be *negated*); hence there is freedom only where that entirety does not embrace *all* possibilities in general, and where what is outside of that entirety is not an absolute impossibility. And man is an individual only to the extent that the *universality* of the possibilities of his being is associated in him with the unique particularity (the only one of its kind) of their temporal realizations and manifestations. It is solely because he is potentially infinite and always limited in deed by his death that Man is a free Individual who has a history and who can freely create a place for himself in History, instead of being content, like animals and things, passively to occupy a natural place in the given Cosmos, determined by the structure of the latter.[36]

Therefore, Man is a (free) Individual only to the extent that he is mortal, and he can realize and manifest himself as such an Individual only by realizing and manifesting Death as well. And this can easily be seen by considering Man's existence on the "phenomenological" level.

Hegel saw this in his "romantic" youth, by analyzing the "manifest" existence of "Lovers"—that is, of two human beings who

---

[36] If an animal, or a man as animal, comes to a fork in the road, it *can* go to the right *or* to the left: the two possibilities are compatible as possibilities. But if it actually takes the road to the right, it is impossible that it has taken the road to the left, and inversely: the two possibilities are incompatible as realized. An animal that has set forth on the road to the right must retrace its steps in order to take the road to the left. Man as animal must also do this. But as Man—that is, as *historical* (or "spiritual" or, better, dialectical) being—he never retraces his steps. History does not turn back, and nevertheless it ends up on the road to the left after it has taken the road to the right. It is because there has been a Revolution, it is because Man has *negated* himself as committed to the road to the right, and, having thus become other than he was, has ended up on the road to the left. He has negated himself without completely disappearing and without ceasing to be Man. But the animal in him, which was on the road to the right, *could not* end up on the road to the left: therefore it *had* to disappear, and the Man whom it embodied had to die. (It would be a miracle, if a revolution could succeed without one generation's replacing the other—in a natural, or more or less violent, fashion.)

transcend their animality and have a complete community in one and the same truly human life (in which the human value attributed to oneself is a function of that attributed to the other, and inversely). He saw that death alone could separate and distinguish these two beings—that is, particularize and hence individualize them. For although each of them could live in and by the other, and somehow in place of the other, each had to die for himself, his death being truly his, and only his. Now, this statement remains true, even if we take it out of its romantic setting, even if we consider Man's historical existence, and not his love life. If in truly homogeneous humanity, realized as State at the end of History, *human* existences become really interchangeable, in the sense that the action (and "the true *being* of Man is his *action*," according to Hegel) of each man is also the action of all, and inversely (*Tun Aller und Jeder*), death will necessarily oppose each one to all the others and will particularize him in his empirical existence, so that *universal* action will also always be *particular* action (or action liable to failure where another succeeds), and therefore *Individual*.[37]

Therefore, Man's freedom and individuality indeed presuppose his death. And the same holds true for his historicity, since as we have seen, it is nothing other than free individuality or individual or individualized freedom.

For Hegel, History does not begin until the "first" Fight for Recognition, which would not be what it is—i.e., anthropogenetic—if it did not imply a real risk of life. And History in its entirety is only an evolution of the "contradiction" (*Widerspruch*) arising from the "immediate" (*unmittelbar*) solution of this first social or human conflict provided by the opposition (*Entgegensetzung*) of Mastery and Slavery. According to Hegel, therefore, History would have no meaning, no reason for existing, no possibility of existing, if Man were not mortal. And it is easy to see that this is indeed the case.

Indeed, if Man lived eternally (= as long as Time lasts), he could, to be sure, have "undergone an evolution," as animals and plants did. But while "evolving" in Time, he would only "develop" an eternal determined "nature," which would be *given* to him ahead of time or imposed on him; and his evolution would be any-

---

[37] What would remain of Christ's *individuality*, if Jesus had not been born and had not *died*?

thing but a historical drama whose end is unknown. Seriousness enters into a historical situation and transforms a given existential situation into a "historical" one only to the extent that Man can definitively fail to achieve his human destiny, to the extent that History can fail to attain its end; and this is possible only if History is limited in and by Time, and hence if Man who creates it is mortal. It is solely because of the essential finiteness of Man and of History that History is something other than a tragedy, if not a comedy, played by human actors for the entertainment of the gods, who are its authors, who hence know its outcome, and who consequently cannot take it seriously, nor truly tragically, just like all the actors themselves when they know that they are playing roles that have been given to them. The finiteness of every historical action—that is, the possibility of an absolute failure—is what engenders the seriousness characteristic of a man's actual participation in History: a seriousness that allows Man who is creating History to do without any spectator besides himself.[38]

In fine, then, human death does indeed present itself as a "manifestation" of Man's freedom, individuality, and historicity—that is, of the "total" or dialectical character of his being and his existence. More particularly, death is an "appearance" of Negativity, which is the genuine motor of the dialectical movement. But if death is a manifestation of Man's dialecticity, it is because it overcomes him *dialectically*—that is, while preserving and sublimat-

---

[38] The solution proposed by Plato, and taken up by Kant, is not satisfactory either. According to Plato-Kant, each man, although eternal or immortal, chooses (outside of Time) a determined particular existence, which he lives for a certain time. But it is obvious that such a temporal existence is in no way truly *historical*. The seriousness inheres, at most, in the "transcendental choice": its temporal realization is but a comedy, of which it is hard to say why and for whom it is played, the content and the outcome being known ahead of time. Furthermore, if the eternal man plays only one temporal role, it is because there is something (in fact, God) that prevents him from playing others (especially if the one he played turns out badly): therefore he is not *free* as eternal. Moreover, it is not clear why transworldly man chooses one role rather than another, nor why he chooses a "bad" role (unless he chooses "by chance"—i.e., precisely without any freedom at all). Thus Calvin was correct in saying that, in the Platonic hypothesis, the choice of role is necessarily *determined* by God, and not by the one who seems to make it. Finally, if each man can choose any role at all, and if the exclusion of the roles other than the one he has chosen is imposed on him by God, it is God who particularizes man's universality, and therefore man is an *individual* only for and through God.

253

ing—and it is as *dialectical* overcoming that it is essentially different from the simple "end" of a purely natural being.

Once more, what is at issue cannot, for Hegel, be an "afterlife" for man after his death; this "afterlife," which would eternally maintain him in given-Being, is incompatible with the essential finiteness of every dialectical being. In and by his death, man is completely and definitively annihilated; he becomes pure Nothingness (*Nichts*), if it can be said, by ceasing to be given-Being (*Sein*). The "dialectical overcoming" of and by death, therefore, is something completely different from immortality.

The Negativity in Being (= Identity) gives it Temporality (= Totality), which exists as real duration of the World and manifests itself as historical Time or History. Negativity is therefore actualized through the negation of Being (which sinks into the nothingness of the "past"). But this negation is dialectical in the sense that it does not end in pure Nothingness: in going beyond or transcending given-Being (*Sein*), one creates the Concept (*Begriff*), which is Being minus the being of Being. The negation therefore *preserves* the "content" of Being (as the concept: "Being"), and *sublimates* it by causing it to subsist in "ideal" and not "real" form. And without Negativity, that is, without finiteness or temporality, Being would never be a *conceived* (*begriffen*) being.

If, then, death is a manifestation of Negativity in Man (or more exactly, a manifestation of Man's Negativity), it is a transformation of his real being into ideal concept. It is because he is mortal that Man can conceive (*begreifen*) of himself as he is in reality—that is, precisely as mortal: in contradistinction to animals, he *thinks* of himself as mortal, and therefore he thinks of his own death. Hence he can "transcend" it, if you please, and situate himself somehow beyond it; but he does this in the only way in which one can "go beyond" given-Being without sinking into pure Nothingness, namely in and by thought.

According to Hegel, Man "for the first time" rises above mere animal sentiment of self (*Selbstgefühl*) and attains human self-consciousness (*Selbstbewusstsein*), conceptual and discursive consciousness in general, by the risk of life accepted without any necessity, by the fact that he goes to his death without being forced to it. For it is by the autonomous acceptance of death that he "goes beyond" or "transcends" the given-being which he himself is, this "going beyond" being precisely the thought which "reveals" this being to itself and to others, by illuminating it as it were from outside and from the standpoint of a nonexistent beyond. If Man were not voluntarily mortal (that is, free, individual, and historical; that is, total or dialectical), he could neither think nor speak: therefore he would be no different in any respect from an animal.

To say that human death, in contradistinction to an animal's "end," is a "dialectical overcoming" (that is, *free*, since it can be biologically premature), therefore, is first of all to say that Man *knows* that he must die. An animal, a plant, and a thing come to an end "in themselves or for us"—that is, only for an external observer. A man's death, on the other hand, also exists "for itself," for he himself is conscious of it. This end "in and for itself"— that is, a dialectical or "total" end—is Death in the proper sense of the word, which takes place only in Man; and it is because Man is *mortal* in this sense that he is truly human and essentially different from an animal.[39]

It is by actually risking his life (unnecessarily) that Man rises to consciousness of his death. And once in possession of this consciousness, he, in contradistinction to an animal, can either die consciously (or voluntarily) or reject death in and by his thought and his will. On the one hand, Man can die "without losing consciousness"; thus he can voluntarily face death as a calculated risk on which he has reflected or in full awareness of the imminence of a fatal outcome; he can even kill himself, for any motives whatsoever he may judge valid. On the other hand, he can negate his death, as he can negate (by deluding himself) anything that is

[39] Epicurus' well-known reasoning is valid only for an animal, or for nondialectical being in general, which can only *suffer* its end without ever being able to prepare it. This being *is* as long as it lives, and it is annihilated after its death. Therefore death does not actually exist *for it*, and one cannot say of it: "*it is dying.*" But man transcends himself in and by his very existence: in living, he is also beyond his real existence; his future absence is present in his life, and the Epicurean argument cannot blot out this presence of the absence in his existence. Thus, man is mortal *for himself*, and that is why he alone can *die* in the proper sense of the word. For only he can live while knowing that he is going to die. And that is why, in certain cases, he can live in terms of the idea of death, by subordinating to it everything that is dictated to him only by his life (an ascetic life).

actually given to him in and by his consciousness: he can declare himself immortal.

But Man cannot *really* become immortal. It is the *being* of what is negated that passes into the negation and *realizes* its result. Thus, by (actively) negating the real natural World, Man can create a historical or human ("technical") World, which is just as real, although real in a different way. But death is pure Nothingness, and it subsists only as *concept* of death (= presence of the absence of life). Now, by negating a concept, one only manages to create another *concept*. Hence Man who negates his death can only "imagine" himself immortal: he can only *believe* in his "eternal" life or his "resurrection," but he cannot really *live* his imaginary "afterlife." But this faith, whose counterpart and origin are the faculty of freely bringing about one's death, also distinguishes Man from animal. Man is not only the sole living being which knows that it must die and which can freely bring about its death: he is also the only one which can aspire to immortality and believe in it more or less firmly.

Thus, to say that Man's death, and consequently his very existence, are dialectical is to say, among other things, that he "manifests" himself as a being that knows it is mortal and aspires to immortality—i.e., that "goes beyond" its death in and by its thought. But Man's "transcendence" with respect to his death "manifests" itself in yet another way than by the mistaken "subjective certainty" (*Gewissheit*) of an afterlife; this transcendence also "appears" as a truth (*Wahrheit*), being the revelation of an "objective reality" (*Wirklichkeit*).

To say that Man is dialectical or mortal, in the strict sense, is to say that he can freely prepare his death, or go beyond his given existence, whatever it is, independently of the character belonging to that existence. This, then, is to say that his possibilities go beyond all his actual realizations and are not determined by these realizations in an unequivocal manner. But this is also to say that he can actually realize only a limited number of his infinite (or better: indefinite, in the sense that every non-A is indefinite) possibilities. In other words, Man always dies somehow prematurely (which to a certain extent "justifies" his desire for an afterlife)—that is, before exhausting all the possibilities of his being (or better: of his negating or creative action). An animal can be annihilated after realizing everything of which it was capable, so that a prolongation of its life would no longer have any meaning: then its death is "natural." But Man always dies a "violent" death, so to speak, for his death prevents him from doing something other than what he has already done.[40]

Every man who has died could have prolonged his activity or negated it; he did not, therefore, completely exhaust his human existential possibilities. And that is why his human possibilities can be realized humanly—i.e., in and by another man, who will take up his work and prolong his action (which was his very being). It is thus that History is possible, and that is why it can be realized in spite of, or rather because of, death. For men know that they are mortal when they educate their children, in such a way that the children can complete their works, by acting in terms of the memory of ancestors who have passed away. Now, this projection into the future, which will never be a present for the one who thinks of it, and also this prolongation in an existence of a past that does not belong to that existence, are precisely what characterize historical existence and essentially distinguish it from the simple evolution observed in Nature.

This transcendence of death in and by History is the *truth* (= revealed *reality*) of the subjective certainty of an "afterlife": man "goes beyond" his death to the extent that his very being is nothing other than his action and that this action of his is propagated through History (which is itself finite, by the way). But man attains this truth only very late and always reluctantly. In the beginning, he believes (or better: would like to believe) in his own survival after his death, and he negates his definitive annihilation in his imagination. But man is human only when he lives in a World. Accordingly he can think of himself as living humanly after his death on earth only by imagining a transcendent World

---

[40] Even the so-called "violent" or "accidental" end of an animal appears as "natural," if we consider Nature in its entirety: this end is always determined, or "justified," by the animal's natural place in the Cosmos. The fact that the animal's offspring merely reproduces its own existence proves that by procreating it has exhausted all its essential existential possibilities. But the "bright son" always goes further than his "father," even if he goes wrong; and that is why the "father" somehow had the "right" (or the human possibility) to live longer than he did.

or a "beyond" said to be "divine" (the divine or the "sacred" being nothing other than the "natural place" of dead men). However, we have seen that where there is *eternal* life and hence God, there is no place for human freedom, individuality, or historicity. Thus, the man who asserts that he is immortal—if he goes beyond contradiction—always ends up conceiving of himself as a purely natural being, determined once and for all in its purely particular and utterly uncreative existence. And if he possesses the idea of historical free individuality, he assigns it to God alone, and thus by that very fact assigns to God the death that he rejects for himself. But man can be satisfied only by realizing his own individuality, and by *knowing* that he is realizing it. Consequently, the man who believes himself to be immortal, or, what is the same thing, the man who believes in God, never attains satisfaction (*Befriedigung*), and always lives in contradiction with himself: as Hegel says, he is an "unhappy Consciousness" (*unglückliches Bewusstsein*) and he lives a "divided condition" (*Entzweiung*).

Man's definitive satisfaction, which completes History, necessarily implies *consciousness* of individuality that has been realized (by universal recognition of particularity). And this consciousness necessarily implies consciousness of death. If, then, Man's complete satisfaction is the goal and the natural end of history, it can be said that history completes itself by Man's perfect understanding of his death. Now, it is in and by Hegelian Science that Man for the first time has fully understood the phenomenological, metaphysical, and ontological meaning of his essential finiteness. Therefore, if this Science, which is Wisdom, could appear only at the end of History, only through it is History perfected and definitively completed. For it is only by understanding himself in this Science as mortal—that is, as a historical free individual— that Man attains fullness of consciousness of a self that no longer has any reason to negate itself and become other.

Hegelian Science culminates in the description of Man understood as a total or dialectical being. Now, to say that Man is dialectical is to say that he "appears" to himself as mortal (phenomenological level); or what is the same thing, that he necessarily exists in a natural World that has no beyond—i.e., where there is no place for a God (metaphysical level); or, what is again the same thing, that he is essentially temporal in his very being, which thus, in truth, is *action* (ontological level).[41]

In summary:
Hegelian Dialectic is not a *method* of research or of philosophical exposition, but the adequate description of the *structure* of Being, and of the realization and appearance of Being as well.

To say that Being is dialectical is first to say (on the ontological level) that it is a *Totality* that implies *Identity* and *Negativity*. Next, it is to say (on the metaphysical level) that Being realizes itself not only as *natural World*, but also as a *historical* (or human) *World*, these two Worlds exhausting the totality of the objective-real (there is no divine World). It is finally to say (on the phenomenological level) that the objective-real empirically-exists and appears not only as inanimate thing, plant, and animal, but also as essentially temporal or *mortal historical free individual* (who *fights* and who *works*). Or, to put it otherwise, to say that there is *Totality*, or *Mediation*, or *dialectical Overcoming*, is to say that in addition to *given-Being*, there is also *creative Action* which ends in a *Product*.

[41] God and the afterlife have always been denied by certain men. But Hegel was the first to try to formulate a complete *philosophy* that is atheistic and finitist in relation to Man (at least in the great *Logik* and the earlier writings). He not only gave a correct description of *finite* human existence on the "phenomenological" level, which allowed him to use the fundamental categories of Judaeo-Christian thought without any inconsistency. He also tried (without completely succeeding, it is true) to complete this description with a metaphysical and ontological analysis, also radically atheistic and finitist. But very few of his readers have understood that in the final analysis dialectic meant atheism. Since Hegel, atheism has never again risen to the metaphysical and ontological levels. In our times Heidegger is the first to undertake a complete atheistic philosophy. But he does not seem to have pushed it beyond the phenomenological anthropology developed in the first volume of *Sein und Zeit* (the only volume that has appeared). This anthropology (which is without a doubt remarkable and authentically philosophical) adds, fundamentally, nothing new to the anthropology of the *Phenomenology* (which, by the way, would probably never have been understood if Heidegger had not published his book): but atheism or ontological finitism are implicitly asserted in his book in a perfectly consequent fashion. This has not prevented certain readers, who are otherwise competent, from speaking of a Heideggerian theology and from finding a notion of an afterlife in his anthropology.

APPENDIX

The Structure of the Phenomenology of Spirit

The *Phenomenology* can only be understood by the reader who is aware of its dialectical articulations. These articulations are, however, only rarely explicated by Hegel himself. The purpose of the following analysis will be to indicate them to the reader.

The *Phenomenology* is a *phenomenological* description of human existence. That is to say, it describes human existence as it "appears" (*erscheint*) or "manifests" itself to the very one who experiences it. In other words, Hegel describes the content of the self-consciousness of man, whose existence is dominated either by one of the typical existential attitudes that are found everywhere and at all times (First Part), or by an attitude characterizing an outstanding historical epoch (Second Part). Since "Consciousness" (*Bewusstsein*) is the general term for man in the *Phenomenology*, Hegel indicates that he is giving a *phenomenological* description when he says he is describing the attitude in question as it exists "for Consciousness itself" (*für das Bewusstsein selbst*).

But Hegel himself writes the *Phenomenology* after having thought it—that is, after having integrated in his mind *all* of the possible existential attitudes. He therefore knows the *totality* of human existence, and consequently sees it as it is in reality or in truth (*in der Tat*). Thus possessing "absolute knowledge," he sees a given attitude, which is partial or historically conditioned, in a different light than the man who realizes it. The latter is concerned with an attitude which he believes to be total and the only possible one or, at the very least, the only admissible one. Hegel, on the contrary, knows that he is dealing with a mere fragment

Edited, translated, and correlated with the Hoffmeister (1952) and Baillie (1931) editions of the *Phenomenology* by Kenley and Christa Dove.

or a stage in the formation of integral existence. He is the only one who sees the links which unite the fragments with each other, as well as the order of the stages.

Bringing these links and this order to light is precisely what gives a "scientific" or philosophical character to the phenomenological description (which otherwise would be purely literary). This is why Hegel frames the descriptions made from the point of view of the one who is being described (*für es*) with analyses written from the point of view of "absolute knowledge," which is the viewpoint of Hegel himself. In these remarks that serve as frameworks, Hegel therefore describes the existential attitudes such as they "appear" to him, or, as he says: "to us" (*für uns*), this "we" being Hegel himself and the reader who understands him. Now Hegel sees the things as they are in truth or in reality, or as he says: "in themselves" (*an sich*). Therefore he says indifferently "in itself or for us" (*an sich oder für uns*), or simply "in itself" or else "for us," when he wants to make clear that at this particular point he is not giving a *phenomenological* description but a philosophical or *scientific* analysis of the situation.

Unfortunately, Hegel often omits the sacramental formula, and the boundaries between the descriptions *für es* and the analyses *für uns* are therefore not always easy to establish. And it becomes even more complicated, because sometimes, without telling the reader, he inserts into the descriptions Notes written from the point of view of Absolute Knowledge (*für uns = an sich*). But, in principle, these Notes should not be there, and each description *für es* should be preceded by an introduction where Hegel indicates the place which the constituent-element or the historical stage in question occupies in the simultaneous and consecutive integrity of human existence; and each description should be followed by a sort of conclusion where he makes evident the "true" why and how of the transformation of the element or stage under consideration into those that result from it (through their "dialectical overcoming"). The "dialectical" transformations which are *experienced* by those who undergo them (or, more exactly, who provoke them) are described in the phenomenological parts (*für es*).

The principal aim of the following Analysis is to indicate the boundaries between the phenomenological parts and the *Introduc-*

tions and *Transitions* which surround them and which are written from the point of view of Absolute Knowledge (*für uns*). The Analysis also brings to light the dialectical (triadic) articulations of the phenomenological parts themselves, while pointing out the Notes inserted *für uns*.

In Chapter VIII, the distinction between *für es* and *für uns* comes to disappear, because this chapter describes the self-consciousness of the Wise Man possessing Absolute Knowledge—that is to say, Hegel himself—which "appears" to that self (*für es*) as it is in reality (*an sich*) and also as it appears to those who truly understand it (*für uns*). At this stage the phenomenological description therefore coincides with the philosophical or "scientific" analysis. However, this coinciding of the *für es* and the *für uns* only comes about at the end of the chapter. Therefore the chapter has a general *Introduction*, and its first Section has an *Introduction* and a *Transition*.

Of course, the *Preface* (*Vorrede*) and the *Introduction* (*Einleitung*) of the *Phenomenology* are written entirely from the point of view of Absolute Knowledge (*für uns*).

[The first two numbers indicate the page and line of the Hoffmeister edition (Hamburg: Meiner, 1952); the last two numbers indicate the page and line of the English translation of Baillie (second edition, London: Allen & Unwin, 1931). "PhG" is used as an abbreviation for the *Phenomenology*.]

PREFACE

INTRODUCTION

FIRST PART (= A. *Consciousness* and B. *Self-consciousness* = Chaps. I to IV):

THE CONSTITUENT-ELEMENTS OF HUMAN EXISTENCE

BOOK I (= A. *Consciousness*; = Chaps. I–III):

THE COGNITIVE ELEMENTS

CHAPTER I (= Chap. I): The attitude of Sensation.

CHAPTER II (= Chap. II): The attitude of Perception.

Appendix: *The Structure of the* Phenomenology of Spirit

	HOFFMEISTER	BAILLIE
NOTE:	121:1–19	202:30–203:12

(3). The *World upside-down*

(a). Introduction	121:20	203:13
(b). Dialectic	122:32	205:1
NOTES on the philosophy of nature:	122:4–13	204:2–13
	122:37–123:3	205:7–14
NOTES on crime and punishment:	122:13–31	204:13–33
	123:3–7	205:15–19
	123:31–124:4	206:8–23
(c). Transition	124:26	207:7
c. Transition	124:33	207:15
NOTE:	125:3–9	207:28–34

C. *Conclusion*

1. Result of Chap. III and Book I, and transition to Chap. IV: the notion of *Life*	125:20	208:10
2. Summary of the first three Chaps. and transition to Chap. IV and Book II: the notion of *self-consciousness*	126:31	209:31

BOOK II (= B. *Self-consciousness* = Chap. IV):

THE EMOTIONAL AND ACTIVE ELEMENTS.

GENERAL INTRODUCTION: The notion of *Self-consciousness.*

A. Summary of Book I and the place of Book II in the whole of the PhG	133:3	218:3
B. Analysis of *Self-consciousness* taken as the result of the dialectic of Book I; theme of the dialectic of Book II	134:6	219:6
C. *Ontological* analysis of *Life* (which normally should be part of the *Logik*)	135:39	221:16
NOTE:	136:27–40	222:8–23

CHAPTER I: The attitude of Desire (corresponds to the attitude of Sensation).

A. *Introduction*: *Life* and *Self-consciousness*	138:21	224:23
B. *Dialectic*	139:1	225:7
NOTE on *Life*:	139:31–39	226:6–15
NOTE on *Spirit*:	140:28–39	227:9–22

SECOND PART: (= C. Reason; = Chap. V.–VIII):

CONCRETE EXISTENTIAL ATTITUDES.

BOOK I (= Chap. V):

APOLITICAL ATTITUDES: THE INTELLECTUAL

GENERAL INTRODUCTION: The notion of *Reason.*

CHAPTER I (= Chap. V, A): The Scientist.

CHAPTER II (= Chap. V, B): The Man of Enjoyment
and the Moralist.

CHAPTER III (= Chap. V, C): The Man of Letters.

Book II (= Chapters VI and VII)

POLITICAL ATTITUDES: THE LOYAL CITIZEN AND
THE REVOLUTIONARY.

FIRST SECTION (= Chapter VI):
Dialectic of the historical *reality*

GENERAL INTRODUCTION

CHAPTER I (= Chap. VI, A): Antiquity: the Pagan World.

CHAPTER III (= Chap. VI, C): The Contemporary Epoch: German Philosophy and the Napoleonic Empire.

SECOND SECTION (= Chap. VII):
Dialectic of historical *Ideologies* (Arts, Literatures, Religions).
GENERAL INTRODUCTION

CHAPTER IV (= Chap. VII, A): The ideologies of societies that are dominated by the Desire anterior to the Fight for recognition: primitive societies and ancient Egypt. (Chap. VII, A, has no equivalent in Chap. VI, for there Hegel does not deal with political formations anterior to the *polis*.)

CHAPTER VI (= Chap. VII, C): The ideologies of societies dominated by *Work* which is posterior to the Fight for Recognition: The Religion of the Bourgeois World (Christianity). (Chap. VII, C corresponds to Chap. VI, B; Chap. VI, C has no equivalent in Chapter VII, for in Chap. VI, C, Hegel already describes the *Ideologies* of the Post-revolutionary World.)